TREE

Melina Sempill Watts

Library of Congress Control Number: 2017900565

ISBN: Number 978-0-9976921-1-2

Our books may be purchased in bulk
for promotional, education, or business use.
Please contact your local bookseller or by email at
publisher@changetheworld-books.com.

First Change the World Books edition published April 2017
Reprinted June 2020

Out of respect and love for trees, this book was printed
on 100% recycled paper stock with plant-based inks.

To Steve Davids, for *Poaceae*

That green things may grow.

FOREWORD

Somehow, despite the fact that I was raised in Los Angeles, I developed a connection with trees. I loved playing with and picking apples from a tree in my backyard, which my mom transformed into delectable cinnamon applesauce.

At age fifteen, I joined with fellow summer campers to plant a small grove of smog tolerant trees in an effort to begin replacing millions of trees that were being killed by L.A.'s air pollution. My teenage experience of making a difference by helping to save a forest, was so potent that it moved me to engage others to join the work, and led to the formation of TreePeople (...an organization that has inspired and supported millions of people to participate in revitalizing city and forest lands in the United States and around the world.)

For decades, I have asked people to tell me about a tree in their lives. What did I find? Every single person has an answer about a special tree and a story to go with the answer.

What is it that people intuitively know about trees?

Dr. Jared Diamond, in his groundbreaking book *Collapse: How Societies Choose to Fail or Succeed,* documented that throughout history, every civilization that forgot its vital connection with trees, cut them all down, triggering a cascade of collapsing ecosystem and human life support systems, which ultimately led to the demise and disappearance of that civilization. Those civilizations that remembered and saved their trees, saved themselves and are still around today.

This message is all the more relevant as global weather becomes increasingly severe, threatening lives, communities and even nations.

For most of us, despite these facts, our conscious relationship with trees, woodlands, forests and watersheds has withered. We've lost, perhaps to our detriment, the visceral knowledge of the gifts of trees, (including life support services of water supply, flood protection, biodiversity habitat, air and water quality protection, stress reduction, and spiritual renewal, to name a few,) and the inherent understanding of our personal ability and responsibility to protect, restore, plant, and care for trees and forests.

Whether through art, science, poetry, spirit, extreme sports or simply walking in the woods, it behooves us to find our own way of reconnecting and rebuilding our personal relationship with trees and nature.

Melina Watts' *Tree* provides a unique avenue.

Tree is an imaginative leap into the private world of a California live oak; from a literary vantage point, this is magical realism at its best. Viewing life from the perspective of a tree activated my imagination and opened my heart.

Reading the book, I found answers from decades of people telling me about their trees.

What I really learned from listening to everyone's stories is that for people who connect with the natural world, reality is magic.

I invite you to step into the world of *Tree*, where plant and rock, animal, sky and water, star, dirt and light unite to share the joy of existence on the page and in your heart.

As Watts says: "May green things grow."

Andy Lipkis, Founder, TreePeople

Much of what drives literature, human culture, art and history itself focuses on the romantic energy between men and women. Related variations arise when people fall in love within their own genders. Our need to connect person to person is powerful. Trees, as entities that do not engage in courtship, that are cross-fertilized by the wind and which stay in one site, static, for a lifetime, have a totally different way of experiencing reality than we do.

To allow readers to access Tree's interior life, the book uses e, a third pronoun for Tree and the other plants which are simultaneously both male and female.

TREE

ONE DAY IN TOPANGA

The tree was enormous, with roots that reached down into the stillness of the mountain. Centuries of rain and drought, of fire and regeneration had brought it an impervious calmness that drew plants, creatures, rain and stone towards it, each hoping to acquire peace from proximity. However neutrality is not the same as peace, and this tree's disdain for emotion was so great that the comfort it brought others was tinged with sadness for this tree's secret message was that there is no happiness. Only serenity lasts.

Late in the fall, bedecked with acorns like a night beach strewn with grunion glittering in their thousands, the tree shed one large, ripe acorn from its upmost, valley-facing branch. This release felt sweet – like watching a young bear off to forage on his own for the first time – and even tree could not resist a little dollop of joy at the departure of this perfect seed. Maybe. How many thousand acorns every year? How many eaten by insects and mold, animals and heat? How many inherently unable to sprout? How many desiccated by summer and so destroyed? How ridiculous, really, to have any feelings for any offspring at all. And yet – the tree felt the large acorn falling through the clear air with a rush and felt the hope like a pretty little indecent thought roiling around an old mind.

And released the thought as soon as it came. An acorn is one of many. How few are chosen. How few survive. How few become tree.

Tree's roots reached deeper into the stone in which they were interlaced and morsels of rock crumbled away, shocked at the sudden freedom from the main of the mountain. The pure rock stood fast against the infinitesimal onslaught. Both rock and tree enjoyed the creep and struggle. Tree's love for big things like sunandwaterandbreezeandstone dominated once again. Love for little things is so dangerous because little things are fragile.

But little things love themselves. And this acorn fell and hit the dead leaves beneath tree with a thud and after a tiny bounce, rolled to a stop. Motes of dust rose into the air, sparkling in the light. The movement attracted the eye of scrub jay, old, fat, with scruffy feathers yet still the proud owner of a strong beak.

Old scrub jay was trying to convince a pretty female scrub jay who had taken up residence on the other side of tree that he was not such a bad fellow, really, despite the fact that he flew less swiftly than the scrub jays her age, despite the fact that his feathers were a thinning a bit and that the once impressive blue-tone barbules that lined each principal feather had faded with little shivers of white through them. He didn't know she had already taken up with his own second cousin, two trees down the way, in fact, was contemplating leaving tree, though she'd rather her beau came to move in with her. Actually, he did know. He knew all about it. The young scrub jay already had two mates who were squabbling with one another and young scrub jay would be stretched thin to fend for a third family. This was not how things were done in scrub jay's time – like most birds, anything but monogamy appeared physically impossible when it came time to raising chicks. Even one nest was almost too much work. This fat acorn would make the perfect present. Surely she would understand that he, scrub jay, knew what it was to love. He grabbed the precious treat in one claw, standing on the left claw, his little nails curving around to grasp into the shiny warm surface. He looked around, twitched his beak and made little cries of "Chaw! Chaw!" as scrub jays are wont to do, and fluffed his tail feathers.

Just in case she was looking.

The movement caught the eye of a fiery red-tailed hawk, circling on an updraft, lazy as a sated rattlesnake, lazy as only the truly tired can be. In an instant, heart bursting with glee, he was diving through the air and slamming talons into startled scrub jay and bouncing off the impact and back into the sky, wings slamming into his torso with the effort to power back up into the clouds. The fwooo sound as the enormous feathers caught the air and the slam as they hit the bird's body made up all the sound in the world to old scrub jay. His small bright eyes filled with tears. Not out of fear, not out of loss of female scrub jay, not even for regret for the one last untasted acorn, still tight in his claw. He remembered the crushing joy of resting his head on his first mate's neck as they slept in the cold of winter, up in their nest, the sparkle in her eye, when she stirred and blinked to look lovingly at him in the moonlight.

Missing her as he did always, a little, upwelled and overflowed from his heart and throughout his whole body in such an overwhelming way that he did not even see how very tiny tree now looked beneath them, nor notice what the high clouds actually felt like now that he was whipping through one. He had never been up so high in his life.

Hawk took great pride in knowing how easy he was making nesting for his mate. This was the second treat of the day. She would be happy and so would he. Enough to share.

As he headed back towards the ridge, knowing that he'd drift down the same updraft in circles back to the perfectly sized cave she'd managed to claim for their nest, he cried out his joy, in the hawk's screech, skipping up a fifth, the same notes over and over again, in feral joy. He knew she'd be hopping from one foot to the other, waiting for food, for him, for her own joy returned.

Startled from his reverie by the rough cry, scrub jay dropped his acorn and twitched. The acorn tumbled through empty air yet again. Hawk shifted his grasp of scrub jay's body and broke the smaller bird's back with his strong talons. He was almost home and scrub jay would still taste hot and fresh and hawk was not willing to risk losing his prey in air.

For anyone who cared, it seemed a long way for such a tiny seed to fall. But the double encasing of outer shell and inner skin protected the future. Acorn slammed into the side of a hill as it slid into valley land, right into the crack wedged into the dirt by summer-drought. Fully four inches into the ground, it might have been a little deep inside the earth for a lesser acorn, but this was no lesser acorn. There was a tree in this acorn, waiting for the future.

The acorn slipped another millimeter into the dust as the drought deepened. Another and another each day. The crack was widening. The grass went from dusty green to gold to a murky brown. The tough chaparral plants – manzanita, white sage, black sage and feathery cowboy sage – hung in there, enduring. The trees reached deeper into the ground, hunting for fragments of moisture with thirsty roots.

Animals crept around low to the ground in the heat. Flies buzzed happily – there were dead things to eat so only they were feeling fat and fly.

From the east hill came the sound of chase. A deer came bounding over the top and crashing down the path, heart pounding so loud that even the rocks could hear it as it passed by. Behind it was a lean mountain lion, intent as a shark with a seal. Aching for contact. The mountain lion had more bounce and verve than the deer and the deer hunched up at the bottom of the hill to leap over the dry creekbed. Anticipating the move, the lion leapt first, landing partly on the deer's back. In a burst of horror, the deer leapt free and the lion fell crashing to the rocky bed of the creek, leaving eight thick claw marks in the deer's skin.

The deer felt it like someone had flung molten iron on its back, which slid in even strips down his side. Electrified, he took off with renewed energy. But he was now so frightened that he was quivery with adrenaline – and not nearly so coordinated. He stepped unevenly on the track and stumbled but kept up.

For her part, the lion, or rather lioness, for she was female from the inside out, was irritated to have been tossed to the ground, which was hard as cement. She didn't like to get bruised, but she didn't mind it because the clear wet black iron smell of fresh blood was on her own claws and she was hungry.

Hungry for her own life, for the life of the deer. Like all lions, for her it was them or her, and she always chose her. Snarling as warning, threat, complaint, pleasure, she could fit a speech into one cry. The deer heard it and struggled to outpace the lioness as they poured through the dry valley.

The lioness gathered up her strength into short, bunchy strides, lavishing on the speed. Pulling her back legs up neatly under her front shoulders, she sprang out into a bravura leap, landing squarely on the back of the deer, who fell with the impact. In a blur of squeals and snarls, kicks and bites, the deer struggled to escape until the lioness cemented her victory in one massive bite.

Without pause she was ripping off sun-hot fur to get to the meat inside. The deer's blood trickled into the cracked earth. Into the dust. On top of the acorn. Cupful after cupful. Pint after pint. Until the crack was a little river of blood, the acorn beginning to float in the tiny sea of deer's blood.

When the lioness left her kill the next morning, the weight of the carcass was spread out over the crack in the dirt, keeping the moisture trapped inside.

And the acorn responded to sudden moisture as seeds do. Things uncoiled and uncurled inside.

* * *

The pressure mounted up as the acorn absorbed the moisture and new cells proliferated in the dark. At last, a thin crack spread from top

14

to bottom and back part way up the other side. A thin finger of white poked out, tiny as the forearm of a baby mouse. It poked into the blood-softened dust and down the narrow extent of the crack, reaching for a toehold in the earth. The deer's own moisture was still trapped in this few cubic feet of the entire extent of the valley, under the weight of the now rotting carcass, bones, fur and decaying meat where once was beauty. But curiously, decay elicits growth and freshness and so the acorn continued to transform into an incipient tree, an embryo of the oak it would become.

The top of the acorn split open and one small shoot came out the top, bland and blond. And optimistic. The first day it was just a morsel. The next day it shot up to half an inch, what would become twinned leaves twined around each other, visible at the top, and then it added another inch.

Then it began to wilt, for without any light, there was nothing to feed the next stage of the infant tree's growth. If it didn't find its way to the sun soon, in a day or so, this tree's future would die and it would become something for something else to eat, consume, digest and use.

But the hungriest creatures in California are always the coyotes. And the drought had wrought havoc with the game.

Starving, a pack of coyotes limped along looking for something to chase and eat. Dead meat was appealing in that it didn't require the expenditure of much life force to acquire. The lead male took a bite of the deer carcass – not to his taste, but food nonetheless and his mate came in next to him to eat. He snapped at her and she moved down to the gnawed over hindquarters. Their half-grown pups and adult siblings tried to move in to share the carrion, but the lead pair snapped at them and chased them off. However the dominant puppy gathered up his siblings and took on the off hind leg of the dead deer and pulled. His siblings joined in. Enraged, the parents pulled back, neatly ripping a leg off the crumbly skeleton. Relieved of the oppositional pressure, the half-grown coyotes found themselves the victors and tumbled back, pulling the deer with them for a few yards. Happy to share the booty, they dove at the remnants in a frenzy. Turning his nose up at the rancid feast and his own ill-behaved brood, the father turned down the trail and kept going, looking for something with a pulse. His alpha female, following his idea, followed him into the bushes, leaving their kids to the carcass.

And in the mid-day sun, the tree, for that is what it was becoming with each passing moment, quivered in the first burst of light it had ever seen/felt/smelt/known. Like all trees and fully sentient plants, tree experienced all the sensations that animals know in a simultaneous burst coming in at tree's core, from every exposed cell in tree's outside. Top, bottom, sides, roots, tree experienced the full extent of being alive in one brilliant moment and then shrank for an instant. It was nearly too much. But tree found inside a hunger for this hot light, for this dusty air, for the sky, that drove tree to reach up and up.

Tree's tiny taproot dove down, open in every cell to bringing in the water from the bloody ground that would grow it up; meanwhile the beginning of tree's trunk strove and unfurled, snapped up teeny and tall, moving up through the crack. At the end of the day, the proto-trunk was still technically just subterranean, but tree's interior core was skybound.

As the sun moved away and tree saw/felt the colors of sundown for the first time, tree felt an aching joy/sadness that felt like love and then a sharp horror when the sun altogether disappeared. How could tree survive without the hot/light? Where was the love? Night grew cold quickly and the sky went from purpley-blue to navy to black, shiny, smooth and immaculate. Tree felt loneliness and fear, and inside tree's core, tree knew the hot/light had abandoned tree forever. The pre-trunk curled down, looking for the comfort of the earth in the absence of sun. But then little blinky lights popped up in the sky like surprise visitors and tree could see/feel that the sky was populated with friendly entities. Not one of them made tree feel fed/loved at core, but tree could feel distant affection and that was surely better than the starving grief of sunset. A big yellowy white globe came out to the sky and tree felt/looked up, shivering in the night, at a kind of pure beauty that had nothing to do with tree's core growth and everything to do with…with…whatever it was that this living thing was about. Tree felt a distant amused warmth and slender affection and asked this large entity for protection and, very quietly asked it to bring back the hot/light. Tree asked the night/globe for the hot/light in the next instant, because it felt better to have help in such a big world than to be in it all alone. And because it made tree feel more hopeful and because tree believed that this was an efficacious act, tree asked again in the next instant. And the next. And the next. And the next. A minute passed. 10 minutes. A slow half hour.

Finally an hour. Hot/light please oh hot/light please oh please oh please oh hot/light hot/light hot/light oh please. Oh night/globe oh beautiful kind oh night/globe oh my lonely friend oh my lonely me oh please oh please ah please –

And such for an hour and another hour and on until night began to wane. The night/globe disappeared over the west hill and tree felt a stab of grief that fully rivaled tree's first pain not so long ago. But the color of the sky was changing in the east to dark blue then to light blue and finally a shiver of deep pink came up along the horizon and a smudge of red and then the hot/light came up, first just an upside down smile of light, then more until a segment of lychee sat along the east hill and then it turned into a whole sun and tree knew pure radiant joy and sent out every speck of love in its tiny core to sun and sun, sun knew.

And showered light over tree and all the others with a kind of generosity that no living being can ever recreate, but only emulate.

Tree's cells multiplied with intense fury in a crazy burst of eagerness to embrace sunlight and full of the heat of growth, of desire, of the need of the lonely to find, keep, have and maintain love, the little sprout peeked out from the drought-crack in the earth and up into the pure air of Topanga as human beings have been wont to call this magickal place of trees and deer and dust and sky and light and dark.

Sun shone down with the very same even heat that had driven all the grass and many of the creatures to death this summer. Full of moisture taken from the life of another, tree just enjoyed the power of summer. And grew. And grew.

The next night, tree was devastated again by sun's departure, but tree spent the whole time communing with the now slightly smaller night/globe and secretly hoping that sun would come back again. When sun came up the same place as the day before, in the same way, tree felt clever and brave and enjoyed the third day in a different way than tree had enjoyed days one and two – with a growing self-confidence and awareness of self. Tree talked to night/globe that night, but no longer with the ardent hysterical prayers of the young, but more in a social way. Because sun would come back. And sun did.

At the end of the first week, something dark red erupted from the tiny greenish-brown stick that made up tree, something burnt purple. That night, the little thing at tree's top unfurled and, in the morning, tree recognized the addition as a tiny leaf, far lighter green in shade than would be tree's adult leaves, but a recognizable California live oak leaf nonetheless, with the curved surface that would enable tree to collect dew on the underside and the little spikes along the tips of each leaf meant to try to scare off leaf-eating herbivores. The leaf was less brittle than the leaves tree would grow as an adult, but that meant it could make and acquire more chlorophyll more quickly, assisting tree in tree's major mission in the next years – to grow up and out, to acquire as many branches and as much gravitas as soon as possible. Tree's new leaf allowed tree to see/feel/smell/taste/know/understand more and to do so more quickly than tree had ever before. With tree's new leaf, tree could recognize that tree was growing in a vast meadow full of many things. Not far away was an enormous rock, granite. This rock interested tree, but apparently tree did not interest rock for tree's best efforts to connect met with a resounding silence.

Tree observed that the ground was hard from drought but underneath, deep underneath, tree could sense hidden moisture. The knowledge that wetness was there for the taking made tree's taproot greedy. It plunged down deeper, sending from its tip a few more inches of snaky tendril, hardly much wider than a strand of coarse hair.

Then the taproot sent out little sideways growing tentacles, slender as baby hairs. Each speck of root had to meander around fragments of dust, or to invade, cell by cell, ambivalent or outright unwilling bedrock, making a place for tree in this world, will it or no.

The moisture called out a siren's song, tricky as mermaids, beseeching tree to come to embrace the water. Tree strove mightily, but tree was little in the extreme and the moisture was very, very far away. And the deer's blood was long gone.

Tree recognized more and more neighbors each and every day. The sage – a tribe of many – seemed so dry and brave, no fear in the face of heat and rainless weather. The smell of the sage dominated every other smell – dust, sweat, dry grass. The white sage with the dusty under note of the so-called cowboy sage was the primary note of summer in Topanga and tree enjoyed the scent of these living plants; the scent was the spirit of the plant released to the world as gift.

Tree wanted to converse with some of the sage but couldn't figure out how to get tree's thoughts into sage or how to capture sage's thoughts and put them into tree. It was very frustrating to smell this wonderful smell and not to be able to mutually commune. In the distance were bayberries and California walnuts, and a hundred hundred other potential friends, but tree did not have the size or understanding to project tree's own voice to these strangers and the strangers did not bother connecting with one fragile oak tree sprout.

As the days crept on, tree gradually stopped growing and started enduring. And eventually shriveling a little, even drooping. There was no more water to provide the tension needed to keep a small young plant upright.

Tree's love for the hot/light was unabated but tree's appreciation for night-time grew. Night-time was cool. Dew fell. It was relaxing after enduring dehydration to at least feel better for some hours. But the moisture below was so very far away. How could tree get moisture? Where was water? Where did it come from? Tree yearned, inarticulate and passionate, for a solution to all this.

And then the Santa Anas came and tree was flattened by these wild winds of late fall that seemed to double the heat and to elicit all sorts of crazy yearnings in the animals that traversed the hillsides. Tree felt it too, that sense that magick could happen, that the future was just around the next instant, that if you wanted It enough, It would be yours, if you only wanted It enough. Whatever It was. The winds poured on and on. For an hour, the little oak sprout was bent nearly to the ground. Sometimes it withstood the onslaught, bending only a little. Two days worth of desiccating welter and tumult and then a stillness. The heat deepened. Tree could feel tree's very life. Already tree had known beauty and love and fear and sorrow. And now it was coming to an end.

The next night was cool. And in the morning, yesterday's turquoisey sky was now completely grey. And cool drops plopped down onto the earth, first slowly and then more swiftly. And tree uncurled, reaching up for the wet in triumph and vigor, just as tree had first uncoiled to hit the hot/light full on. When drops fell on tree, tree's thin bark and leaves (two more now) sucked them in pure.

And as the ground grew soft and then liquid, tree's root puffed up like the tummy of a pregnant bunny, fat and white and full of good things. The littler tendrils snaked down and around, embracing this portion of earth ever more deeply. From the center of tree's core, tree cried out to the Universe, "Life is good." And the rain came down like laughter.

WET

Tree was grateful for the length of that taproot because the deluge was so profound that tree soon found the creek had revived from what appeared complete death and was flooding its customary borders. Tree eself was standing in six inches of water. As tree was only eight inches tall, this was considerably challenging. The long taproot and the binary and tertiary roots that had sprung off in random directions did their job and held the little tree fast as the water swirled on by. All in all, it was a considerable adventure. A southern steelhead trout actually swam by tree on its way upstream – the local steelhead trout that live partly in sea, partly in freshwater, home at last to spawn. The smooth-slick of the fish's scales on tree's young bark felt eerie and delicious. Tree reached out to connect to the fish, but she was gone, flipping her tail to hurry faster.

The rain came down, striking tree's five little leaves and rolling on down to rejoin the mass of water, reuniting with the collective person of water. Tree was a little concerned that the rain might never stop, but so far, the sun had returned every day since tree sprouted, and rain had come when tree was near dead from thirst and so tree concluded that the rain would stop when tree had had enough. Or so tree hoped. On the fifth day there was a light drizzle and as the creek kept on rushing to the sea, the water now playing with tree's leaves receded down to tree's middle. To tree's surprise, e missed the embrace of the temporary lake in which e had been housed, it had been rather cozy in an elusive kind of way. The drizzle felt like fingers reading hidden messages on tree's bark and leaves – so pleasant.

The next day the sun came out in full yellowy force and the sky was cerulean blue. The creek rushed on, gurgling and fat, but now the size of a small river instead of the foreshadowing for some apocalypse. Everywhere the dead grass was smashed flat into the muddy ground. As a herd of deer came down to the creek to drink, their feet sank in the mud up to their knees and hocks. Indeed the little ones panicked and wouldn't come down all the way, thirsty or no. A buck came close to tree, seeing the crunchy green leaves as a treat in this hungry time before the great growth of the fall/winter season. Tree innocently looked at the big head coming closer, still young enough not to put two and two together, even as the mouth opened and the big creamy teeth came in kissing near. But just as tree was recognizing e's peril, the buck started and the whole herd fled in slow-motion through the mud and back up the hill, struggling for speed in the morass of mud.

Tree shivered in bright light. A plant's life is difficult – deer can flee or pause and eat or roam for water. A tree must take what life gives e and find enjoyment, meaning and value in wherever it is that the acorn happens to sprout.

As the sun dragged down to the embrace of the west hills, tree saw something startling in the brown mud.

Little flecks of light green. Hundreds of them. Tiny little things. Tree was delighted by all the new specks of life. 360° of them extending as far as e could see, in all directions. From tree's core all the love e had stored up from the hot/light, the compassion from the night/globe, the yearning for water, the happiness from rain, it all came out in a jumble of shared emotion, radiating outwards, showering affection equally on each of the miniature sprouts. And to tree's surprise, an answering burst came at tree in tiny sparkly shards, tiny as shattered glass, but as shimmery and pretty – the little sprouts were loving tree back. Thrilled past all measure, tree pulled up from the tips of every strand of root, up into the taproot, up into the core and then out through bark and leaves, an even louder answer. A tinier, thinner answer came back from the new grass. Tree realized: they were busy sprouting and sprouting was hard work as tree recalled. So tree turned down the volume and sent out gentle waves of affection that required no answer – and when the sun set and the whole herd of grass panicked as a unit, tree sent out as best e could a vision of the long first night and the coming dawn. And the infant grass sprouts understood and settled in for the night. Tree was glad that e had been able to share this gift, to protect these new lives from fear and bewilderment. Tree fell asleep, content.

The next morning, tree woke up at dawn to hear the chatter of the grass as the sun rose, each thanking tree, by the by, for the promise that came true. Tree was tickled to be a local hero. It was obvious to tree that all the grass loved tree and tree was happy to return the favor. From right near tree's biggest lateral root (a big five inches now, itself as skinny as new grass), came a big voice.

"Good morning!

Tree startled to hear thoughts spoken so clearly – especially by one so young. Tree was embarrassed because tree had never spoken like that and wasn't sure what to do back.

"Good morning!" repeated the voice. "Don't you hear me?"

Tree grunted out an answer "Uh, yeah."

The littler voice laughed. "You're not nearly as articulate this morning as you were last night. Thank you for telling us all that sun would come back."

At a loss, tree asked, "Who are you? What is your name?"

There was a pause. The voice had to think up the answer to both questions.

"I am grass. These are all my siblings. But I am grass. One. My name is Univervia."

Tree felt an interior smile. What a brave little spirit.

Tree had already figured out that many grass never got taller than tree was already and trees, well, trees could touch the sky. But Tree could feel that Univervia already felt e was touching the sky and this enthusiasm, this confidence was a tonic to tree, who was, at core, rather shy and timid, despite the fact that e had spoken to hundreds of grass last night without hesitation or fear.

Tree thought for a while.

Univervia interrupted Tree's reverie. "Well? What's your name?"

Tree thought and thought. Humbly, Tree answered. "I am tree. I am a tree. And…my name is Tree."

Univervia laughed, but in a friendly way. "O.K., big one. Tree. Shall we be friends since we are growing together in this space of dirt?"

Tree felt e's sap race. A friend. That is what tree had needed all along! And with such a one as this! A Mexican sprangle grass, Univervia's stem was already thin and straight, shooting up faster than all the other stems of the new grass. And Univervia was a soft green with a shimmer of grey overcast. Univervia was aiming to be tall and had a delicacy in structure that made e beautiful. Tree was certain that Univervia was the most wonderful blade of grass that ever grew. Tree felt a bit overwhelmed by this realization. This blade of grass had asked tree to be a friend.

Univervia waited patiently. Tree was a bit slow.

Univervia's thoughts were as fast as chubs darting after mosquitoes. First Univervia thought Tree wanted to be friends, they were, after all, chatting. Then Univervia thought Tree was too big, too snobby, too tree to be friends with a blade of grass. But then why had Tree been so kind to them last night as the sun set? Maybe Univervia had misread the whole situation! Perhaps Tree liked the grass and didn't like Univervia! Univervia's core cringed and twisted inside. Univervia really admired Tree and wanted Tree to like Univervia back.

But Univervia was a brave sprout of grass and Univervia decided that it didn't matter. Univervia could have a good life without Tree. Gathering dignity and pride around eself like a bobcat self-grooming after a slight, Univervia jumped back into the conversation.

"Fine. I mean, that's O.K. We can just share dirt. We don't have to…"

Tree rushed in to interrupt Univervia before Univervia changed e's mind.

"Univervia! Please be my friend. I would be honored. I was so honored I was having trouble finding the words to agree to your suggestion. You'll have to be patient with me. I am not used to talking."

Univervia's clear laugh rippled into Tree and made Tree's leaves curl tighter, the spines sparking with the sound/feel.

Univervia, having next to no inhibitions, conceded quickly, "When you took so long to answer I figured you didn't want to be my friend. So I was preparing to retract my offer. We'll have to figure out how I can communicate more slowly and you can communicate more swiftly or we'll drive each other crazy."

Tree felt a big tree smile rumbling in e's roots. "Oh, I hope so."

The non sequitur felt like a satisfactory answer to Univervia.

Tired with all the chatter, Univervia focused on eating light and dirt and wet and growing. Tree watched over all the grass, but especially over Univervia and noted as Univervia's central leaf/stem shifted over the day to follow the course of the sun. Tree could see/feel Univervia growing/expanding rapidly, could feel the tiny explosions of energy as individual cells within Univervia grew, divided and grew some more. It was like re-experiencing Tree's own sprout-hood.

Univervia could feel Tree's warm support and it helped Univervia to grow faster, stronger and greener. By the end of the day, Univervia, was a full two millimeters taller than e's peers.

The whole herd of grass settled in to rest for the night.

Tree stretched outward, relaxing gently into the cool moonlight. Beneath came tiny sighs of oxygen from all the grass. Tree could feel one particular puff of grass-breath coming from Univervia and it felt peaceful.

It rained briefly in the night and in the morning, Tree released a puff of oxygen and Univervia glistened from root to tip with drops of water and Tree felt again that Univervia was purely the most beautiful blade of grass ever. And Tree's very own friend, no less.

UNIVERVIA GROWS

After several days of light rain and patchy sunlight, the grass was half a foot tall. Tree was terribly impressed with how quickly the herd was maturing as it had taken e weeks to get that kind of height. But when e looked at the trunks of the grass, they were fragile as could be. Tree worried that the first strong wind would destroy such ephemeral looking plants. Tree kept these worries in e's core as Tree did not want the young plants to be afraid.

That night a soft wind came tickling Tree's bark and Tree thought "This is it. The grass is done for."

But when the hot/light came back, (not so very hot at the moment) and Tree could see/feel the wind, Tree was surprised to see that when the wind pushed against the grass, each strand bowed down but then bounced back up, straight as ever. Tree braced eself as the wind grew stronger, small and erect in the face of the brisk morning.

Then Tree looked out over the meadow as the wind accelerated, to see that the whole field undulated in waves along with the wind in much the same effect as a waves rippling across a bay to fall in froth and back to smooth jade. It was just so over-the-top pretty. Why did grass waving in the wind exist? How could Tree capture and hold this moment forever?

Univervia was eavesdropping on Tree's reverie and e laughed at Tree's melancholy. Tree was chagrined to realize that e had almost no privacy in the face of Univervia's friendship for Univervia could listen to Tree's every thought like a pregnant mammal feeling every movement subtle or large from an unborn infant, each curl and uncurl, kick, punch and slither or swim.

"You'll just have to remember," Univervia asserted, "For as long as you live." Tree pictured the wind rushing a current through the standing grass and felt the same sense of unsatiated pleasure as in the moment of seeing it and sighed out a pop of oxygen. Tree thought for a bit and then answered Univervia's easy wisdom, "Univervia, you don't know how alone I was before you sprouted. For how long. You have always been a part of your herd. It is different to sprout all alone, to have no one to talk to but the hot/light."

Univervia's blades snapped in the breeze in agreement. Surely it was nice to be a part of the herd.

Hesitantly, Univervia whispered (e wished the herd were not always there, always listening, *chismoso* about everything Univervia said and did and felt/thought,) "Tree. It is pleasant to be grass. Our roots interlace back and forth against one another in the dirt. I am touching a hundred of the herd at any one moment, day and night. I love them all. But…" Univervia petered out, suddenly timid.

Tree couldn't stand silence in the face of Univervia's usual constant stream of chatter, Univervia's open prairie policy towards revealing every fleck of a feeling/thought. When Tree went to try to reach into Univervia's core, it was sealed as tight as a seed. Tree felt a prick of hurt but e's curiosity outweighed the worry about rejection. Tree spoke very quietly and realized the rest of the herd was oblivious to this kind of subtlety. They were alone in the crowd. "Univervia. What were you about to say? You can say anything to me."

Univervia cringed, shy. But Tree caught a whiff of thought/feeling and voiced what e had heard. Tree spoke again in a whispery voice "You like the herd. But you like me best of all." Tree had suspected as much all along, but to find such an explicit depiction of primacy in Univervia's own core was perfect happiness to Tree. But Univervia curled and coiled in discomfort. Tree picked up on the discomfort and still whispery soft, apologized, "Am I too close? I am sorry. But now that I am here, I cannot figure out how not to listen. I am very clumsy, compared to you, Univervia."

For answer, Univervia let slip out the thought e had been holding on to tightly as if it were something that might drive Tree away. Univervia's secret fear was that Tree would suddenly recognize that Univervia was grass and Tree was tree and would pull away from their friendship. Of course since Univervia was Tree's first and only friend, Tree could not even see/feel this thought when it was right in front of e. For Tree, Univervia was It. But for the moment, Univervia was feeling Tree's unbending enthusiasm and so revealed the request e had been formulating in the last few days. "Could you grow a root in my direction? I would like to grow together."

The warmth in Tree's core was all the answer Univervia needed. It would take days and several false starts but Univervia knew that sooner or later, Tree would push several roots out in e's direction and meander around in a self-defined maze until brushing up against one of Univervia's very own roots. Univervia anticipated the first contact with pleasure. It would be like talking, like sharing thought/feeling but it would be cozy now. And once roots are set, they don't move. So this would be a forever thing. And Univervia, growing fast as growing fast as an adolescent, was craving forever.

Tree could not follow all of Univervia's mercurial moods and was perplexed as to why e had them. This forever thing? Tree was not even sure what the concept meant. Tree concluded it, along with the mood swings, was a grass thing, something alien that must be embraced as an incomprehensible but inherent part of the other. For Univervia's part, Tree's inability to understand Univervia's hot and cold feelings was a continual source of torment – it felt so logical, so clear and obvious to Univervia why Univervia was upset, happy, dismal, overjoyed – why wouldn't Tree understand such lucidity?

But Univervia recognized that Tree was different – and that it didn't really matter because Tree's unmoving loyalty was something as splendid as sunshine. Univervia slowly turned e's blades to front the sun as the wind let up. The day warmed up and Tree's leaves, now increased to ten in number, twisted in the light to catch the rays. Together, both plants joined the whole field in soaking up sun and oxygen and creating green, green and more green. It was a beautiful day and both Tree and Univervia felt united in the shared creative endeavor of creating more tree, more grass.

Days and weeks fled by in this effort. Resting at night in dewy moisture and growing in the bright light. Univervia stretched up and up, one day passing Tree in height. Tree laughed a rumbly laugh, for when Univervia was a sprout, it had never occurred to Tree that a speck of grass could and would be taller than Tree! Univervia laughed the confident laugh of the adolescent, sure that the universe was e's for the taking. Tree, still in the plant-world equivalent of prepubescence, ages away from acorns and all that that would represent emotionally, could only watch e's newly tall friend grow taller, layering in more stems, more strands, a green intensifying towards neon lime, with leaves underlaid with a sandy taupe, more beautiful and more feisty, and wonder what had become of the timid stem with delicate new blades that e had once known.

But Univervia had a generous core and felt Tree's overwhelm and reached out and put comfort into Tree. "I am grass! I am nearly grown! You are tree, you will catch up with me."

Tree focused on growth but felt e would not even begin to catch up with Univervia, with grass. Frustrated, e sat in a snit, temporarily paralyzed. Univervia asked gently, "How are your roots? Are you close to me yet?"

This was a sore point for the task that Tree had thought was an easy gift was quite complex. It took extraordinary focus to ask the roots (and asking didn't mean the stubborn things would do what had been requested) to grow in any direction at all. And when Tree finally got three roots to drift over, cell by cell, towards the patch of dirt where Univervia grew, one stumbled into a rock and grew around it and then would grow no more.

As Univervia and Tree moved cell by cell towards one another, slow as the idea of time itself, things moved quickly in the world around them. Within the herd were those who were jealous of Univervia's height, Univervia's unique voice and above all – distressed by Univervia's unusual friendship with a tree. Most of the herd was friends with other grass, with the herd itself. Small fescue spoke to Pacific foxtail spoke to slender fescue spoke to Six weeks three awn and all these annuals spoke to the grander perennials who spoke back to them kindly; purple needlegrass spoke to giant wild rye spoke to poa spoke to stipa spoke to rush and back to small fescue and Mexican sprangle grass, but grass was grass and really all such distinctions were not so important. A California live oak was an altogether different thing. And while Univervia united with the group and had a few individual friends within the herd of grass, clearly e's attention was with Tree. And so discontent grew. In particular, one plant who grew near Univervia was most upset. Dant. Dant was nearly as tall as Univervia and brighter and deeper in green tone. The rest of the herd recognized Dant as a centering voice within the group.

Univervia – growing only a few inches away from Dant, appeared oblivious.

Dant had tried to chat up Univervia by discussing the quality of the dirt they shared, which was the abysmal shale typical of Topanga. It took a great deal of life force to force a root into the dirt which was like powdered dust compressed into rock, unless rain turned it into claylike mud. Neither way was it a treat. But Univervia was regal about the hardship, sharing out the plant truism that a plant must grow where a plant sprouts, which offended Dant for it made Dant, a powerful half-grown witchgrass, look like a lightweight for experiencing the work of growing through the soil as a struggle. However, Dant sucked it up and tried to participate in Univervia's grass-songs, but Univervia did not notice the subtle harmonizing, the beautiful low undertone Dant provided when Univervia was scatting up and down the notes woven into the wind by Univervia's enthusiasms. So for Dant, e's musical efforts then felt pointless.

Another grass nearby suggested, discreetly, that Dant should find other grass with whom to play, grass who would appreciate Dant as Dant deserved. Looking at the scrawny little wretch who had made this observation, Dant, already half the height of e's species, tall and vibrant, bent e's stem. Whatever. Dant was not going to state what seemed abundantly obvious: Univervia looked perfect and Dant was sure that Dant looked perfect. They were meant to grow together.

Dant took to singing to eself, looking to distract eself from the failure to connect with Univervia, but also hoping, eventually, to impress Univervia.

To Dant's surprise, one day Tree observed that Dant's grass-song was truly a marvel. Dant turned e's central blade abruptly away and shut down the sound. Tree felt the snub and asked surprised, "You do not like me?"

Dant responded, "You are not grass."

Tree, recognizing that haughtiness was all that could protect eself in the face of such hostility, responded, "I have been a friend to grass, a friend to this herd, since the day you sprouted."

Dant shrugged a slim blade. "You are a tree. You can only love other trees. I do not know why you bother us."

Shocked and hurt, Tree retreated into eself and shut down so that only internal growth could be felt. The little roots moving downward. The rocks far below them. The quiet of the earth.

Univervia was busy intersinging with the whole of the herd and had missed the exchange.

Oblivious for hours, e did not notice Tree's absence until sometime after the hot/light had set and when Univervia asked what was wrong, Tree could not admit out loud that e had been rejected by a member of Univervia's herd. "Nothing." Univervia pressed the point and Tree stiffened up, "Nothing, Univervia. Nothing." Univervia backed off, hoping to get to the bottom of it later. But there was a hairline fracture in their friendship and Univervia was acutely aware of the tiny flaw, the glitch that prevented the formerly fluid exchange of raw emotion back and forth. And the more Univervia felt it the more the invisible crack widened. Tree felt it as if Univervia was siding with Dant and Univervia felt it as if Tree was bored with Univervia. Univervia took to intersinging with the herd when the crack surfaced, leaving Tree feeling very other indeed.

Still, Tree maintained the mission e had set earlier, hoping that a physical connection would help to remind Univervia of Tree's abiding affections. And hopefully, e's own lasting feelings. But as Tree's other two roots grew millimeter by millimeter forward towards Univervia, the herd of grass grew aware of Tree's intention. Many of them razzed Univervia endlessly, "Tree-lover, Tree-lover. Too big for e's own herd!" Or worse, "Wanna-be tree. You're no part of this grass herd." Univervia was tough and rose above it, but Tree cringed to watch Univervia's own siblings and cousins turn on poor Univervia. Still, a few brave grass spoke up. "We like Tree. We like Univervia. Grass must have friends in this field besides grass." A little yarrow spoke in a tiny flowery voice, "All plants are one." For a moment that hushed the herd. The horrible comments abated, but never entirely ceased – an intermittent theme of grumbling popped up every now and then in the constant chatter of grass. It was difficult because up until this point the herd had been cohesive and had shared thoughts about sun and rain and wind and insects and the grades of dirt through which they grew in a social mass. But now that the grass was maturing, each grass was feeling angst and pressure and inexplicable feelings of yearning and some of them handled this with considerably less grace than others. Some used these feelings to create grass-song and both Univervia and Tree enjoyed the soaring beauty of solo songs, the joy of all day long intermingled chanting.

But all this political turmoil over Univervia had two serious side-effects. One – some of the grass roots near Univervia wanted to punish Univervia as insufficiently grass-loyal. They wanted to stop up Univervia's root-growth until Univervia gave in to the norm. But others disagreed, thought that Univervia brought variety and dazzle into the herd. The two sides waged a battle and counter battle underground fought in such a time lapse that the movement of a slug would look water down-hill fast in comparison. Dant sent out a long root with the intention of encircling Univervia's taproot and there was nothing

Univervia could do to resist the looming assault. Univervia tried to sing to Dant of friendship and herdness but found that Dant and Dant's friends interrupted e and out-sang Univervia's buoyant voice. Shocked, Univervia fell silent. Underneath this display of raucous cruelty Tree's voice reached out, "Univervia, I am still here." But Univervia did not hear Tree and Tree and Univervia were sad in different ways, separate.

For Tree's part, Tree's own advancing roots were helped and hindered through the two sides. Several times other grass roots claimed to be Univervia, which was quite embarrassing to Tree. But Tree was stubborn and Tree had promised Univervia that e would interlace roots and Tree would keep this promise. Besides Tree was bigger than the grass roots and thus could afford to just bludgeon forward day after day, cell by cell.

A day later, still in the middle of this mess, a younger grass, a small fescue, spoke up. "I am Viciam. I am grass!"

The phrasing of this expression made both Tree and Univervia smile – and they recognized this independent spirit as a new friend. After greeting the youngster and promising e the sun would go down but then come back, they left e to sprout and grow. Viciam quickly absorbed the history and gossip of e's herd and then, for a plant only an inch and a half tall, spoke up in a surprisingly loud voice, dominating the conversation of the entire herd. "Grass. Do you remember the first night the herd sprouted? The beauty of sun? The onset of night?" As the whole herd relived these first hours, Viciam rushed to the punchline, "Who told us the hot/light would come back? Who befriended us all?" The entire herd had to agree that it had been Tree. "So," Viciam continued "Univervia is the wisest of us all for e has made best friends with our best friend. And Univervia has not stopped being a part of the herd just because of this friendship. So, though I am young, I must speak up. The root battles must stop."

But Dant outshouted this eloquence, "You are a tiny sprout. After Univervia, I am the largest and oldest and wisest of the annuals. Univervia must cease this ridiculous friendship. Our roots are enough for us to intermingle with ourselves."

Univervia, hot and dark green, snapped out, "Do not presume to tell me what to do and what not to do, Dant. I am an individual grass plant, not a cell in your own stem. Boss yourself, but leave me be."

Dant could feel everything going horribly wrong. Now Univervia did not like Dant, which was never Dant's intention, Dant just wanted to convince Univervia to behave how Dant thought grass should. Univervia's fidelity to Tree in the face of public opprobrium was more than Dant could bear. "If you won't turn your blade on Tree and give your core to us, we will make you."

Univervia laughed. "How can you?"

Solemnly Dant made the threat. "We will root-choke you. You will be dead in seven days time if you do not choose us over Tree."

Slender and proud, waving over the sturdier Dant, Univervia repeated eself. "I love my herd. I love Tree. There is no choice to be made."

And...slow as grief, the roots began the war.

Eventually, Dant fought past several friendly grass and wrapped a key root around Univervia's tap root. Then Dant began to tighten. At first there was no effect but within days, Univervia begin to droop.

Tree was beside eself. Finally Tree burst out, "I will stop speaking to Univervia. Do not kill Univervia! I promise."

But Dant, enjoying the heat of power, declined in a growly voice. "This is not between us and you. You are an outsider. This has to do with Univervia's loyalty to us. Univervia must choose us over you."

Obdurate, Univervia spoke in a cramped and narrow voice. "I choose both."

And while the herd of grass was intensely engaged in this battle, wondering if Dant would do such a heinous thing to a sibling blade that everyone but everyone knew Dant had loved so much, a second herd of deer was on the hoof, wandering through the meadow.

The grass had known the prickly unease of deer herds before: their hooves severed the top portions of grass off and crushed young and old plants, causing the need to grow back over weeks' time. And...they ate the tops of plants and sometimes they uprooted grass and that was just that. They were blandly violent, oblivious to that which they caused.

A velvety brown mouth came near the patch of grass which included Dant, Viciam and Univervia. A big bite took out Dant and Dant's pack of friends, severing them off at an inch above the roots. There was a universal shriek as the creature began grinding them down into food and the silence of a noble death thereafter. Dant, suffering a mortal wound, clung to the earth by e's roots, shivering at the disappearance of 90% of e's stem and blades. Univervia spoke softly, "Dant. You are still alive. Don't fall asleep. Don't give up. Grow. Grow! You can heal and thrive."

Shocked to the core by kindness from Univervia after having put e under a grass *fatwa*, Dant cried. Univervia continued, "Grow. Grow!" And Dant clung to the command and put out a wish to form cells along the severed edge, oozing precious wetness into the air. Dant began to reconstruct.

And in that moment the deer's mouth came back in and neatly chomped out half of Univervia. Tree was electrified. It felt like e's own core had been cleaved.

To Tree's surprise, e could still feel the blade of Univervia that was on the deer's tongue. And the feelings that came at Tree were fast, intense and surprising. The whole blade lay languid, surrendering as the tongue mashed the strands of grass up to the roof of the doe's mouth. Then the deer twisted the grass sideways and ground teeth into the grass. As the grass was destroyed, each cell popped and gave shots of grass life-force into the hungry deer, in little pops of ecstatic release. The whole thing happened as swiftly as a string of firecrackers going off into light and smoke, leaving behind a dull residue that gave no sense of the evanescent beauty that had been enchanting the air only moments before. Tree felt this chunk of Univervia embrace willful dissolution and then suddenly all these little pieces that had been integrated into Univervia were separated into something like *ananda*, the joy which powers the universe and then…then the grass was deer.

Tree looked at the deer with newfound respect. On a fundamental level, the animal was grass. The deer itself was plant. Boggled by the insight, Tree could only be, still and erect, and watch the marauding deer move on.

The cry of the half of Univervia which remained tore into Tree like watching a lover plunge off a cliff.

Tree gasped out as a last-ditch effort "Univervia!" and Univervia grasped at the contact.

"Am I alive?" the shortened grass shrieked.

Relieved to have made contact, to have heard a voice, Tree spoke with the majesty of a grown tree, completely silencing the entire bustling herd of grass. "You are still here. And. You. Will. Grow."

Frantically, Univervia clung to this demand and promise and began pouring every speck of energy into healing the glistening top, pushing liquescent green from the top of the severed stem and blades. Ironically, a chunk of the deer's saliva had hit the ground right near Univervia and as it sank into the earth, Univervia hungrily used it up to water eself.

Released from the pressure of Dant's encircling root, Univervia grew down into the shale further, looking for moisture.

Tree's third root which had been sent weeks ago on the venture to connect to Univervia suddenly found the way clear as Dant's pack's roots moved a smidge aside in pity for everyone and Tree reached forward only a decimillimeter but it was enough and at last e's root touched Univervia's taproot.

Univervia recognized Tree's feel instantly though it was the first physical contact they had ever shared.

"Oh!" said Univervia.

"I am here." said Tree quietly.

Univervia whimpered, humbled by the last few minutes. "I am not what I once was. I am just a half of a strand of grass."

Tree spoke very intently and quietly so that no one in the rest of herd would hear. "You are my friend, whether you are alive or dead, a sprout or tall grass. You will grow back and I will be here beside you."

In the shadow of other members of the herd, Univervia wondered if e would ever again be so tall, so deep in green, so full of blades and leaves.

Tree heard the worry and asserted again. "I do not care if you are tall or green. You are my friend. You are alive. And that is good."

And grass realized that e could have been eaten down to the last dollop of root filament, that it could have been the end of everything. Instead, here was a chance to grow up again, a chance to live and shine and be grass.

"Alive is good." Univervia agreed in a shaky voice.

"Yes," agreed Dant.

And Viciam, at eighteen inches, now suddenly taller than the two older grass, agreed. "Alive is good. And grass is good. And Tree is good."

"Yes," murmured Dant, full of a sudden sense of the fragility of all plant life.

Univervia and Tree didn't say anything. They didn't need to because their roots were touching and Tree could literally feel Univervia working to grow back to beauty.

Tree sat still all day, feeling life pour itself up and down Univervia through the power of Univervia's own passion. And Tree's.

BLESSÉ

The next morning Univervia spoke just to Tree, "When I was eaten… it felt like stars and lights and fizzy water and burning pitch inside my core. No more talking."

Amid the dew, Univervia lay collapsed, limp, with no more pride left than a rain soaked opossum. Then Univervia's wounded blade tilted sunward, already growing.

All around Univervia, Tree could hear the dazed sound of recuperating grass. Reviewing yesterday's event, Tree realized that mouthful by mouthful e had heard similar expressions of euphoria as the grass acquiesced to moving from coherent form into a mass of cud, cell after cell bruised open to spill the juice of life into each deer.

Tree was humbled by the grass herd's willingness to give up everything or even nearly everything just to grow a herd of deer. Tree wasn't sure that Tree knew how to be so generous, so self-sacrificing. Tree wasn't sure e wanted to be. Tree spoke to Univervia, "Next time I don't want you to be so accommodating. Next time I want you to move and bend and stay out of the way."

Univervia just laughed. "Nonsense. I love that feeling of giving up, giving in, just giving. Now I am deer AND grass."

Tree shrugged off the nobility and wished that e could find a way to protect Univervia from everything. Tree was worried. What if the Deer had uprooted Univervia? What then?

For now, Univervia stopped talking to rebuild, as eager and innocent as a sprout. Again.

The jagged tops of Univervia's strands sealed over in the next few days. As the sun passed overhead, Univervia's whole body turned to track the sun as before and Tree found this very comforting. From nearby, Dant struggled to seal e's own edges. To e's surprise, Tree felt compassion for the damaged grass. Dant had been a large and dangerous presence in the herd, a big grass, and was now reduced to nearly nothing.

Tree found eself hoping Dant would make it.

Brash Viciam spoke up, "Don't worry about Dant. Dant is a survivor." Dant's voice, a crushed fragment of e's former melodic tenor came out basso profundo, "I am here!" It was all Dant could manage.

At night-time as dew gathered on the grass, Tree recalled Univervia only a few mornings ago at dawn, then still tall, glittering in the first sunlight with drops of water on e's skin like crystals caught in sunlight. Looking down at Univervia's shredded leaves, gathering equally beautiful plum-round drops of water, Tree said under the noise of the sleepy herd, "Univervia. You are still beautiful." Univervia mumbled, "Just you wait." And fell asleep.

The next day, Univervia tried to put a brightness into e's song that would sweep all the strain of mass renewal away.

It was late afternoon and Tree was lazing in the sun, luxuriating in the companionship of the whole field of grass, Univervia in particular of course. The stream gurgled on, steady as the drone of a beehive. Univervia was tilted sideways to gather more light in e's central stem. The sunbliss was too much for Univervia and e had started to sing a grass-song which no creatures could hear, but which amused all the plants in listen/feel distance. Univervia burbled up and down the scale, reiterating the key point of happiness in sunlight, weaving in appreciation for plant camaraderie, for the treat of dirt, for the gift of air, slight nostalgia for rain and then coming back to the sun thing over and over again. It was quite repetitive but the song changed just enough each time to hold everyone's attention. Therefore, Univervia had set the mood for the whole meadow. Everyone was dazed by sun and late spring and the good things in life.

Suddenly a group of humans – several families – came running down towards the stream. A little girl with even flat bangs and smooth long hair came running in heavy steps, not looking where she was going. Just as she was surely about to step right on Tree, a man grabbed the child and lifted her up a few feet up in the air and dropped her back down again. "Tuhuy!" he said, in a tone of reprimand. This was not the first time they had had this conversation. As her feet landed on grass, the little plants sighed. The feeling of being crushed was not unpleasant but always a bit surprising. It would force them to grow and flex and move and heal and this was pleasure after the first moment of discomfort and anxiety. Above them, Xus gave his daughter an earful. None of the plants could understand him. Chumash, Tongva, the calls of birds, – it was all exterior sound, talk and song alike. The grass weren't focusing on animals, on people, anyway. They had each other, they had the passion of their own young growth. There was tree, some nice insects, some awful ones. They were busy. But Tree was intrigued by birds, animals and these people. They moved. They interacted. It felt like plants' emotions and interactions going at blinding speed. If only they would move more slowly, think more loudly. Perhaps someday e would understand.

Shamed now, Tuhuy caressed Tree's topmost leaf and then looked up placatingly at her father. He could not resist his child. He reached down and rubbed the tip of his nose against her forehead and she smiled. He picked her up and put her, big as she was at four, onto his shoulders. She wove her fingers into her father's hair and smiled.

She was forgiven.

Tree re-examined the feeling of the little girl's fingertips on e's leaves. Was she expressing affection at e? Tree tried to recall little shivers of feeling at that moment. It was hard. She felt/talked nothing like a plant. What was the point of her action?

As they walked away, Xus repeated his lecture, totally unheard by the plants who were the beneficiaries of his diatribe. He explained to his child that she had almost stepped on a *ku'w*, a first-year California live oak tree. Oak trees gave acorns, the primary food for their family and people. If she protected this little tree, gave it water in a drought, watched over it, it would feed her children and their people. And, if *Chupu*, the earth, allowed it, her children's children and so on into the 8th generation.

Sobered by the idea of such distant progeny, she fell quiet. Xus patted her leg and pulled on a piece of her hair and she laughed.

Tree heard the laughter and wondered at it. The human child reminded him somehow of Univervia.

Univervia heard the thought and scoffed.

"There is no one like I!"

Tree laughed. "That is true. There is no one like you Univervia."

As the human herd moved away, it seemed that Univervia was feeling social and feeling social for Univervia meant loquacious. Luckily for both Univervia and Tree, trees are listening beings and Tree loved nothing better than to relax in the hot/light (or the night/globe) and listen to Univervia as she filled the world with her thoughts and wishes and desires and wants and wonders and wonderings and affection and little bursts of pique and even wrath and then regret and forward-thinking and gossip and such. Tree valued it all as being the benefit of being near Univervia – for Univervia had that rare ability to let others into e's core at will – and then to retreat into the core eself so that no one else could come in. And the only plant that Univervia nearly always let in was Tree.

Today Univervia started off about the dirt around e's roots. "I can feel the particles moving around my roots. They like me growing in, around, about and even through them. Dirt lives for grass." Univervia amended, "And trees, of course."

Tree grunted, amused. Univervia kept on unfurling with more talk, "But Tree – have you noticed the ants?" In fact, until that very moment, Tree, focused on all the variety of plants, on the taste of sun and dust, Tree had not actually even seen them. Suddenly Tree saw first one and then another ant and then was astonished to realize that as many blades of grass as there were, there appeared to be individual ants. "True." Univervia interjected, reading Tree's thoughts. "But they belong to a field of ants as big as our field of grass. They move back and forth the little paths between the grass herd. Carrying bits of things. The herd says there's an underground collection of them."

Tree could not keep track of any of the ants for more than an instant because as soon as e focused on one it was gone and distant. Univervia was sympathetic. "Trees think and see and feel more slowly. Try to flutter like a blade of grass. You will see more ants. And will see them moving."

Tree tried to imagine being as light and fragile as a blade of grass but the effort was exhausting and Tree slouched down. But as Tree gave up on watching the racing insects and trying to see them as they sped about their business, and Tree rested eself, Tree became aware of the feeling of the movement of the ants as they zipped about gathering food and making new trails. The effect was like being surprised by a loud noise during a complete sleep: startling, mandating instant focus. Tree exclaimed, "Oh!" Univervia laughed, "Now you know what it is like to be me." That was a nice idea. Tree liked Univervia so feeling like Univervia was inherently pleasant. Tree decided to reverse the gift. Tree wanted to find a way to show Univervia what it felt like to be Tree. Tree thought and thought. The sun crossed the horizon and begin to edge towards the nightly snuggle with the mountains. Still no closer to an idea of how to go about this, Tree thought slowly, comfortable with e's own tree pace.

Univervia interjected, "I wish I could feel inside your roots. All the roots of the grass herd twirl and intertwine. I can feel dozens of my peers at any one time." Tree felt a twinge of jealousy, was that one root contact too little? But plants grow where they do and e guessed that there is nothing any plant ever can have or ever will do about that. So Tree did the Tree-thing and accepted the distance. And sent out an arc of affection through the air. Univervia wiggled in the fading light and Tree felt happy. Univervia was always so easy to interconnect with. A true friend.

A few days later, Tree felt something different as the hot/globe rose. E looked over at Univervia. New growth, came out of the top of several of the broken strands. Tree was as happy as a near-fledgling on the return of a parent bird. From the broken strands, the new growth looked to be about a third as wide as what was left behind, and was in part the same light color as a childish sprout and in part a sandy gold. By evening, an altogether new stem came up from the base of Univervia, a new node sliding up out of the old, tiny as a new grass sprout.

The new versions of the lost blades grew up in tall over the next week, making Univervia a rough-edged waif, even taller and skinnier, with leaves that formed a lacy pattern at the tops. Then the new stem grew up and out, opening up a bit wider, as once all e's blades had been.

As Tree steadily added on e's first new branches, Tree could only stand amazed at this rapid reconstruction, this need to achieve height at speed. For Univervia was on a bigger mission then just the mere idea of returning to former glory as the tallest of the annual grass in the herd (apparently unaware that the California wild rye, purple needlegrass and other perennials had long surpassed everyone else.) Univervia was feeling something that did not translate when e tried to share it with Tree. Univervia was ravenous for something mysterious and near in e's future. It fueled this swift growth. It made Univervia's grass-song wild and plaintive, it made Univervia alternate between picking fights with grass and tree alike and lavishing honeyed attention on anyone and everyone. One evening, Uni said suddenly, "I do not know what I want, but I sure do want it a lot." Tree mulled on that as the stars turned the night forward.

For e's part Tree found Univervia's continuing general moodiness irritating yet fascinating. The next day, Univervia got wistful and said in a moment of somber grey, "Tree. I can't talk. Anymore." And fell silent.

Tree wondered over what caused this retreat.

No amount of witty anecdote, nostalgia or fantasia could elicit a response from Univervia.

Finally after a week of abandonment, Tree launched into Tree-song, that rarest of melodies – slow as mountains fading. Tree-song is nothing like the Scarlatti cadence of grass-song; it is the beauty of the held note, of the heart-stilling silence, the resumption of the same note, the eventual slide into another note. It is slower than *butoh*, as nourishing as the chanting of Tibetan monks and, in this instance, as lonely as the song of a lost whale.

Dant tried to bring levity to the song by inserting an alto fluting of I'm-still-alive euphoria into the tune, but the swift bubbles of grass-sound left only a soft dry mossy patina on the heavy core of the music.

Univervia smiled to hear Tree sing and Tree noticed that at least Univervia had heard e.

Tree kept on after the hot/light set, far into the night until even Tree fell asleep.

The next morning, something frothy and pale was quivering at the top of Univervia's primary stem.

The wind was waving this about and Univervia wore it like a prize: coy and proud. Tree gasped at the implication, "Are you growing seeds?" Univervia, husky, "I am grass. It is time." Transfixed by the sight, Tree forgot to grow, forgot to turn to eat the sunlight for hours at a time that day.

Soon the whole field was awash in such frippery. All Tree wanted to do was to watch the miniscule grass-flowers as monarch butterflies landed and flew about the field, scattering pollen from one stem to the next, hovering over milkweed, bouncing back to grass, carpenter bees tracking labyrinth dances from one scented flower to the other, as the flowers grew bigger and tiny petals fell away and the seeds formed. Univervia made every effort to speak to Tree daily, even hourly, as e remembered when e spoke to Tree in a constant stream of interaction from dawn to dusk.

But the whole flowering thing made Univervia indolent and sleepy, as if building this ripeness took nearly every speck of e's life force, leaving nothing for song, for chatter. Only a languor as heavy as darkness during night-fog.

Other grass also built seeds, but poor Dant was not even half as tall as once e had been.

But Dant asserted bravely, "I am alive. I am grass. Your seeds are my seeds. We are siblings. We are all alive together." And to Tree's surprise, Univervia, who had never really come to care for Dant even after Dant was humbled, agreed. "My seeds are your seeds. We are grass."

And Viciam came out with a shiver of flowers and Univervia, regal as a monarch, approved of the young heir's new crop; the smaller grass' flowers were transitioning into seeds much bigger than those of Univervia. Everywhere the grass was congratulating eself, each other and Tree felt the difference between being grass and being tree more sharply than ever before.

Everywhere grass was marrying itself, each other and Tree was still struggling to sprout a third tiny branch. A separate branch was a huge effort. The idea of seeds was literally something e could not picture how it would be for eself – how they would look, how they would feel. E had no more memory of life as an acorn than a human baby animal has of his or her own conception. And, the whole process of procreation seemed a bit hazy to Tree, though the idea of seeds seemed pretty clearcut: seeds sprout into baby grass, right?

As summer got hotter and the days outweighed the warm nights by hours at a time, Univervia began shedding seeds like a rich boy giving small coins to the poor.

Such unanalyzed generosity! One small and shining seed after another, where they lay glittering dulled silver in the dirt, one after another.

Regally, Univervia cast off another and another in clumps at a time while Tree watched in silent admiration. Univervia was so clearly adult in this moment. Tree could only wiggle e's deepest roots and watch. What would it feel like to create new life from e's own self? Clearly, Univervia felt it was the gravest pleasure in life itself.

Tree missed feeling that e was the biggest event in Univervia's life and Univervia, even in this day of glory, heard Tree's private thought and took notice. Univervia pushed e's roots up against Tree's own root. "Oh Tree, e are my best friend. Enjoy my seeds with me – I would never have been able to create them without your devotion throughout the summer." Tree felt good to the core to hear such a serious compliment, and felt at the same time that it was only true. Tree had been a growing companion to Univervia through their whole life together. Univervia continued, "I hope you love them as much as me for they are me."

Tree assented, "Of course Univervia, of course."

And then the seeds were all scattered and Univervia stood tall in the forewarnings of the Santa Anas as dry winds rustled through the grass herd, encouraging every stem to drop each remaining grain.

The rustle of the grass sounded different than it did before but it took Tree a few days to figure out the difference. With e's own roots deep into the ground still finding memories of moisture to feed e's core, e had not considered how hard and compact the dirt had grown at the surface of the land. How exceedingly warm the hot/light was day after day, how scant the dew. The sky was hot blue, not a cloud in sight. And then Tree realized the whole herd was changing colors in an abrupt few days like a snow bunny molting in the fall. From deep green, to a dull green to grey green to brown. Or to green to olive to tan to gold to blond. The transitions were different but the cause was the same: there was not enough water to feed the herd of grass.

Aghast at the realization that drought was not just about to return but was now in fact here, Tree tried to figure out a way to give some of e's own stored water to Univervia. But though their roots were interlaced, there was no way to suck water from e's core and to put it into Univervia's. E's root could not fuse with Univervia's root to download moisture into the other plant.

And Univervia's change was sudden and shocking. From green to brown to amber to brass and then to the blanched yellow of beach-sand. Tree could hear the strands of Univervia were hollow when the wind whistled through. And the grass herd had fallen silent. No more grass songs. Tree sang to keep the herd company and the herd sent back silent appreciation. Now they all had the patience to listen to such slow songs.

At night Univervia whispered to Tree not caring who heard in the broad silence.

"Tree. Tree."

"Yes?" Tree jumped at the sound, knowing full well that Univervia was conserving energy by silence. "I am not sure if I am still alive, I am so dry." Tree could feel Univervia's roots, slender and fragile as dried corn silk.

Univervia rushed ahead, "I have been green and tall. I have loved the hot/light and the bright rain. I have had the pleasure of growth and have survived becoming deer. I made flowers and I have made many seeds. And I have had one true friend. You. And now I must go. The wind is calling me. Us. The herd. Good-bye Tree."

Tree was too ravaged by this speech to find an answer. From e's core came out huge, torn pieces of love, ripped from eself and thrown out wildly at Univervia and the world at large. Shaking with the extremity of emotion, Tree spoke as awkwardly as a new sprout, "Wait. Stay. Don't leave me." As the chunks of Tree-love came straight at Univervia, e felt them as deep as rain inside. E shivered a bit of affection back at Tree and then Univervia disappeared. In e's place was a strand of dead grass.

All across the field for the next few days, there were similar little shivers as grass after grass left this life. Tree stood immobilized, unable to grow or feel or understand. The silence was awesome and the wind sounded loud in the absence of the herd. At last near Tree, a small voice came out. Dant, having never grown much bigger than the height the deer-bite left e at, had lasted the longest. "Tree. Tree. You have been a good friend."

And then another shiver and that spreading ripple of loss. One less grass in the world.

Completely alone, Tree felt the Santa Anas coming in and did not care. More heat. More wind. More dry. What did e care?

Tree saw the dead grass encircling eself and felt lonelier than e had before e had known anyone but eself and the hot/light. From roots through core to bark and leaves a cry rose up loud enough to be heard all the way to the sea and into the sky, "Univervia!"

And no one answered. Tree sat still in the empty field.

DESOLATION

The wind made a song of its own through the silent field of grass and Tree listened mutely to the rustling absence of grass song. A velvet ant, red and black, looking for something to eat came off the trek beside Tree and crept up Tree's trunk. Once such an exotic experience would have been fodder for much contemplation about the differences between animal and plant, and Tree would have attempted speech with the little zig-zagging being. But grief had immobilized Tree's thought processes. So the tickle on e's trunk barely registered. Finding nothing of note, the ant went over the cleft between Tree's branches and marched down the back-side of the little trunk, moving back onto the ant-trail, looking for portable treats.

Tree started a yearning-song, but e's own voice was painful to hear and Tree was sure no one was there to listen. There was a hungry void in e's core that surpassed thirst, light-craving, warm-wanting, any feeling of need e had known before. And the truth was that only Univervia could fill this emptiness and Tree was tormented by the fragile string around one root representing what was once Univervia's fine and healthy tertiary root, by the sight of a clump of blond straw that had once been Univervia, green as life itself. Like a cast-off piece of snakeskin, the form of the dead grass evoked the memory of the being who once inhabited the empty shape.

Tree discovered that if e turned inwards, e did not see the world outside, which was a nice relief for the colors spoke of drought and sadness. But the sound of the wind in the dry grass came percolating through anyway like a lamentation.

At first Tree tried to speak to Univervia as if Univervia were nearby but as there was no answer that Tree ever heard, Tree eventually started to ask the bright-light to watch over Univervia's spirit and the spirits of all the desiccated herd. Tree wanted to rejoin Univervia or to have Univervia rejoin Tree, and Tree considered a visitation of any kind by Univervia worth any and everything. This solution was not forthcoming. Tree prayed to join Univervia, by death if necessary, but Tree's taproot was too deep for Tree to die – water came to Tree whether Tree wanted it or not.

Gradually Tree's inability to connect to the dead, to connect to the bright-light, to connect to any other being became dominant in a kind of constant blur of pain. So Tree began to pray to feel nothing – not knowing that e had blundered upon the secret of e's own parent's sanity, longevity and inaccessible appeal. But Tree was not capable of feeling nothing, or at least not for more than a few moments at a time…so Tree gradually came to admit that what e really wanted was oblivion. This felt like a firmer commitment to death than the fantasy of rejoining Univervia through dying. Tree stopped turning towards the sun, stopped e's internal push to grow, tried even to stop pulling in more water. Tried to stop participating in life. Through this abeyance, Tree dropped two leaves. Then a dozen. And as the drought deepened, Tree fell into a kind of miserable somnolence. Neither awake nor asleep, never out of pain, but never quite feeling anything either. A few smaller ants tried to speak to e once but Tree heard nothing. Hawks soared on updrafts in the heat, Tree saw nothing.

After a brutal hot day, two human children, Tuhuy and her older brother Helek, came down the hill carrying a large empty basket that had a layer of asphaltum on the outside, each holding one side. Because he was the taller, the basket was tilted at an angle, bouncing as they walked. Without talking they went down to the creek, which was dry in parts, and found a pool of water. Careful not to take in any fish, they half-filled the basket, lugged it up the low bank and over to Tree. They poured it onto the small oak and Tree felt ill. Had they done this a month ago, would it have saved Univervia? The ground was so dry that the water sank in quickly. Tree cringed to feel damp seep into e's roots. E consoled eself: it was only a little water, maybe the drought could still take e from this empty world.

Some of the perennial grass, stoic as trees, ringing the meadow, still here and there in the field, individual islands of brown stems and faded green leaves standing sere amidst the crushed straw of the annuals, felt compassion and tried to reach out to Tree but the younger plant had not connected earlier with California wild rye or purple needlegrass or any of them, and blocked by sadness, could not hear them now.

Days came and went like broken promises and Tree did nothing. The dryness of later summer was nothing compared to the dryness in Tree's core. With each miserable day, Tree felt incrementally closer to the goal of a release from this life.

So absorbed was Tree in this self-centered focus on finding an escape from daily pain that e did even see when the wind succeeded in mashing down the season's dead grass in a permanent slump to the right, interweaving what was once Univervia, so thoroughly with the remnants of e's herd that Tree would never see even a shadow of Univervia's one-time corporeal existence again. All that was left of the grass was crushed straw and desiccated seeds perched upon a parched earth. With one skinny young tree standing above it like a stick stuck into the ground.

SECOND RAIN

When the rains started up again, Tree's first sensation at the pelting of drops on e's leaves was of disappointment. E had not succeeded in disappearing like Univervia. Instead of experiencing rain as gift, sensual pleasure, food from heaven, Tree felt it like being forced. It was invasive, even violent. The world forcing life upon the living. And will e or nil e, e's roots soaked up the wet through the mud and e could feel cells popping anew and e's young trunk building up further towards the sky. Nibs of leaves formed in e's branches. And as nourishment filled Tree, e woke from that half-dormant state of near-neutrality and again Univervia's non-presence cleft e's core like an ax. The song of it burst out from Tree, and trees clear on the other side of the meadow had to hear this big voice from a new tree, for over the course of the drought Tree had doubled in height, moving out of the range of grass, taller than sage, and Tree's long-silent voice had grown to match. Even as every other tree in the meadow celebrated the onset of rain, Tree's tale of love and loss came pouring out, taking them into Tree's private world. The rest of the Trees were silent, in respect. Tree eself did not realize that e's audience had expanded. All Tree knew was that the sky was listening – and from the sky Tree heard that this grief was as old as life itself and that it had to be endured – and yet sky offered a cool sympathy that felt better than the rain itself. Finally Tree felt a morsel of comfort. Tree sang all through the night, through driving rain and fell into exhausted silence the next day, taking on the rain as if it were a continuation of e's own emotion. Halfway through that second night of rain, e fell into the first real sleep e had had since Univervia died. When Tree woke up the rain had turned into a drizzle with patches of sunlight. To e's distress surcingled with pleasure, the ground around e was suddenly dotted with bits of emerald.

E knew: this was the next year's new grass. A new herd. Tiny voices popped up from the mud and underneath the drenched straw, each saying variants on sentences Tree could still remember from last year, "I am grass! I am here! My name is…Grass!"

To answer any of the little queries sparking in the air around Tree felt like it would be forgetting Univervia, like trying to replace e with a new blade of grass. So Tree said nothing. Not one word. Even when one scrawny blade nearby identified eself as "Aristida!" and asked Tree for Tree's name. The grass was insistent, certain that Tree could hear, and finally gave up, hurt, that a bigger plant would ignore e.

The quality of the little grass' upset was so similar to the moods of Univervia that it gouged at Tree like root-rot, a persistent aching kind of thing.

Tree retreated to an interior place and ignored the new sprouts. And when the hot/light moved to the edge of the mountains and dropped off, the little sprouts shrieked.

Truly, Tree wanted to tell them it would be all right. But Tree knew without a doubt that the whole herd would be gone in a year. And the idea of befriending these sweet little plants and then watching them grow and die was unbearable. So Tree let the whole herd whimper and talk to itself all night, trying not to feel any empathetic joy as the whole herd rejoiced as the hot/globe came up over the opposing side of mountains. The little green dots' little sparkles of pleasure were impossible to ignore though, and Tree could not decide if the little bits of grass-happiness bombarding e's trunk felt good or bad. Stuck between two emotions, e wavered when suddenly a tremendously slow and stately voice spoke from nearby.

Taking nearly the morning to get through a few sentences, the voice unrolled its being's message, "I-----a-m-----s-t--o---n---e. S----o----o-o-----o-----m---u-c-h------o--l-d---e---r-----t-h-a-n---l--i-t-t-l-e---y---o-u.--R--o-c---k---i---s---n---e---a----r----e-t---e---r-n-a--l.--F---r--o---m--d---i---s---t--a---n---t-----m--o-u--n---t---a--i--n--s---r----i--v--e---r----w---a-t-----e---r----b---r-o-u--g-h-t-----m--e."

"Oh." Said Tree, startled to hear a new voice, a new style of speech. A non-plant-being. "I did not realize you were alive." Tree said tactlessly, adding on respectfully, "Oh, Old Rock."

Rock's voice rumbled with humor. "A---l---l------t---h---i--n---g----s-----a---r---e-----a--l--i-v---e.----F--e---w----k-n--o--w.----N--o-t---h-i--n---g-----l---a---s---t--s----f--o-r-e-v-e-r.----L--o--v-e----w---h--a---t-----y--o-u---h---a-v---e----w--h--i-l--e---y---o---u---h---a--v-e-----i---t."

Tree was startled to find images in e's core that were not visible in the world around e. Enormous lizard-type creatures. A fern as tall as Tree. The green of the fern was portrayed with such vibrancy, such care, that Rock's feelings for the long-dead fern came through like heat from a true kiss. Tree froze with surprise – Rock's memory felt just like Tree eself felt about Univervia. And it was clear the Fern was long, long dead. But the love felt as new as sunrise. Tree tried to understand how such a thing could be.

Tree tried to ask Rock, but Rock was now as silent and as impenetrable as e had been for the entire year of Tree's life up to this point. A brief burst of imagery came at Tree as an afterthought and Tree was overwhelmed by the amount of time Rock was trying to summarize: enormous snails, lizard-monsters, little flowers, bigger flowers, sabertooth tigers, and grass. And Univervia. And Tree. And then the rest of the day came back at Tree loud and clear and as usual as every other day of e's life.

For the next few days Tree tried talking to Rock, then e tried talking at Rock out of sheer loneliness. Tree also listened to the point of practically flattening e's leaves with the strain of trying to hear some whisper of Rock but there was nothing. Tree surmised, correctly, that for a being as ancient as Rock, speech came only every hundred years or so if that. Curious about this idea that everything was alive, Tree tried talking and listening to the earth, to the worms snaking around underground and to the air itself. Tree could feel an affectionate warmth coming up from the whole of the earth, a constant steady embrace available if Tree was quiet enough but e was having trouble connecting with much of anything past that. Diaphanous white clouds slid across the sky and thickened into puffy mounds and heaps of silvery-grey and white drifting through the blue, placing seductive thoughts of rain into the middle of the hot day, but the clouds did not appear to hear Tree in the least. In the midst of this feverish listening and talking Tree had forgotten to be sad and had forgotten to think about tree and grass and it was at this point that a clear voice, sounding like little bells came from across the way.

"I am Elderberry. Sweet as berries, young as grass. I am Elderberry. Are you you?"

Startled Tree asserted, "I am Tree. My name is Tree."

Across the way Elderberry heard the smaller voice, "Ah. You are Tree. Your name is Tree." A pause. "Are you sure? You are awfully small for a tree. Especially a California live oak!"

Tree was offended but determined not to turn a potential friendship awry. "I am...young."

Elderberry answered with a smile in e's voice. "I know. I was teasing. You will be much bigger than me some day."

A third voice came into the equation, sounding like a tenor and bass gamelan. Transfixed by the beauty of these tones, Tree could not even understand the words. Torrents of sound came at e, healing as the caress of a young mother. Tree drank it all in, unable to move in the hypnotic welter of noise. At last a particularly lucid note transformed into words and the California black walnut spoke to Tree, "Tree! Little big Tree! Ah. At last I see you understand me. I have heard your song. We have all heard your song."

"At first we thought your love for a grass was silly. Trivial to love such a little being. But then we saw that your love was not little and that it was we who were silly and trivial to think that only trees mattered. We have shared your grief now for months but you could not hear us. We are many but most likely it will take years before you can hear all the trees in this meadow. For now we two are here for you."

And the Elderberry spoke on top of the California black walnut and together they sent back an intermingled song of condolences, of the reflections of the bright green they saw in Tree's memories and Univervia lived as if in the shared pages of a book that the three were reading together and Tree was so overwhelmed that others cared about eself, about e's love for a dead piece of grass, about Univervia eself that wrenching cries came out of Tree without any ability of Tree to control it, but the sounds wove into the music of gamelan and anklets, making it something more beautiful than before and when the song meandered off into silence Tree's core was full. Full of something new, not the same as what e had shared with Univervia, but something good. And this new feeling did not replace or supplant the old feeling, it was just new life inside Tree. And Tree decided that while e was alive, e should experience every feeling, every idea, every possibility to the largest degree conceivable, so that this mysterious thing, living, sentience, should not be wasted. It was what Univervia had done. And to move forward engaging in all possible ways with the known universe was to celebrate the life of Univervia and the life of Tree.

Tree sent out a passionate ping of love into unknown realms. Somewhere some shadow of Univervia felt this ping and knew that the love of this life on earth had been a true thing. And then this sliver of glimmering spirit went to a place where our ideas cannot and Tree knew this time that it must be so. Tree stayed rooted to e's dirt and felt a piece of e's core expand and go and e let it go. Along with the grief, the love, the memory.

SECOND YEAR

It was going to be a wet year, which meant that the next months had as many rainy days as sunny. Twice the creek flooded. Lacking a best friend, Tree was not as chatty as e had been the summer before. But having persisted through grief, e had changed anyway. The urge to connect and communicate was dampened. The only thing that seemed to matter now was to grow large and strong, to take up the amount of space e was destined to be granted. To focus on living. This time, Tree made no effort to dictate root growth or turn leaves towards sun, e was big enough that it was no longer necessary. E took on every day as an opportunity to do better, to get bigger and stronger. From across the field, Elderberry and Black Walnut watched as Tree doubled again in height, as branches layered outwards, and, when the rains stopped, admired, as the slender trunk begin to fill outwards. Tree's increased girth grew to width of a sunflower and started to move towards approaching the diameter of a big gopher snake, and e's silence added to the sense of tree-like gravitas that others might get from being near e. In Topanga, an acorn can go from sprout to the height of a man between the downpour of two rainy seasons.

When the rain finally stopped for the year, the grass was twice as lush as the season before. All the creatures in the woods had extra young and the snake population doubled from the quantities of tiny rodents available. Tree found the feel of a rattlesnake slithering past the dirt and over e's prominent roots evocative of the feeling e had when Univervia's own root had laced around Tree's own root. The snake was gone in the time it took the thought to form and pass. Deer grazed nearby but had no interest in Tree's prickly leaves given the wealth of young green food all around. Tree was somewhat oblivious to the intertwined agonies and pleasures that this gave the grass. Every doe had a fawn and every fawn played in the hot/light as if this was the first day of life for all things. Older deer watched tolerantly the gambols of the young and mountain lions plotted how to consume the playfulness so as to feed it second-hand to their own nursing young.

Through all this, Tree focused purely on being, not on talking, learning or interlacing with other beings, and through this state of neutrality, e came closer to Rock's approach to existence. Sometimes their non-thoughts merged and strange things floated through this emptiness like big fish in a still lake. Later on, Tree would try to understand these amorphous visions, but for now e observed. From this state of detachment, Tree would sometimes hear the clear ring and echoing clatter from Elderberry and Black Walnut as they engaged in conversation with e-other and other trees.

One day a human boy came by, Helek, with arrows cached in a quiver, made from the dried, hollow flowering stalk of a yucca plant, on his back and Tree noted that the arrows were made up of dead mulefat stems lashed by deer sinew to pointy rocks of monterey chert. Idly e wondered if the rocks and branches had been friends first or become such now. Other human children followed him, intensely silent and watchful. Helek hissed back at the children in a whisper, "*Kniy!*" All eyes darted to the field, where a fox hunched down in the grass, trying to disappear from view.

When Helek nocked an arrow and took down the fox with the stone/deer sinew/mulefat stem, the idea that e's own kind could be involved in a carnivorous act left Tree chilled. E had certainly watched much killing and eating and defecating going on all around e for the last year, but these acts had been something that other beings did. Helek ran off in glee to grab the fox and his friends caressed the dead animal, admiring the pretty pelt and the clean shot. Tuhuy grabbed at the fox and, Helek, older than she, let her have it, to the envy of the rest of their friends. But she was his baby sister, so the fox was not a prize anyone else would win. She carried it carefully and they all went running across the field and up the path on the hillside to show off this catch to their parents and the other adults in their near-distant village.

Tree replayed the scene in e's core and concluded that the stem had been dead, long separated from e's own tree. The dry stem held no responsibility for the act. And then, Tree rationalized, even for the human child, there could be no real guilt when it came to taking the life of a fox, for foxes kill to eat so there's no shame in killing a fox for the human boy and the littler furry/scaly things that foxes eat, eat grass and seeds and nuts and berries. Tree ate light, but who is to say what it feels like for light to be eaten? Tree wondered if light was sentient and if so, how could e communicate with it? Was using it as food a kind of communication itself?

Tree replayed the scene a third time, somehow fascinated by the whole thing and finally the biggest secret in the moment was revealed to e: the child had whispered "*kniy*." And then all the children all looked out to see the animal crouching in the grass. So – "*kniy*" meant "fox" to the human children. "*Kniy*" was a sound that represented a creature. These word-sounds were how human beings communicated. Tree reflected over the many years of human voices echoing through e's valley, soft, loud, adult, child, solo, together and imagined that all those sounds had *meant* something.

This idea left Tree quiet for several days. Without a new wave of sorrow, Tree thought to eself that Univervia with e's speed and sparkle would have begun to acquire more word-sounds each time the human group passed by. But Tree eself found it difficult to follow their movements, nearly impossible to understand their darting feelings and the word-sounds came with such speed and rapidity, e figured e might never learn more than the word for fox itself.

Frustrated, Tree reminded eself that e had other friends with whom to occupy eself. E could try to speak back and forth with Elderberry and Black Walnut. Some day e expected that Rock would speak again. Why would e want to befriend something so alien, so other as a human? They were impossibly different. But then Tree remembered that Trees live for so many years…if e only learned a few words every season, surely in a 100 years e would understand big chunks of what they said.

E replayed the scene a fourth time and recalled the image of the children, boy clutching his dead fox, running across the field. E wondered how it would feel to run. Or for that matter to fly. To swim. These were dizzying concepts and elicited anxious feelings after even a little thought.

Movement itself looked seductive, but the idea of actually leaving e's home gave Tree a sick and hollow feeling. For Tree had fallen in love with e's place. E's dirt and rock and the creek down the way and the mountains that surrounded eself. There could be no more perfect place in all the world. In all the universe. The center was here and Tree would never, could never leave such a spot.

Content to have named this truth, Tree fell asleep before the hot/light sank. At home.

RENAISSANCE

All around Tree the grass chitter-chattered. Sometimes a voice would be directed at e, purely out of curiosity.

Though Tree was following the sun and hoping to befriend other trees, e left the grass alone with the same regal indifference that the other trees and Rock had treated Tree eself as a sprout. To love ephemeral beings is just too challenging, Tree thought to eself.

That instantly identifiable rumbly voice came creaking out of Rock again. E---v--e--r---y---t-h--i-n-g-----i--s----e--p-h—e-m-m-m-m-e-r---a--l.---E--v--e---n-----t--h---e-----h---o--t--l-i-g-h-t----w---i-l---l---p-e--r---i-s--h.----L----o--v-e----f----e--e-d--s----.

The voice broke off in mid-sentence, as if it took far too much energy to speak.

A tiny voice came out of the new field of grass, half way across. "What was that?" said a new grass, fascinated. And Tree considered that from Rock's perspective, e was shorter-lived than Univervia. Yet Rock had been kind to e.

So, e would be kind to grass. Not friends, but kind.

"Rock." "Rock?" said the little teal love grass in tones of complete disbelief. Tree found eself mimicking Rock's terse style of speech. "All things are alive." The little grass was too young to see much past eself, yet, and clung to the known.

"I'm alive! I'm alive!" said the new grass. "I can see that –" said Tree gently.

Tree retreated from the conversation of the herd, but felt better for having acknowledged them. Who was to say whose life had more or less value? Perhaps grass, raising generation after generation of eself, is the backbone of life as we know it. A few trees more or less, a rock large or small, carry their own weight in the world. But each blade of grass is part of an incomprehensibly enormous community that creates oxygen for animals, food for animals, loosens and binds dirt, houses insects, flowers and in short creates the texture of living on the earthen skin of this world. Suddenly the idea that some of this herd were the children of Univervia struck Tree and Tree said nothing for a week. It was a sufficiently big thought.

From across the way, California Black Walnut's bell-strewn voice created a welcome intrusion into Tree's solitude. "Think less, grow more – " advised the older tree. "I grew four branches my second year."

Elderberry chimed in, "I grew seven."

California Black Walnut talked on top of Elderberry, "Yes, Elderberry, but you're somewhere between a bush and tree so of course you grow quickly in the beginning. Big trees take time."

Elderberry kept on blithely, "I bet you can't even grow five."

California Black Walnut was firm, "You must work on this and nothing else. You will not be sure to survive until you are thick as two rattlesnakes and too tall for a deer to eat your leaves all up in a dry year."

Overwhelmed with the idea of such hugeness, Tree shrank into e's core.

Elderberry spoke up, "Don't let Walnut scare you. You are strong already. But you must grow with passion now if you are to survive a drought year."

Tree spoke up proudly, "I have survived two droughts already. Once when I was a sprout and once again, well you know, when the herd died."

Both Elderberry and Walnut laughed. Elderberry explained, "Droughts can go on for years. You just don't know." Walnut pushed the point, "Grow. And grow more. It will rain tonight. Use it."

And it did. And Tree pushed every cell to suck in the water and by the end of the year, had four new branches added to the trio of the year before. E was as tall as the head of a deer.

UP

When the Santa Anas came roiling around and the second round of Topanga summer hit in October, Tree braced eself for the wrenching departure of this herd of grass. Standing the height of a nearly grown man above the shimmery blond grass, however, had the effect of helping Tree distance eself from the dissolution of life after tiny life. From this height, e could see the grace and symmetry to the disappearance of lives well lived. E could also see the fallen treasure of grass seeds, some being wrestled with by packs of ants, others eaten en masse by dusky-footed woodrats, squirrels and bunnies, but many left waiting for someone to lay greedy claim to the past. The seeds helped e listen to the whisper sounds of wind in dead grass.

And…the other voices e had come to rely upon, Elderberry, Black Walnut, the alternate language of the tribes of sage, chamise and manzanita, the bolder grass that persisted like cattail and deerweed, these helped. And when violently hot days inverted into cold nights, e's mass protected e from last year's fear that e's sap would freeze.

Sometimes at night, e would whisper the name "Univervia," quietly enough that none of the other trees would hear e and the word left a sweetness in the air. As Tree matured, this memory was becoming a source of nourishment rather than remaining an open wound. Univervia lived on through Tree's core.

This third year there was dry cold and the winter grasses did not come up in December, January or even February. Tree was starting to wonder if this lengthy absence of rain was what Black Walnut and Elderberry had meant when they had spoken of "drought" but one night, e was awakened by the familiar speckles of cold rain upon e's leaves. All across the woodland e could hear the plants sighing in relief. With five main branches splitting off from e's trunk, and several dozen secondary branches, all well-leafed, the rain impacted Tree in so many places that e could not easily differentiate an individual drop as e had when e was very young. Now it was more of the effect of a shower than a one-on-one thing. Water's ability to be solitary and part of a mass and back again in moments of time intrigued Tree. Was water a unified entity or merely millions of happily integrated miniscule spots?

After a few days of drizzle spotted with actual rain, dots of green came up in the damp ground and Tree observed carefully that what had once seemed to e a mass of grass was a welter of species as different as e was from Elderberry or Black Walnut. E started to pay attention to the minutia, to the differing languages, to the disparate shapes and e noticed that coming up within the pack of grass, were individual flowering plants. E had been so busy with loving – or ignoring – or coming to terms with the species of grass that e had overlooked these little wildflowers. One with an intriguing rootmass like an anorexic onion, popped up between two of e's primary roots, creating a ticklish sensation that would be an intermittent distraction for months. This little creature popped out with language a few days after sprouting, "I am a blue dick –" announced the future flower, self-aware as any good plant on earth. Then, shamelessly, the sprout turned to Tree, "What is blue?"

Tree reached a thought down into the little sprout, a picture of sky in all e's permutations and, stunned by the vast imagery, the little nascent flower asked Tree, "I will turn into blue?" with a picture of pure sky attached. Tree tried to explain that e was referencing the color, not the thing, but it was too much for the little green plant to process so early on and the sprout returned to obsessively stretching the little roots growing off e's bulb down into the ground. Tree left e alone for a few weeks.

Across the way Elderberry exclaimed, "Hello/how are you/am fine/missed you lots!" in a burst and Tree responded more leisurely, "You surely did grow quiet between rains."

"Was afraid –" came Elderberry's immediate response. Tree was surprised as e had not been afraid even when e thought it was a drought. But Elderberry flashed the feeling of e's own roots out at Tree and Tree realized e reached, already, to a greater depth below the surface of the earth than did Elderberry's roots. They were different beings. "Hear the willows?" Elderberry asked and Tree conceded e had heard little but, as the arroyo willow and narrowleaf willow responded to the renaissance of the creek with hundreds of the cutest little leaves and new grey-green bark and all sorts of self-referential whispering. Tree laughed, "I don't think they talk to oaks. Or elderberry."

"No," Elderberry answered, "they are a world to themselves."

"I have been feeling rather self-referential myself." Tree said with some chagrin. Elderberry laughed with a sound like water hitting slick rock, thin and tinny. It made Tree laugh back. "We all feel that way sometimes," Elderberry responded, "it seems to be part of growing up. And later, it will be part of making berries. Or acorns, I guess in, your case."

"Up," responded Tree thoughtfully.

NUTS

When Tree woke up, e noticed the herd of grass beneath e was acting silly and moody and wild and Tree knew from past years that this meant that seeding was right around the corner.

From across the field came the feisty banter of Elderberry and Tree wondered if Elderberry was also about to go to flower. Black Walnut was also full of this amorous energy and Tree broke e's long silence.

"Black Walnut. Black Walnut, how are you?"

A sigh came sliding across the field. "Fine, I guess. Actually, wonderfully, excessively fine. But I am hoping the bees come out today."

Elderberry spoke up. "We all need the bees to help our flowers come to fruit, but it is much harder for Black Walnut. E has partner trees and without the pollen from the flowers of the ones dusting the flowers of the other, there will be no nuts."

Completely unclear on what Elderberry had just said, Tree answered, "Oh, of course. Like Univervia?"

Irritated, Black Walnut spoke up. "Not like Univervia. Like me. Like my own self. But different. And neither of us can make more trees unless we intermingle each with the other. And I yearn for e and e yearns for me but without the bees…" Black Walnut did not finish. E broke into a song of blue dreamy melancholy. From further up the hillside several other sorrow infused voices spoke up, syrupy and melodic through the haze of glum.

Tree said, "I hear…other black walnuts? Missing you while you miss them?"

Elderberry whispered, "Oh yes. They will sing like this for weeks until they all go into flower and cross-pollinate,"

Tree asked, "You don't sing sad songs?"

Elderberry's smile was audible. E spoke quietly. "I can feel my buds forming. Flowers are coming. And I have no doubt that I will be pollinated or self-pollinate or that my fruit will form. I am meant to be what I am. Being alive is just a treat."

Tree mumbled, "I just don't feel that way. On good days I do, but other days, it seems there is so much sorrow, or I am so alone, or that I have no purpose or that I am miserable, that I lose track of how to enjoy life." Elderberry was kind, "I am a naturally happy tree. You are prone to melancholy, but it goes with having a long life and with intelligence. I envy you your intelligence, but then it comes with a propensity for sadness, so I'd rather be exuberant, short-lived and less than brilliant and be me. But that's not much help to you.

What I'm really trying to say is…you will understand my feelings, Black Walnut's feelings, when you have acorns.

But you're still growing. You won't have acorns for three or four more years. So you just have to enjoy what you do have. Me. Black Walnut. The children of your Univervia, even if you don't speak to them. Rock. Hot/light. Your spot of dirt."

And Elderberry broke into song and retreated into e's own world of pre-blooming and sun-eating, unable to see past the tips of e's own leaves.

Something had broken open in Tree and new voices were popping in all across the valley, Husky chanting coming in a chorus from the scattered pack of white sage, black sage, purple sage. The dusty muted sharpness of their parallel scents came across loud and clear with little teeny pricks of sweetness from the honey-scented tiny violet flowers some of them were already sporting. Hot powdered sandstone cowboy sage floating clouds of cowboy perfume. The raspy laughter of cattails thinking about forming fuzzy batons filled with a veritable megalopolis of seeds. Frogs calling out. Crickets. The vain little moans of willows growing near the creek. A hawk keening for a mate to return home. And a sound that made e's sap stop for a moment – a low voice – from a distant hillside on the west not visible by sight. A California live oak coming into flower. And with all the frantic pre-procreation growing on around, Tree simply laced e's roots in lower and deeper into the hard earth and reached e's branches up higher and filled out e's trunk, looking to dominate e's own attention with growth.

Again, e retreated into some space of silence inside where only quiet reigned.

Within this stillness e stayed for a day and a night and then days and nights and weeks. The hot/light poured heat into each day and the flowers came and exploded and beauty overtook the world but Tree was oblivious. And bees and beetles and hummingbirds enjoyed pollen and shared the gold that had been given them with the plants which were giving it and things went to seed and Tree was startled back into participating in the shared world by the luxurious bass tones of Black Walnut and Black Walnut's kin.

Black Walnut spoke, "You are acting more and more oak-like. These long retreats into oblivion. Elderberry misses you when you go!"

Tree was surprised that Elderberry had noticed. "You all seemed so busy with flowers."

Black Walnut's voice rumbled in amusement. "Oh we've all moved on since then. Elderberry has berries, red as cottontail blood, hundreds of them. And I have walnuts. Hundreds and hundreds. I have more trees on me than the field has strands of grass."

"But if you grow so many trees, and then they grow trees, how will there be room for grass or all the creatures or us even? That's overwhelming. And wonderful and beautiful, of course."

Elderberry spoke as birds picked off e's ripe berries. "The nuts and berries are not just for us. Not just for tree-childrening. Creatures eat them. And we must give them up. Gifts."

Black Walnut spoke at the same time, "Can you see the squirrels which live in my trunk? They eat my walnuts. They pick them and hide them in me, in the ground, all around. I will be lucky if one tree sprouts and lives from me this year."

Elderberry, "And I as well."

Black Walnut continued, "But the creatures love us. After they have eaten us, you see…they are us. Mobile trees."

Tree found this too much to fathom, but Elderberry laughed a small little laugh sounding very young.

Tree turned inwards and was growing lost in eself again when a big slow voice came up.

"M---e----a-g-a-i-n-.---Q--u---i--t--a-c-t-i-n-g----l---i---k- --e-----w-h-a-t---y-o-u-u-u-u—u-u-----t-h-i-n-k——--i-s-----a--- --r--o---c-k.---O--n--e----l---i--f---e----.---L---i--s--t--e---n-- ,---f--e-----e---l."

Rock sent a fragment of feeling recalling the day that e's friend Fern had died and Tree pulled back from the communication like a human toddler who has stepped on a bee. The silent shriek Tree was trying to hide from e's tree-friends was interrupted by Rock who somehow wedged into Tree's core and plucked out the pain like a stinger from a red hillock of stung flesh. "Y---o---u------m---u----s---t---g---i---v---e---l---o---v----e------t---o-----g---e----t-----l---o----v---e." And suddenly Tree could see a flash of a tiny Fern frond uncurling and the delicate little tendrils of love shooting all around that charmed everyone near Fern, including one stolid, uncommunicative Rock. Tree could feel Rock retreating again, exhausted with the effort of speaking quickly enough for a Tree to understand.

Tree decided that Fern and Univervia were the same – beings capable of spewing affection without regard for the outcome, creating little pockets of happiness wherever they came to grow. Rock and Tree had loved these pretty little beings back, but had not yet learned how to give with no expectations, to just release internal goodness out into the wild for the simple joy of sharing. Rock's approach to Tree had been out of compassion and empathy. But Tree determined to be like Univervia. To just...

Hours passed while Tree sat in emotional paralysis. A butterfly fluttered by and Tree tried this new trick out on a mobile being – a safer creature than a plant because after all, mobile beings move on. Any act one might try on another plant had the potential to create an indefinitely ongoing and evolving relationship. With another plant one had to be sure. With a butterfly, well, Tree was not even sure the butterfly would hear e. Tree released a small puff of admiring affection at the butterfly. Momentarily startled, the creature backed from Tree, looked up and down the oak, and then flew on, apparently unfazed. Had the butterfly heard? Tree had no idea. But...Tree had been brave and daring and Univervia-esque. E hoped that Rock had shared the experience.

The next morning Helek, Tuhuy and their friends came down to the meadow with their mothers, all of them with woven baskets in their arms or strapped to their backs via a leather tumpline that went over their forehead.

Laughing and singing rowdy songs, a few dads brought up the rear. All of them scattered up into the low-lying hills and some of the children and their fathers shimmied up the California black walnuts and threw the nuts down to their mothers and siblings, while the others reached the low-lying nuts and picked them and put them in baskets. A few grandmothers went to work cracking nuts and the others would sometimes take a break and scamper over to her to eat handfuls of buttery young walnuts. And each black walnut in dulcet tones gave off that same powdery emotion of love-with-no-purpose that Tree had tried to download upon the butterfly. Tree noted that each of the black walnuts was almost but not completely denuded; some few nuts remained. E deduced that this was intentional on the part of the human beings. Perhaps this was for the purpose of feeding the squirrels or out of some kind of kindness to the trees themselves, but still the rapid removal in a mere morning of nearly all the walnuts from all the trees in the valley and hills left Tree trembling.

That afternoon, baskets heavy, the whole group of humans left. And the walnuts broke into the loudest interlaced song that Tree had ever heard them sing, of a unity.

And Tree was humbled, perplexed and moved. Out of the fullness of e's core, Tree finally spoke to the field of grass, a full yard below him, telling the grass how beautiful they all were, how green, how gorgeous their seeds were, how much e had loved their parents. The field shimmered in the praise of the oak, preening and waving their seeds and Tree felt that the life of grass was so swift and charming that e could not bear it, and the warmth of the field of grass was like and unlike Univervia in equal parts, making for a bittersweet ending to a long day.

RUSH

Sxa'min was one of the older humans that Tree had noted walking in and out of e's valley; today she came through on her own. She sounded cheerful, singing. She went down to the creek and caressed the cattails on her way as if they were old friends and went straight to the rush, which stood slightly taller than she, healthy and vibrant green. She talked to the rushes quietly and Tree strained to hear and then watched as she cut them, near the base and took armfuls and lay them next to her in orderly heaps. Tree could feel that sense of luscious acquiescence that e remembered from seeing grass in the meadow eaten by deer. The rush gave in to the process and the low remnants of the plants remaining rooted in the cool creekside mud began an intensely concentrated effort to regrow. She had brought string made from Indian hemp and tied up bundles as large as she could carry, which she picked up and carried easily back through the meadow up towards the hill.

Earlier, Tree had already surmised that the things that people picked up and down to make them able to carry more than any other animal were pieces of rush stems. Was this cutting and taking away a part of that? As Tree saw Sxa'min meandering up and away, e had a sense that e was missing some part of this. Or not missing it. How did the rush become the carrying? It was not eating. It was… it was…

Tree abandoned the thought and sent good growth thoughts to the rush on the stream bank. Their ground was wet. They would grow. Grass would thrive. Still. If the humans did not eat the grass, why cut the grass? The thought sat in e's core like an insect gnawing into new bark: an irritant that must be accepted.

UP AND UP

Despite the ideas, memories and emotions braided into e's core, up was still the central word which had been driving e through the last two years of e's life, and which appeared to be dominant again this year. It was as if e craved to stick e's branches into clouds and until e's leaves were caught up in the fluff of white fog floating in sky, nothing else would do. Tree wondered how tall a Tree could be? How tall could a coastal live oak get and most specifically of all – how far would e get to go up?

This year, Tree resolved, e would chitchat with any plant – or rock – willing to be social. But e determined e's primary goal would be to grow upward. E began with obsessive intent, soaking up water, eating light, moving roots and core, branches and leave in this one direction. But then an interesting thing happened after e noticed the grass about to seed, halfway as tall as it was going to grow.

Flowers.

Now some flowers had been in the field each year of Tree's life so far, but Tree had been too caught up in everything else to notice. Tree had no way of anticipating that this was going to be one of those insanely bright years for wildflowers. The first violent bursts of violet from the arroyo lupine blooms left e speechless.

And the crowd of tall bluey-purple flowers noted that they had had an impact on Tree. Finding e's attention flattering, they determined to seduce e once and for all with their voices combined in mass and from them burst a joy to the world ode. Tree's branches unfurled in the wealth of sound, leaves popping open with the glee. "We are here –" sang the flowers in harmony.

"I see." responded Tree. Noticing the carefully ordered deluge of sound, Blue Dick let e's own bud open, sprinkling a soft light blue into the sunlight. "Oh," said Tree. "You are blue." And then the California poppies burst out with orange-coated sugar and the red of the Indian paintbrush, the soft faded orange of the sticky monkey flower, the pale pinks of Catalina poppy, the wan pink of rock rose, the blush of the wild rose, tall and skinny cliff aster, little dots of daisies in white, the double-edged intoxicating and even fatal charm of datura, the bright of many tongued canyon sunflowers in yellow with dark eyes snapping, the nodding complexity of Chinese pagodas, all of them competing for a slice of Tree's devotion.

"Stop!" cried Tree. "I see you all! You are all wonderful! I cannot do this all at once!"

"But you must!" shouted the California poppies. "We are here for such a short time! And we are all so beautiful – " added the lupine "and beauty for naught is worse than not having lived at all."

"We must be loved – " cried out the flowers with one voice. The grass had been sedate compared to this cacophony of color, the brightness only underlining the passion and feeling in the field. Tree shrank before the onslaught. To e's gratitude, voices came from down by the creek. "Pipe down – " said a willow. "We are all wonderful and brief and deserve and require attention. But no one can enjoy interactions that become assaultive."

"Yeah – " agreed the oboe-y voice of a cattail.

"We are not assaultive," said one arroyo lupine in a tone of elegant offense, each stellar flower retreating to e's cool green core.

"We do not need you," said California poppy sulkily.

"We adore e-each other," asserted the sunflowers.

"Don't go away – " said Tree. "Just…speak to me softly."

One arroyo lupine voice popped up from the rest, a shadowy whisper that found its way to Tree's core while the rest of the disparate flower voices crashed and interlaced like waves coming in at cross purposes to a common shore, alternately painful and enticing. This voice was as soothing as a dusting of pollen to a solitary flower. "Tree," said the secretive little voice.

"Yes?" answered Tree quietly.

"We are all going to seed. It makes us crazed."

"Mmm," answered Tree.

Lupine asked so quietly that Tree could barely hear. "Tree. Tree, what is it like to live for so very many years? I will only live for two seasons. What does longevity feel like?"

"Easy question, flower. I have only been alive for three years. So I don't know."

"But you have the expectation of such a future. What does that feel like?"

Tree tried on the question. For quite a while. "I don't know," Tree finally answered. "I only know that it is beautiful and sad to see so many pretty lives come and go. Rock tells me that we all will come and go, rock included. If it helps, I will remember you."

Lupine laughed. "You do not need to remember me. No one has ever lived as much, thought as much, felt as much as I. I have put more into my six weeks than any creature alive can imagine. When I go, I will go with no regrets. My seeds will be the beginnings of flowers even more beautiful than I. Who could want anything more?"

Tree grunted agreement. What could e say after such an outburst?

Lupine continued, "Have you had seeds?"

Tree's silence answered the question.

Lupine answered kindly, "Oh. I see. But your day will come."

"Let's talk about something else." Tree suggested. E was tired of mortality, tired of seeds. E wanted to explore the universe, not to obsess over progeny that might never come. "Have you ever spoken to animals of any kind?

Lupine thought about it. "Very difficult to describe," Lupine finally answered.

Tree assented. "Once I tried to communicate to a butterfly. But it flew away."

Lupine shivered. "Imagine leaving one's patch of dirt. How awful!"

Tree agreed. "I thought I understood a human once. And another time, I believe a large human stopped a small human from stepping on me."

Lupine projected a horrifying image of a human as tall as a cliff coming to step on Tree and Tree rumbled a laugh. "No, no. I was a sprout back then. Shorter than you."

"Oh." There was a pause in the conversation while the afternoon went by. As the hot/light was sinking, the whispery voice of Lupine entered Tree's thoughts again.

"A human picked my first flower." The feeling of being separated from eself, of being in a human fist, of being passed into another human fist, the gaping wet tear in the stem remaining behind all came exact as sensation into Tree.

"Goodness!" Tree blurted out.

"Actually, I think that was sort of the idea," Lupine ruminated. "I believe that one human was communicating an emotion we would call love by using me to express the feeling the human could not emote in a lucid way. My flower became the human's plant-thought. When the other person took my flower, it was as if e took a piece of the other human with e. I could feel the second human's happiness far more clearly than the first."

"Then what happened?" Tree asked.

"They walked away. With my flower. And I lost track of e's experience because the flower was separated from me. But it was interesting. To them, my flower is the meaning of friendship, with no strings attached."

"What do your flowers mean to you?" Tree said foolishly. The answer came in a blur of emotion and language and sound and color which left Tree utterly unable to communicate for several days. By the time the sugary communication-coma had cleared, Lupine's largest flower had gone to seed and was waving softly in the wind, Lupine looking very proud and graceful. Even more softly came that whispery voice, "Am I not perfect, Tree?"

Tree laughed. "Too perfect for me, friend. You must speak to me more softly or I will burst apart into little pieces of Tree, flung across the valley like the volcanoes that Rock once showed me."

Recognizing that Lupine did not understand the concept of volcano, Tree demonstrated the vision that Rock had once given e, of rock as liquid-volatile as the creek in winter, rock so anxious to be free of earth that it would run up the center of a mountain, leap out into the sky in bursts of fire and come drooling down the sides of hills, chilling into black rock along the path. Such a vision made Lupine cringe and Tree quickly comforted Lupine, "Such a thing is rare and we shall never see it. Nor our sprouts nor their sprout's sprouts." Lupine sighed in relief. Lupine sent an image of e's seed pods popping and the little seeds rolling about to find each a niche in the dust and then fell asleep as abruptly as an infant tired of crawling, leaving Tree by eself, talking to no one.

Rock piped up, taking all night to share a mere sentence and two fragments. "G--o--o----d----v--o-l-c-a-n---o-. ----S--h----o---u--l---d---h---a--v---e----w---a-r---n---e---d---y---o---u---a---b---o--u---t----f---l---o---w-e---r-r----s--s-.---W---a--t---c--h---o---u---t----f---o----r-----s--t-a---r-r---s-s---!" For Tree alone, Rock revealed e's feelings after e was emotionally flattened by a mere drop of starlight and Tree was silent for a month in contemplation of this momentous event. When Tree returned to society, all the flowers had gone to seed and the world was a different place. "Oh my goodness." thought Tree. It was dusk when Tree started re-engaging with the world and the first thing e heard was the yipping of coyotes on the west side of the mountains and the answering howls on several other fronts on the east side of the hills. E realized that the coyotes were talking, planning and plotting for the evening's hunt. Such a realization was another move outward with e's ability to understand others other than eself and other plants. E thought of the coyotes as plants with feet. Happily e looked skyward where the night/globe lay shining like a semi-translucent poppy seed, a perfect half-globe glistening with white pollen.

Each of e's leaves sparkled up to the stars in gratitude for the beauty of the evening, though e shrank a bit at the intensity of rock's one-time experience with befriending a star. But a general noise came back from the stars as a whole, "We are far. You are far. You are there. We are here. Hello. Hello. Hello."

So e responded, "Hello."

"Hello. Hello." As the night progressed, Tree realized that other trees were having this exact conversation in different spots all around and past e. The interlacing of star and tree chitchat seemed a wonderful thing and the next morning, e realized that e was taller than the humans, taller than the deer, taller than some of Elderberry's kin, than many of the willow, taller than all the sage and the scrub oak. E was feeling very tree indeed. And it was at that moment that e felt something strange and weird inside. And all of Univervia's moodiness came flooding back and Tree understood in a flash. E was joining the rest of the plantworld in the race to create more more. It was so intense that e could only embrace e's own core and comfort eself through the momentous process.

One cold dawn in the spring, the thick cool mud snuggling around e's roots like a rabbit in a well stocked burrow, Tree shivered with an unnerving new feeling. A scrub jay came down out of the sky and hit a branch with both talons, giving a coarse blue screech to the hot/light peeking behind the mountain.

And after a season, e had six acorns, five after one dropped prematurely. E was proud and tremulous and full of hopes that one or more of these pretty things would turn into tree and e would have a lifelong companion, perhaps a tree with a soul like Univervia. E craved a little plant-life to nurture as e might have wished to be nurtured when e was a sprout. E could feel the trees hidden inside the acorns like a thought secreted unspoken inside someone's core. E wanted these thoughts to be spoken, these trees to sprout, these lives to be lived! Too full of this emotion to be silent, e burst into song and heard Elderberry and Black Walnut break from e's own songs to join in Tree's songs in celebration of e's first acorns. The grass below sang along with e and e felt connected to the other plants in the race of life more than at any time before.

And then Tuhuy came walking by the path that deer and people and lion alike used to walk through the grass to the creek and back to wherever it was that they wandered when not in Tree's valley. Her father's name for her like winds riffling mulefat branches. Tuhuy. E remembered this human girl from when the girl was much smaller and had almost stepped on e and then the girl's father had picked up the child and put the child on his shoulders. They had walked off and Tree now recognized that the elder human had saved e from the younger human. E remembered when she and her brother had brought water to e.

All Tuhuy's hair was smooth as water running down her back, the even black color reflecting light like a bobcat's eyes at night. She was wearing a skirt made of strands of twined cottonwood bark which made a soft hushed sound with every movement; tied to each strand was a tiny shell and these tinkled with each step.

This girl was nearly as tall as the human adults and had the poise of an adult. The girl saw Tree and cocked her head to look at the young oak. A smile lurked on her face. "*Ku'w.*" she said. Tree felt electrified. Was that a word for Tree?

Tuhuy circled around the tree and caressed e's bark. She said some things that went by Tree faster than a rock going downhill.

Tree had no idea what the girl had thought or said, but when she turned to go, the feeling of human fingertips remained on e's bark all day long.

The next day, Tuhuy returned with her father, mother, brother and a number of other adults and young people from her village. Today, she wore a fancy skirt made from the fuzzy part of thistle flowers that had been twined around strands of yucca string. These hung past her knees, each decorated with the white down from a duck's breast, and twined at the bottom with red and black feathers. In her arms, she carried a basket, similar to the woven grass and junco *'esmu* that she wore like a crown on her head. She stood over Tree's roots and her father started a song and her mother joined in. The parents, their solemn daughter, their neighbors danced around Tree, giving the young plant the same dignity that would be accorded an enormous tree. A child reached towards Tuhuy's gleaming black hair, swinging in the dance, and was pulled away by her mother. The young woman looked back at the toddler, very serious, though a smile was in her eyes. Then she shuffled forward through the grass to Tree. She leaned forward and embraced Tree for a long time and was followed in this act by the others of the group.

Was this a good thing, like when e's roots met and mixed with the roots of the grass and flowers?

Or was it potentially deadly? Or something more ambiguous, as when the young coyote brush down by the creek was overgrown by the tufts of witches' hair dodder, long delicate strands of orange string, that clambered over the half-grown coyote brush which soldiered on nevertheless?

E shivered. Was this girl going to take a bite out of e like the deer did e's leaves?

Tuhuy began singing, the other people following her, swaying, stamping. Then it was silent. One person after another reached up and plucked three of the five remaining acorns. One they left for Tree and one they left for the other creatures of their world. The chant came to a rumbling stop and then everyone filed off, the thing ended, everyone on to other parts of the day. Tree did not understand that they had claimed Tree for their village for Tree could only understand that e belonged to eself.

The departure of the humans, acorns held within their mobile branches, felt like some pieces of Tree's core were going with the girl, her family and friends. E followed the people until they were small specks on the path of the western hillside and disappeared into the edge of the forest.

Tree felt very strange. That night, a dusky-footed woodrat found one of the other two acorns and took it away. The next morning a squirrel took the last remaining acorn. Yet Tree did not feel bereft. It was true what they said about being eaten: rat was tree and tree was rat, and squirrel hid away his acorn, leaving the future of both squirrel and acorn intertwined until some unknowable future.

Two days passed and then Tuhuy with the shining hair came back with her crew of kith and kin. She took some still warm acorn mush, and put a tiny morsel of it each in everyone's mouth, sweet, smooth. Tree could smell the acorns, even cooked, so as they each ate, Tree felt pieces of tree being taken into them, e felt that all of them were now e's humans. E was in the inside of this group of people and e determined that e would learn to understand them.

They left going up the path they had taken and Tree realized that the benefit of being a Tree is that e would, over the next however many years, grow more acorns than e had yet had had thoughts. And surely one or two of these acorns would become trees able to surpass eself. But for now...e was content just to be. A part of the world. Plant and animal and rock.

E sang a variation of Lupine's seeding song, low and slow as only an oak could go and e was content.

SKIN

On a cool fall afternoon, some of the older Chumash boys came up to Tree. E could feel their focus on e and wondered why – the acorns were gone already. The acorns were in them.

The youngsters grabbed hold of e's bark, using sharp tools to help, pulled off some long pieces which they added to a basket of oak bark they had in hand and went away. The taking of the bark came right before a new layer started growing in and was uncomfortable; e's trunk felt uneasy without this thick protection. Why this assault? Tree was too far from the *aps* to be able to smell the scent of the bark when it became fuel for fires at their village.

One of the boys lay a hand on e's new bare wood and whispered, "*Kaqinas.*"

ACORN PEOPLE

In the ensuing years, Tuhuy, Helek and their friends and relatives came many times to harvest Tree's acorns. Each time Tuhuy stood looking at Tree before and after. Tree had this feeling that e was special to Tuhuy but could not say how or why – but e was certain of this. For Tuhuy, Tree represented a moment in time with her father, when he told her about oaks and acorns and people and she heard him deeply and it stayed planted in her heart.

For Tree, these moments of ritual contact felt fleeting in tree-time and e was never able to decipher language or emotion from the human, except for a vague feeling of appreciation and affection.

One year, Tuhuy came and Tree noted that compared to how she used to look, she seemed horribly distorted. Sadly, Tree wondered what kind of wasp would make such an enormous gall on such a small human and Tree wondered if the human would survive until the larvae inside the gall either were eaten or ate their own way free, to become independent wasps. Whenever she came by the path to go to the creek or to cross over to the other hillside or any such thing, e observed the spectacularly swift growth of the gall which seemed to occupy her entire middle third. However, she did not happen to come by during the rainy season and the next time e saw her, she had a small human tied in some kind of basket on her back.

Aghast, Tree realized that inside the gall had been her own offspring! Furthermore, days later, when the human infant began to cry, the woman sat down, took the baby out of the back-basket and held it up to her chest. Even from 100 yards away, it was clear to Tree that she was feeding the child her own sap! This bizarre life cycle completely flummoxed Tree and Tree attempted to retreat from thinking about it. But then Tuhuy took something out of a purse attached to her waist, a thick flatbread made of crushed, leached and boiled acorns, and Tree had to acknowledge that now e was a part of this little baby through the method of woman ingesting tree and baby ingesting woman.

She put the baby upon her shoulder, patting his back. The baby spit up some milk and the woman was ready – she had a few sycamore leaves, tender-fuzzy on one side, for the clean up. Quickly she packed up the now happy child, layering in some dried rose petals against the baby's bottom before swaddling him, and resumed her activities, stopping by to caress Tree's trunk, further underlining her familial claims upon e. However, Tree had had some momentous experiences in the last year, more momentous than becoming part of the human community. For some of e's acorns had sprouted. E had told the little trees that the hot/light would return and they had rejoiced, but the sprouts were all beneath the growing canopy of e's tree, so Tree could see the little ones struggling to endure in the shade. Then, during a drought, deer had uprooted and eaten every one. And Tree had become old enough to know that few acorns become Tree, but still it had been a brief and passionate voyage. Grief echoed like a distant bell repeating.

LONG NECKED DEER

Then something came into the valley which was stranger than any nursing baby. Humans, again. Encased in some special kind of husk made from leather, from the fur of animals and shredded and reconstructed bits of plants, so complex it was hard to imagine the animal body that was hiding under these husks. There were many of them, and Tree recognized that these were different than e's humans because they seemed attached to a second creature – as if two species were mating, or the human were considering eating the second animal and holding itself in abeyance or maybe as if the human were the baby in the basket being portaged by the first. The other species were tall deer-like creatures with elegant curving necks, who stomped their feet and impatiently grabbed up bites of grass as soon as they had crossed the creek. Tree opened every stoma to see/feel/hear better and more, for e was unsettled. The humans had the tall deer tied up in leather straps, and struck the restless creatures with more strands of leather. They circled in the meadow, bashing down piles of grass and then stopped to let the long-necked deer with heavy round hooves drink at the creek and then the people separated from the tall-deer and took off layers of husk from the long-necked deer and from themselves and they built a fire down by the creek where the animals and humans had worn a bare spot in the earth through so much transit to and from the creek. They cooked meat over the fire and drank something that made them loud until long after the stars and the night/globe had come out. They fell asleep in heaps, but two of them stayed up late, looking out over the grass and the woods as if they were anxious.

Tree could hear Tuhuy and her kin at the periphery of e's dirt, for their village was just a steep walk up behind the California black walnuts, the scrub oak and ceanothus stands. Apparently the new humans did not realize they were being watched, for the two watchers paced up and down periodically all night without interacting with the people who ate acorns.

As the hot/light rose, the visitors were greeted by a stately procession from the adjacent village. The Chumash stopped, in a half circle on the hillside, awaiting their guests. They were carrying baskets filled with many foods, a blanket made of rabbit furs, necklaces and tools. Tree could hear the wind catching the shells on the edges of the skirts of some of the women, a glitter of sound edging the quiet morning.

Surprised by guests so early, the men rose up from the dust around the burnt-out fire and began putting the husks back upon themselves and their long-necked deer. Tree was surprised by this, as e had never seen a plant or animal that shed a husk put it back on again. When a bird dropped a feather, a snake shed its skin or deer rubbed fur off onto e's trunk, they left the detritus behind. Yet further proof of the strangeness of man. Tree could smell the remains of urine and defecation in the damp places behind the willows – and e realized the local humans had kept their excrement far from the creek, far from Tree's valley. The men with extra husks on their head came to the front of the group. The men with less husks strode behind them and they got in a line, like a quail with her babies, running down a path.

From the hillside at the far end of the meadow, Helek, once a child who killed a fox and now a man to take on all the fears of his tribe, stood forward. Paxaayt, Tuhuy's first love, her husband, the father of their child, a Tongva originally from several watersheds south, stood behind her brother. Tuhuy and the other men, women and children stayed silent in their half circle, quiet.

They had heard rumors of these people who looked and smelled so different, of the tall deer, they had heard dark stories of a visit from similar men from their own grandparents. Why were they here on this land? Used to the power of trade and conversation in many languages, Helek stepped forward. Clearly in charge, one Spaniard stepped forward, Capitan Juan Bautista de Anza. He gave a slight bow. Helek repeated the bow, assuming it a greeting.

Tuhuy had a new blanket of rabbit fur, the softest colors of dust and brown, and she stepped forward to pass it to her brother, though just the night before, it had had kept her own son warm. Behind her, Paxaayt had a spear in one hand and his bow in the other, gift and threat, to help to define the intent of these odd people from an unknown tribe.

Helek called out greetings and stepped forward with Tuhuy's gift. His brother-in-law's hand tightened and relaxed on the spear as he resisted down repeating waves of impulses to defend.

De Anza reached towards the blanket. When he took it, he rubbed the soft fur on his face and smiled. Tuhuy smiled back. Cautiously. Tribal elders with the most linguistic agility stepped forward and tried out a number of languages from neighboring peoples. The Spanish leader looked towards his men, focusing on the soldiers from the peoples of Baja California.

Sxa'min's spoke in Cahuilla, welcoming these visitors to the valley and the larger grove of trees on the hills behind them, their home. She called it *"meki'i'wa,"* the place that waits for me. One of the soldiers smiled at the phrase which spoke to him like family of the oaks from his childhood visits to an uncle he had not seen in years and the luxurious warmth of acorn mush in the desert, and called out to his *capitan*, explaining that she had welcomed them to their *arboleda*. Jesús, his natal name floating to the surface of sound and desire only in sunlit dreams and memories of the time when he was Cochimí first, walked up to the front. Leadership on both sides skipped the rituals of trading: this was first contact. Gift-giving.

Juan Bautista De Anza explained the ship, the trek on foot and horseback, Spain, Christ, the claim to the land, hopes for brotherhood, aiming for a tone of warmth, strength, friendliness and slight threat. When his foot soldier spoke with considerably more brevity, De Anza was not sure how much the soldier had managed to translate to the older woman. She took somewhat longer to narrate his version of things into Chumash. People asked her questions which she answered. Then she spoke directly to De Anza, not as a translator per se, but as an elder of her people. Jesús stood ready to jump in and explain.

De Anza's dog, a Spanish mastiff who had wandered off trail the day before, came leaping up, late again. Seeing strangers and feeling the unspoken male-male primate bristling, the dog began to bay. The dog outweighed a grown man and had the teeth of a predator. De Anza put out his hand to silence the dog, just as Tuhuy put out her hand to stop Paxaayt from launching his spear. There was an uncomfortable pause.

Tuhuy determined to smooth things over, and stepped forward and burst into song. Behind her, other people joined in. The Spaniards relaxed. When she paused, one of the *padres* caught De Anza's eye, who nodded.

The *padre* stepped forward to explain about God and Christ and the crucifixion and love as he understood it. His young translator boldly forged ahead. Sxa'min translated. Her explanations fell awkwardly into the crowd, so that a number of people laughed. Jesús looked mortified and the *padre* who had spoken was not happy. De Anza reiterated what the *padre* had said in a loud ringing voice to dead quiet. His intensity caught people's attention even though they did not know Spanish. Jesús tried again, with much care and pause, so Sxa'min did too. This time people looked distinctly uncomfortable. New gods, new powers, new countries, distant lands, perhaps claims of primacy.

Tuhuy intervened again; clearly food would help make mutual understanding easier. She asked Sxa'min to ask their visitors join them for a meal. De Anza took this as a respite from the conversation and accepted with grace. Time enough to share gifts, to answer questions, to let another *padre* tell their stories after everyone had eaten.

Capitan De Anza, the three *padres*, twenty soldiers and most of the eleven servants followed the Chumash up the hill towards their village. The movement gave room for their following herd of cattle, horses and pigs that had been downstream to move into the meadow in which Tree grew, filling the now empty space.

Heads turned to see these animals, large and new, obviously herbivores, being managed by people. The cattle were longhorns, intimidating as wild beasts and the horses were only slightly calmer, equally capable of defending themselves. A thousand miles through desert and scrub and mountain territory had given the animals physical power that caught the eye, while the few pigs tagging along at the end were daunting, the boars especially. The servants shouted and moved them into a huddle on the grass. Tuhuy reached out for Paxaat's hand, her brother Helek put a hand on her shoulder. Plenty to talk about later. They saw the animals responding to the people and the herders interested them even more than the brand new animal species. They turned to head to their homes, to food, to conversation with a two or four language gap, to growing some kind of understandings with these men with hair on their faces, animals that appeared to do their bidding and new weapons.

As they walked the three *padres* intoned a prayer and their hosts felt the weight of it; the only other sound was the crunching of leaves as they walked.

Only a few of the servants remained to watch over the mixed herd of animals. Tree watched as the strange animals grazed the grass and nibbled on low-lying tree leaves, some of them standing in the creek in the heat of the spring day. There were thirty-five mules, sixty-five cattle, a dozen pigs and 140 horses, so looking for more room, the servants managing the herds pushed the animals upstream and out of Tree's valley.

Tree did not feel right at the moment, but these new humans had left e's patch of dirt. The fire they had built had not spread. The sun was shining. What could one do but grow?

TINY BLACK SEEDS

The Spanish stayed through the night and for a breakfast sumptuous enough for a wedding between the heirs of two nations; they left gifts and promises of a return. When the soldiers and servants packed up and left, the herders followed pushing the animals after. At the end of the group, a man with a soft brown husk, no metal that Tree could see, had some sort of soft basket, a seed-pouch, inside which were hundreds of tiny round black seeds with a sharp smell which Tree had never before encountered. Mustard seed. As the soldiers took off, the little man at the end of the line strewed a handful of seeds every few hundred yards or so.

The soldiers began to sing a dark melody, leaving a whiff of gloom that sifted slowly through the sunlit air as they walked away.

Upon their departure, an uneasy silence fell, akin to that which comes over the landscape during a lunar eclipse.

PURPLE NEEDLEGRASS

Later that afternoon, Tree caught sight of a grass that had been shredded by the livestock; about three-fourths of its stems were gone and e had been crushed around the base. Retroactively, e remembered the plant had tried to reach out to e after Univervia's death; e had not understood the grass at the time.

Tentatively, Tree asked, "Purple needlegrass? Is that you? How are you faring?"

Purple needlegrass grunted an affirmative. As answer, Tree felt a nudge low, on e's taproot. E was startled: did the grass have roots that were eighteen feet long?

Tree was pretty certain the plant might die of these injuries. E knew that grass could face such a thing with serenity but e also felt the need to say that e saw, had seen, had cherished, would cherish – as e formulated e's thoughts to share with the grass, an answer came at it in multiple voices all laid upon one another in identical tones, though their pacing did not line up. It took a few minutes to disentangle the separate ideas being shared together. To Tree's amazement, each of the grass speaking claimed to be Purple Needlegrass. Not as in, members of the same species, as in – the same plant. The deepest voiced one started again and the echoing versions of eself fell silent. "We are so very old. Older than a tree. Nearly a thousand years if you care to count this way. We began as one and then our roots create more us, more me, me, me, and each new me sprouts up, as like as we. And we share feelings and conversation and memories and fires and droughts and rains and here me we are."

Tree could think of nothing to say back. Was it many or one? The purple needlegrass heard, "Yes. We are one and many. We grow seeds and young new plants, like your dear friend Univervia, but mostly, we persist. Our long roots give us life that is long. Like you. And not like you."

Again, Tree struggled to for tact and coherency but the grass could feel where Tree was going before Tree found words.

"The one that caught you at the core – this me that was eaten and trod on – we me think I us this one will survive. But regardless, there are we me in spots all over this meadow, one me near enough to touch roots with you. We me have been here before and me we will be here after. Rest easy. I us will be fine. Even if those new creatures come back."

Tree finally found e's voice. "Nice to meet you. Though I think I knew you before, I did not know you. Now I will come to love you one and all."

The multiple voices raised up in almost matching unison, "Oh we me are so glad that you see us I."

Tree went silent, trying to track down which voice went with which part of the plant or plants. They were spaced apart like deer grazing – not too close, not too far. E wondered if Univervia could have...

The dominant voice intervened, kindly, "Univervia was a one year grass. We are an every year grass, a many year grass. She lived in full." That last, Tree knew intuitively.

The purple needlegrass began to sing and Tree found eself enmeshed in a choir of grass and history, wondering if rock knew and understood all of this.

Tree's old grief ached like an unhealed bruise that has been struck a second time. Tree said nothing.

WESTERN POND TURTLES

The next day, as the hot/light slipped towards the center of the sky, Tree heard a tiny sound like a rabbit trying to squeeze through a too-small hole. From the creek came the faintest scratchy sounds. Through the bright of day, Tree strained to pick up on what creatures had tiny little claws, yet seemed to bear disproportionate weight? What was the wet slurpy sound going with it? As the sounds came closer, Tree could see a half a dozen turtles heading out of the creek and up the slope of the valley, and under the awning of the chaparral. The turtles moved step after step, slow and steady. Then first one, then another, seemed to find a special favored spot.

Miner's lettuce shone emerald green in the silty mud. Cattail arced in tall spires towards the sky, bent over here and there by the fuzzy chocolate batons packed with seeds that gave them their name.

The first turtle stopped to pause under the canopy of the sage and began to accelerate the walking movements and Tree realized the turtle was digging, frantically, creating a pit in the still slightly damp soil. When the turtle had nearly completely disappeared, the turtle emitted little near-silent distress cries, as if being eaten. Tree could not see the turtle because the pile of dirt was between plant and creature, but the strain evoked birds in laying season and Tree put two and two together. The first turtle lay four eggs and her friends each lay three and eight each. As soon as the turtle nearest Tree had released her last egg, she lay resting, panting on top of her progeny. Then she released a quantity of water, stored up for this purpose and she swiftly covered her future in dirt, which became mud due to the pile of water in which the eggs lay nestled. Tired, she joined a sister on the trek back to the creek and gradually, the other four turtles turned homeward, leaving the eggs hidden away, with hope as grand as mountains, walking slowly back again. One by one they slipped into the water, to rest and dream.

As the afternoon continued, the hot/light completed the work of the turtle-mothers, baking the surface of the underground nests so that as the day progressed, the earth looked undisturbed, the kind of texture that makes shale seem invincible.

AFTERMATH

The first rain after the visit of the foreign men and long-necked deer, many new things happened. Plants no one had ever known came up in the meadow, a cosmos-altering side effect of the most innocuous thing imaginable, the horse's dung. From feed grain to gut to ground came soft green wild oats, eager European rye, Timothy grass, alfalfa and wild radishes.

Something else arose as well – a path of light bright yellowish green, composed of new sprouts. It began across the creek and then extended along the side of the creek and away up towards the hill over which these creatures had last disappeared from view. With sun and time and more water, these new plants grew like proverbial weeds.

Mustard.

Mustard had stems that were long and had spiky little growths like would-be spines growing off them. Underneath the ground, their roots gave off a pungent oil which irritated and disgusted the local grass and flowers so much that they gave ground and would not share dirt with this new plant. Emboldened by this space, the new plants grew up to the height of a man in a season and burst into flower all at the same time, leaving the visual equivalent of a yellow fire trail, the very reason they had been sown in the first place. The mustard-path would give the Spanish a roadmap made of plants of the way to go back after a season of exploration.

Tree spent a lot of time that summer looking at the new biota. The new grasses. Entire communities of plants bent and retreated before these invaders.

Mustard. Oats. Radish. The world was forever changed.

A new color yellow, a new color green, a new world.

RAINFALL

In this last outburst of the year's winter wet, Tree welcomed the water on e's limbs and trunk, on every leaf, which drained and caught water, quivering on the curled underside, ready to release a second shower in days to come after the storm. A deer and her fawn crept in out of the pouring wet to nestle into the duff, creating a nest under e's trunk, the mother coiled around her fawn. Within the first ten minutes the soil sighed and began to absorb as best it could before the run-off commenced; the smell of this damp collision came off in a gently opiatic miasma and all the plants relaxed and opened to receive. There was a pause while the initial cloud drifted on and sunlight came into the clearing and the fog came off the skin of the earth and drifted skywards like archaic prayer. The deer got up and went off to graze, a watchful eye on her sleepy fawn.

The air felt like youth, like a drinkable potion.

At the periphery of Tree's canopy, grew a snarl of wild rose. Tree had been watching in the preceding weeks as damp and wet caused the plant to hide additional rosebuds tucked under leaves and coiled their pre-nascent progeny back and around branches; the plants' secretive approach was charming. The rain had hit the plant at core and suddenly it just let go and bud after bud burst into tiny, potent flowers, each one rimmed in a solitary necklace of petals, the scent disproportionately sweet. Carpenter bees the size of a man's thumb came stumbling and jumping through the air, with flight patterns invisibly depicting a skyline of jagged mountains. They buzzed in and out of the small flowers they dwarfed and looped over to the hummingbird sage, whose jammy scent and large erect flowers evoked the smell of an exceedingly ripe pineapple. Next to the wild rose grew poison oak in profusion, leaves of three in this season, garish red and orange, a few dots of dark green foretelling the summer's more somber shades. The roots of poison oak circled down and around and up and around Tree's own roots. And in the closest ring, girdling e's trunk and laying over the roots of all these close-lying companions was e's own duff, the constantly growing litter of leaves and branches and fallen bark, habitat for a zoo of snakes and rodents and salamanders and bugs, constantly in a process of transformation by bacteria, fungi and insects into a veneer of soil for eself and, given wind and gravity and weather and rolling animals and time, enrichment for the plants growing in the meadow and beyond. The mycorrhiza took up nutrients from Tree, and held on to water and soil, creating long strings of fungi under the surface of the soil connecting Tree and other symbiont plants, like toyon and manzanita, aiding Tree to thrive, though Tree was no more aware of these hidden assistants than a horse might be of the friendly microbial festival living within his gut. The scent of the wild roses reached up to Tree's crown, out through the meadow and along the creek, an olfactory shout, persisting through nightfall and daybreak for days a time, still wisping outwards in heat and bright light as the weather transformed.

Under a layer of cracked mud, hidden under toyon and manazita and elderberry, were the four turtle nests. (A slower sister turtle had added her own nest a few days after the first three laid down their eggs.) The contents of the nest under toyon had been raided by raccoons, gleefully gorging on four servings of protein that could not run, swim or fly away. It had gotten too dry under elderberry, so the embryos in the highest-placed nest had not matured. The other two nests, however, had survived weather, predators and the fortunes of inheritance and the survivor eggs were full of bulge and texture, rippling and bumping. Energized by sunshine and incited by the abruptly empty larders within their shells, the new reptiles used beaks and tender claws to move from solitary worlds of egg interior into the big wild world of earth. The first one to pursue the shock of the new, a male, had a nose escape, then a left foot, a right. Forcing his one and a half inch long body through the narrow crack, the eggshell, softened with age, gave way into an open chasm and the little turtle pushed up and fell forward, head down, onto the dirt edge of the nest. Kicking the egg free with his back legs, he felt a driving urge to move, to go, to explore, to find. The scent of creeky water called him down the hill, around, under and through the mixed stand of willow, mulefat, coyotebrush and mugwort. Behind him came a sister, two brothers, then five half-siblings cousins from the nest under the manzanita. The other turtles heard their brother's descent, smelled the water and struggled over rocks, logs, cracks in the earth, terrain ten times, a hundred times their size, they took on one sturdy little step at a time, legs quivering in the air and planting firmly in the ground, dragging each tiny body, shell and mind towards a watery utopia. The leader found himself looking down a muddy slope at the gurgling creek and made the choice a child of nearly any species would: he sledded down the mud and plunged into the water. The cool wet covered his head and filled in the space between his body and shell. Bubbles rose up as the gap between flesh and shell disappeared.

Closing eyes and mouth, he relaxed, stretching out four legs and head into the water. Being within the fluid evoked eggness, but the coolness, the difference between liquid and viscous, the bigness of it, the lack of enclosedness made it all new. He wiggled and found himself jutting forward. Kicking extra with his back legs he rose to the surface and grabbed a bite of air. The splash of a sister and brother entering the same segment of creek caught his ear and he turned towards the sound. With eyes still adjusting to being outside the shell, he blinked. There was a murky suspicion of sameness and his sister came bumping up at him; he bumped her back and there was a further sense of rightness. Together they meandered with the pull of the water and landed onto a root wedged into the creek bottom.

With scritching noises, they toddled up the side of the root just out of the current and sat watching the water go by, looking at insects land and lift off the surface of the water, curious to know what came next. The other turtles continued their epic half inch by half inch amphibious invasion, completely committed to v—i—c—t—o—r-…

TIME

Day after night, warm after cool, dry after wet, a summer moved into the hot endings, where the air was still and plant and animal alike minimized expenditures of energy and growth, retreated, rested, and when that failed, died. Tree felt e's leaves coiling tighter and some dropping, end branch tips going dead to conserve water, e's tap root straining deeper to access the sullen groundwater. E had played this waiting game before. It was always longer than e remembered.

The slide into cool and then cold was a mercy e welcomed. Rains came again and e watched life spurt up again to celebrate and then enjoyed the loud of crickets and treefrogs, grasses and new unflowered wildflowers rustling in the wind. Spring with a hint of summer was the time to feel *ananda*, "the joy without which the universe would cease to exist." It prickled at e's imagination and spirit, made e to dream of seeds and the past and the new and to wish for starlight after dark.

CERDOS

The second summer since the Spanish had come and gone was underway when a part of the Spanish visitors came back, yet again: a solid ribbon of neon yellow flowers ran across the landscape.

The visit by the Spanish men had made a small hole in the ecosystem of the valley after the initial impact. Then there was a spiderweb of cracks. And a slight crackling as seconds turned into minutes and mounted into hours until finally the once smooth surface was transformed into thousands of pieces clinging together in memory of the whole they once were.

The inner sanctum had now opened to the exterior, the new species taking up larger pieces of space, chasing old species to smaller and smaller niches. Tree realized looking at grass and flower in profusion that there more new plants growing in e's meadow than familiar kinds of flower and grass.

Three of the pigs the Spanish foot-soldiers had herded along while they trekked to provide easy meat had eluded their captors and bred and stayed in Topanga. And they and their squirmy progeny were making repeated contact, every day and every night. Because pigs adore acorns. Black walnuts. Berries. Carrion. Mushrooms. In fact, nearly every food that the people and the animals and birds of Topanga might like. Tree watched the pigs rummaging into the duff underneath e's crown and realized that they hunted, sniffed and dug and wound up finding and eating nearly every acorn e produced, unlike the humans, who took their portion only. E wondered what e's humans would eat now that the pigs had come and gone; e had seen animals starve in drought, were the pigs a kind of drought on legs?

The largest impact, however, had come from the horses who had merely walked and run, eaten and shat, as mutually innocent and rapacious as any herbivore. Hidden within the soil compacted in their hooves, deep inside their guts, had been all those seeds. Those seeds of oats and wild oats, seeds of mustard, wild radish and scarlet pimpernel, European ryes and cheatgrass and all the grass and hay and weeds that had fed them and bedeviled them in Spain and in the boats across the wide seas and in the bags of grain carefully allocated to them after long days at night. As the horses digested them and returned them to open air, those seeds were enclosed in the most perfect fertilizer known to the world and it had only taken one rain after the departure of the Spanish to inspire some them to sprout, grown in a similar but not identical terrain back home, to take root and grow, delighted with the new space. Tree had watched a few of these plants dotting the meadow, by the creekside already.

But after opening rainfall this full year later, these European annuals now found empty spaces between the stately perennial grasses that occupied the valley like chesspieces scattered on a spacious board and took over the blank spaces and pushed hard on what remained. And mustard is oleic, giving off an oil in its roots that made all the other plants in the vicinity stand back. Now there were many more strange new plants intermingled in the meadow. Tree sent out tendrils of communication and was put off by the brassy sass of the mustard, as thoughtlessly enthusiastic as an incoming war party. The already ubiquitous wild oats were different in character – gentle and loving; Tree enjoyed the way they brushed against each other in the wind. The overwhelming chitchat of multitudinous new flower species left Tree a bit aghast; it would take many seasons to decipher who was who. With all this new life there was less of the old. E was reminded of the giant lizards and towering ferns evoked by Rock; Rock had once tried to express that other rocks underneath e had once even been part of a different world with water where Tree knew air.

Tree had pictured a world entirely filled with algae, trout and chub and had been mystified.

* * *

By the third year, wild oats rippled across the meadow and the eastern hill was covered in waves of bright yellow mustard, transforming the color and smell and living communities of the land. Within this altered landscape, Tuhuy raised two children to adulthood and then they buried her. Tuhuy's one daughter came every year to collect the mast from Tree. One year she didn't come and neither did anyone from the tribe. Without knowing why or where they had gone, Tree noted their absence. There were plenty of other species eager to make use of the mast. It was not something to be stingy with – acorns were to be given to bird and squirrel and rat and man and insect and wind, and now, pig. In the midst of all this profligacy, individual seeds were lost, dropped, hidden, crushed, rolled, moved, wedged. And some, Tree had since figured, became tree. The process of acorns sprouting was completely beyond e's control. So e was generous with, bestowing grace and winningness on all and sundry. Tree had come to understand how grass might come to welcome yielding to predators. Without these beings taking e's offspring away, surely every single acorn would fall under e's canopy – doomed by the high roof of leaves and twigs, to miss nearly every jot of sunlight. Sprouts in the duff under e's own encircling ceiling never made it to three seasons in age.

It was the lost that were found.

E wondered where Tuhuy's people had gone – were they lost or found?

TREE

CABALLERO

Tree woke one dawn to the sound of grazing in the valley.

Not deer. Not long-necked deer. Something like deer, but stouter through the trunk. A lot bigger. Long sharp horns curving off their heads like a human with arms extended in greeting. Cloven hooves, hides in various patterns from red to brown to black to mottled white with grey and black.

Big dark eyes. Heroic males, strong females and the sound of stomping, ripping, chewing, tails swishing. There were a lot of them. Tree didn't count per se, but understood the volume of animals at about 100. For the sake of all the meadow, e hoped they would move on before the sun got much higher. Some of them stood knee and hock deep in the creek, blissfully letting the water run by. Tree had noted that every other species of animal crept down to the water and then split, eager to escape lions and bears and coyote, all prone to lurking optimistically in the bushes. These creatures did not have the apparent wisdom of low-running constant fear. One came up and began leaning into Tree, rubbing e's hide into the rough bark. Tree thought it was good to be full grown – this would take out a sapling. The animals lowed and began moving more closely together, heads jerking up, eyes looking wild, anxiously leaning down for a bite of grass and waiting for something. On to the scene burst a quartet of *vaqueros* – men on long-necked deer. Tree noted that the bark of these men was different than the ones who rode the long-necked deer last time. They had leaves on their heads that made canopies big enough to shade them entirely. The bark on their limbs was covered on the sides with stripes that waved like a row of short grass. The main difference, however was the speed with which the long-necked deer moved, galloping down the pass between the western hills like a flower rolling into swift bloom on the first hot day. The men were whooping and yelling and the difference in their cries from those of the Chumash struck e, as different as coyotes from bobcats or bobcats from coyotes. As they came cantering into the valley they split two a side and came encircling the herd. They

95

had pieces of animal hide, long and elastic like grass in a storm. They moved their limbs and as they did so, the leather-grass snapped and popped, venomous, not deadly, like a California scorpion. The stout deer responded to it with the alacrity of real deer fleeing a mountain lion. Tree realized though that the men were not hunting so much as playing, they were convincing the whole of the herd to clump together and then the men and their long-necked deer, now foamy with sweat, chased the stout deer back up the hill from whence they had come, amidst laughter and shouts.

It was quite silent after all the noisy animals had left, only the constant soft bustle of moving air on still grass, the trickle of the creek in summer. Gradually birds started chirping, bees buzzing, lizards flicking tongues.

Tree heard the grass convincing eselves to keep growing – the whole herd had been hit hard by the stout deer with the long horns. Not only had a great mass of the grass been eaten, most of the stand had been broken, crushed and pushed into the ground. Tree wished it would rain to give the field a fighting chance but it was May – there was only the smallest chance of water. Big and stalwart over the edge of the field, e broke e's usual silence and spoke to the whole herd of e's admiration for them. E told them to grow and thrive. Feeling the crushed grass fading after the first compliment, e made up a song about Univervia and Tree and tried to sing it in a pace swift enough that they might follow. The herd fell silent, feeling the story a balm like rain.

From the herd spoke up a set of voices nearly a 100 strong, in varying stages of raggedness and strength. Tree remembered: purple needlegrass. They said their name was Nassella, a grass alive at the same time as Univervia, before Univervia, alive now, they were all each Nassella still, older than Tree, old enough to remember the sprout of every tree in this valley, they explained. From e's roots came out sibling roots and sibling grass – each an offshoot of their first self, completely identical in form, linked in spirit, idea, language tone and soul to that one. For the first year after their sprouting, they had been one plant. The second year, two new. Then Nassella one died. And they kept going. Creating children that were eself. They now grew in a self-perpetuating ring, still spewing seeds in the hope of new life, still repeating their own world view, their own existence in an intimacy of relatedness that simply couldn't translate to an animal, but which

Tree understood as stump-sprouting, something e had seen a young black walnut do after getting knocked down by animals in a tussle. They spoke of eternity and the unity of all grass and this story seemed consoling to the field. Voices from mustard and radish dissented; they could not go on in a facsimile of eternity in such a fashion – they were reliant upon seeds. They had to love their seeds and give up their existence. Grass, however, enjoyed knowing eself in such a way and began to talk amongst eself determining who was which was what. But Tree felt again somehow betrayed. The last time the purple needlegrass had said Univervia had not had such kin, but…

"No," the pack of sameness demurred, "Univervia had been seed-born and died solo."

"Not solo," Tree said fiercely. I was there." E realized that this grass was so insular, so self-referential e could communicate just barely with the whole of e's own herd. Only Tree's fluency in grass allowed it to capture this story. Why did e feel such jealousy? Such anger? E remembered from Rock. Nothing is eternal. So e reached deep to let go of envy of their sense of immortality. Univervia's life and been full of joy. The purpose of life was not to have the most of time but the best of time.

E felt the root that had once been twinned next to Univervia's push and shiver in the ground searching for e in memory. E's branches, leaves, roots and spirit each reached into earth air and sky yearning yearning yearning.

Each particle of air and light and soil and water and *ki* felt like white light, incipient rainbows, tears and joy. Oh for more life.

DOUBT

While Tree reminisced, the present came roaring on apace, as the cowboys came bolting down the hill again to round up lost cattle that had ambled off down near the creek. Only one thing could make them ride this rough – the subtle smell of smoke from who knows where. The horses swirled around the cattle and drove them hard across the creek and up the opposing hillside.

WHERE THERE IS SMOKE

The run of horses in apparent pursuit of cattle, brought Tree into awareness of the intensity of the hot/light. E smelt a familiar smell of wood-burning overlaid with the dusky murk of sage smoke. Nothing new. The humans burnt things all the time. But as the sun rose up the smell intensified and the air itself seemed beige, brown then finally a blackish grey and the smell was overwhelming and Tree felt the hugeness of real fear for the first time since e was a sprout. E did not need to hear the muted shrieking of the worried sage, the panicked yelps of toyon, the husky failing optimism of the willows and the steady weeping of the black walnuts to translate. The high-pitched bagpipe droning of the grass translated directly into Tree and e knew.

Wildfire.

Soon the whole valley was invaded by herds of unfamiliar wild-eyed deer, two bear, a mother and clingy cub, rabbits, coyotes, a bobcat, slithering snakes and even a pack of bees, all coming helter-skelter in advance of the flames. Two men, a woman and a baby, the last of the Chumash residing near Tree, came out from the hills and ran down the dry creekbed towards the solace of the sea, but the animals fled blindly in advance of the coming tsunami of flame, without plan or vision, looking only to run to a place where they might breathe and rest.

Next came the wholesale shriek of plants on the other side of the east hill – plants that Tree had supposed might be there but that e had never spoken to or connected with even once. United first in the murk of smoke which made transpiring difficult, then in unspeakable heat and finally in the burst of flame that killed them, they kept up a steady noise of fear, pain and death. One might suppose the noise would abate in the absence of life, but the fire moved forward, finding new victims to replace the voices of the dead, moving forward at ten feet a minute. Unable to escape, even to imagine any kind of salvation, Tree retreated to e's core and then tried to take e's feelings down into the core of e's roots, but each leaf fluttered in the hot wind, itself a prick of fear and unwilling anticipation. E could not escape from eself, though e tried.

From the time e heard the dreadful noise, it took an afternoon, a night, a day and half a night before the fire was near e's distant food-roots, the one's laced all the way down into the dry creekbed and out into the beginning of the western foothills.

The duff caught fire and, e's lifelong protector became the giver of the flame – and soon the fire was lapping at Tree's trunk, racing up the sides and catching on the surface of the limbs, the branches, the leaves. Soon the pain of burning was like an arrow through an animal's head – unavoidable, ongoing and intensifying pain in one's most central part. There was no escape, e's bark burnt, several layers of wood in burnt and e's roots smoldered under the burning duff. The heat made e's sap hurt like drinking melted silver; e's leaves went up like sparklers, e's branches caught and held fire like a nightmare. E yelled in forthright agony, unable to hide e's pain. The sky pulled back in dismay; this was not bearable secondhand. Tree wondered if e would perish and hoped for a fast death. Instead this became a test of endurance. The fire took on the meadow, the other bushes and trees and Tree was aware of the screams of e's friends. Something shifted in e's core and turned the rabid pain into harmonic shrieking and the other plants tuned their agony towards Tree in a cacophony that became order, like an organ played with hammers. Music to miscarry by. The heat crept inward and Tree felt on the edge of a precipice, like e would fall into eself and disappear, the opposite of a star shining as night rose. Like a woman blacking out in childbirth, e's consciousness elapsed and e felt smelled heard saw nothing.

PHOENICIAN

For the next day and days and week and weeks and months, the landscape looked lunar: variegated grey veering into black. In a few places the dirt cracked open and light tan soil was visible under the crust of black on the surface.

Manzanitas, oak and sycamore were black-trunked.

Piles of soft white ash showed where grass and flowers had stood. The creekbed had a surfeit of ash and sediment and moved sluggishly in the aftermath. A pile of bones where a deer had succumbed to smoke inhalation and staggered to kneeling in the effort to escape, lay still. A pathetic blasted corpse of a squirrel, empty in the middle.

But the land was not dead. Birds came to perch in the trees, calling to each other to discuss the possibilities. The creek kept running. Pieces of desiccated bark fell off the sides of the manzanita revealing the skin-smooth red bark underneath, shockingly alive. The first twenty-four hours after the fire had raged through and fled far away to torment other acres, Tree had felt a burst of life in e's sap and had exploded and ejected fat acorns all over the ground, shedding every hope. Squirrels and scrub jays alike came in to take this rich harvest, shockingly abundant in the empty field. In the hot daytimes, the fine ash rose off the surface of the ground making the air smell like a morning-after campsite. At night there was a cool dank exhausted scent of old smoke, crushed dust and wet charcoal that rolled out of the valley and off to greener fields, a warning to anyone who would mock fire.

A few weeks shy of winter solstice, distant storms shook the Pacific Ocean into tall dreams of waves and Hokusai fury, which circled around and poured north and then down eastward, battering the Channel Islands and the California coastline. And the wind came roiling in, meeting the rising warm air from far off inland deserts in a collision that created a cloud cover as tall as a tale of new gods and old in conversation. The result was thick white moisture held in abeyance for only a few hours of angry conference; then the clouds gave up holding on to their heavy loads and began just releasing the water collected from sea and sky in drops so large and fast it felt like an enormous pot of cold water being dumped onto the earth. The ash was ground into the soil and the combination became wet and then mud.

Animals, lizards, birds, insects found whatever cover they could. And seeds, inspired to germinate by the very heat that had killed off so much in the mountains, burst from a waiting state that was neither alive nor dead, neither germinated nor extinguished, into the very definition of life. And every tree with even a tenuous hold on life took in this onslaught of water and pushed it through whatever roots and interior passages that were still functional and nourished eself with this wet.

The first to return, canyon sunflower came in the dips of the land where water gathered, making leaf after leaf of warm green hearts.

Black Walnut, who anyone but anyone would have claimed for dead, moved through roots and abandoned the dead trunk to begin to stump sprout at the base of the once-tree.

Manzanitas chose which branches to allow to remain grey and dead and which to restore to burnished red, pushing for new branches and leaves.

And Tree eself felt the nubs where leaves would come swelling and popping, new nubs for young lithe branches, two spots at e's base where e would also stumpsprout.

What had looked like obliterated mistletoe at e's crown found eself in the nonstop wave of wet and began talking cells of eself back into life.

The storm broke by midday and yet the moisture stayed on in valley and hill alike; clinging in the form of a low-lying fog that lay attached to every living plant and standing rock in its path, giving the appearance of a smear of mystic watercolor to the landscape, every whisper of wind, bird cry, crunch of a step, amplified by the relative silence. In such a balance of wet and dry, where the daylight is obscured by the shadows of water held in the air, magic is newly conceivable. In such a time the mercilessly blasted land wins the war after it so thoroughly lost the battle: tiny green dots come up in the landscape. Nusella of the many and the one lifted new sprouts from ancient roots.

Tree could see the meadow restoring itself, feel the landscape coming to life after just a kiss. The living fabric of the land was new to Tree, though. Dots of fire-loving wildflowers came up first: Indian paintbrush and scarlet pimpernel. Purple nightshade came up, moving fast to the height flowering required. Then lupine and sticky monkeyflower and others more rare. In the muddier spots, wild morning glory made soft white flowers like hopeful baby faces looking for approval from the sun, the wet and passers-by.

A handful of familiar grass bravely shot out sheathes from damaged rhizomes; some deergrass, down by the creek, some giant ryegrass, a few spots of California melica, and stipa. But Tree was having to search to hear the voices of these familiar tribes. Mustard, radish and hemlock, its pale green stems stippled by a light lavender-violet polka dots, proliferated, as did masses of slender wild oat, annual bluegrass, a bunch of tall fescue, red brome and farmer's foxtail. The new species' songs dominated the valley and the old species attempted first to sing their own familiar songs and then, vainly to interweave, when they were just outshouted.

Tree turned e's back on the meadow's song and felt the mist rolling around e's trunk and branches, a healing balm of moisture. E could hear the sound of running water in the creek, falling down and down and down to the sea, which e could only imagine from the songs of birds, from whence the clouds had come only hours before. E could feel the groundwater growing underneath e like a promise saved. Deer came over the black hills on the east wanting to drink deep from the fresh creek, looking thin and hopeful.

The rain dumped in again after the night/globe came out; most of this rushed down into the creek, some of it sank more into the perched water under the hillsides and some sank directly into the open stomata of Tree. E had not felt such relief, such emotional release since the morning after e's first time alone with the night/globe, when the hot/light returned and all felt right in the world. The whole of the land was uncurling and leaping into hope and new. Tree wondered at the cruelty of fire and the kindness of rain, surely the world was a mélange of hurt and pleasure that a plant could only endure and celebrate, a mystery of emotion and stubborn persistence. E would grow. E would thrive. E would survive.

MINE

As the *vaqueros* herded their cattle, so they themselves were run by the *ranchero* who had been deeded the land in gratitude for an episode of bravery some twelve years before, down in New Spain, in México, where he had been raised. Some days he felt the huge arrays of acres at his disposal as too large a gift for something he would have done for free, other days it seemed his right, as much as the love of his wife for him was his right, the natural outcome of being a man with spirit. Other days he wondered at the injustice of it being his, when once, clearly, a host of pagan Indians had lived on it together. But he told himself that the Spaniards brought these poor people Christianity – such a gift clearly worth the loss of land and freedom. Or so people said. Standing apart from forming a personal opinion about something so completely out of his hands, he focused on running cattle, the children he aimed to have and the rhythms of being *Californio*.

So far, he decided he had better grazing lands on both the east side of these mountains where a vast valley stretched like an open countenance before the sky and to the west, where there was more savannah to the oakland savannahs and less shady forests and steep hillsides. After completing his house and his barn, every week or so, he made it a point to just take off riding so as to explore every nook and cranny of his lands. Thus he found himself tired in the heat of midday, riding his pinto alone down the western hills that edged Tree's domain. Looking down over the watershed, the largest tree in the valley called to him and his horse as the most shaded site for a graze and a nap.

Already having re-discovered the misery of a roll in poison oak growing discreetly under a *roble* (it had been worth it – the side effect of a romantic picnic with his wife under a California valley oak in the early days of their marriage), he saw a clear space perfect for settling down under this *encino*. He thought about the quintet of *tacos* tucked into his bag, each one snug against each other. He saw the meadow around Tree would be a nice place to run a few animals, perhaps a nice place to build a small house, but it was not a good spot for his large herds. In his own creekside adobe, a canyon north, his pregnant wife was probably in the kitchen. She might be napping too, a thought that made him nostalgic in advance for the hours after dinner tonight. She called their house the house of the pumpkins. He had tried to point out that the knotty little coyote melons were not *calabasas* when they first built the adobe home but she told him some day she would have *calabasas* and *limones* and all sorts of good things, including babies. That particular conversation had ended well, as he remembered. He smiled.

Tree, focused on the sweetness of groundwater and hot summer light, had not even noticed when the man had come riding at a slouchy jogtrot down the hill. E became aware of this person sitting on e's roots, eating, and tried to reach out. But the man's heart was elsewhere. Part of the way through the tacos, the man thought again of home, gathered up his horse, remounted, circled his mare, looking over the valley, and rode briskly back up the curving path the Chumash used to use all the time to mount the curve of the northern hill. The man and horse went over the crest of the mountain, through the divide and into a place unknown to Tree.

SMALL WORLDS

At the edges of Tree's canopy, grew mugwort, pale grey-green, with leaves that ended in a serrated pattern of five that looked a lot like the imprint of a raccoon paw. For any human foolish enough to snuggle up to poison oak, these were the promise of salvation – rubbing fresh mugwort leaves was a near guarantee of freedom from the dreadful symptoms of poison oak. Tree liked the poison oak and the mugwort equally. E noticed the first showing of *Phtophthora ramorum* in e's roots with trepidation – e felt the fungus in eself like an itch, or an argument gone wrong, constantly uncomfortable, vaguely frightening. Bursting out of the side of a trunk grew some sulphur-shelf fungus, it went up e's roots and interlaced in e's core, giving off prolific growths that jutted out of e's sides like giant yellow mushroom halves; sort of edible even to people, who optimistically renamed it chicken mushroom. And in e's duff grew *chanterelles*, priceless treats to a Frenchmen, or to the wandering pigs, hunting around in the duff for something before the acorns matured. Most essential were the mycorrhiza, which intertied Tree to all the plants e thought of as friends, in a tiny network of nutrient and moisture exchange, hidden under the duff; but like bacteria in a healthy human gut, Tree could not see or feel these friendly tag-alongs, upon which much of e's personal nutrient economy was based. They just were; when they created fruiting bodies big enough to catch e's attention, e was surprised by the sudden appearance of mushrooms and e understood the emotionality of these mushrooms just about as well as the wandering cattle understood Tree eself; which is to say – a little.

SAPLINGS

Looking over the duff underneath e's canopy and the outlying growth before the ecosystem of the meadow commenced, Tree realized with a start e was no different than the other mature trees had been to eself when e was a sapling – that is to say mostly oblivious to the children trees in e's own domain. Upon reflection e knew it was self-defense; it would be sad to see a young tree not thrive. However, this morning, e heard two young trees, California live oaks, like eself, one a big three to four inches tall, the other a towering seven inches, about a foot out from e's own canopy, making a go of it in the meadow, having the good fortune of having started up right after some aggressive cattle grazing and rolling cleared out a big patch of the mustard, wild oats and foxtails which took up the light in the meadow blocking many lower growing species. They were talking to each other, not to the grass or mustard or oats. Tree could tell from their conversation that they had not understood other plants yet; had just been celebrating sun and water and dirt and each other. Squabbling.

"I am most tall." said one, smug.

"I am most beautiful." responded the smaller tree.

"I am stronger." underlined the first.

"I am very strong, too." asserted the other one, insecurity crunching in the air as e spoke.

Tree had been listening to this one-upmanship for half the morning and finally interrupted. "You are both wonderful saplings." said Tree.

They cringed and searched their understanding to figure out whence this new voice. Tree explained. "I am Tree. Look up. Really up. I am like you will be in forty or fifty years."

The smaller one asked, "You are like us?" in evident awe.

Tree put warmth and comfort into e's voice, "Absolutely."

The larger sapling said, "You do not know what it is like to be us. You are too grand and grown up." Tree chuckled.

The younger sapling agreed. "We are very small. The meadow is very big. The cattle come and we feel very timid. We want to be big."

"I am bigger!" the larger asserted.

Tree stepped in, "You are both the right size for saplings; you will both grow big. Consider this. Of all the thousands of acorns every oak gives off every year, it was you two who sprouted. You are lucky."

Tree could feel them agreeing with this assessment. "And you are lucky to have each other in the same patch of dirt. You can be friends. The grown oaks nearest me are on that distant ridge over there and I rarely hear them speak or they me."

"Friends would be good…" said the older one.

The younger one mumbled something conciliatory while e's skepticism unfurled in the air, a smaller rival country.

Tree told them that when e was a sprout e's best friend was a grass and e could feel their shock; then e sent them a bright blast of memory of Univervia and e was pleased to feel them understand. And the bigger sapling sent a tender greeting under the louder story directed just to e's meadowmate, and Tree heard it. And felt the younger sapling, delicately accept the offer of kindness. And Tree was happy to have facilitated this sweetness. Their rivalry put aside at least for the moment, the truth that drove it out of them surfaced – they were afraid of what each next day and night could bring. And so Tree sent gentle stories of night and day and rain and drought and the sensation of growing to e's own grandeur, taking a pace only slightly swifter than that which Rock would use and e felt the littler trees easing up on their anxiety.

E stepped back into silence to give them room to grow and could feel the tenor of their conversation without tracking the actual words; their interactions batted at each other, their roughhousing a kind of affection, and they drew strength from each other's bravado. Their enthusiasm to take on life was a tonic to Tree.

A few days later, Tree tried to slip back into conversation with the saplings and realized e could not, their language was tightening into a mutually comprehensible dialect for two. As they dug into the ground with their roots and reached upward with their tiny limbs and trunks, stretching leaves for more light, Tree figured that this tight little pile of emotional life would branch out more largely at some point – or it might not. And that there were many kinds of happiness. Perhaps if e had grown with another sapling, e would never have known grass. Or Toyon. Or Elderberry. Or Rock. Or heard the humans once.

IN THE EAST

Pert dudleya perched on the rockface below the eastern ridgeline, finding purchase on impossible locations. The biggest one had taken up residence in the tiny cave that had housed a pair of mating hawks and their children some forty years plus before; now the dominant dudleya took up the circumference where the nest had been, reaching with a kink in e's stem out the hole in the rock, skywards. In the winter, the dudleya boldly sent up spiky stalks for tiny flowers and their succulent leaves puffed up with vigor. In the summer they deflated a bit, getting lanky and even saggy with the tips of their leaves growing pointy with want of water. Tree noted that with the exception of the cave-dwelling plant, the dudleya grew pretty much perpendicular to the hillside, unlike any other plant e knew. On the lower face was a combination of grey lichen, pale orange lichen and dark and drear moss. One good rain and the whole thing would explode in rainforest colors.

It was above this that Tree saw the *ranchero* riding his same pinto come in. He had on chaps, a leather coat and leather gloves in the heat. Having come to understand the clothes phenomenon in part, Tree wondered why any animal would add extra bark on such a hot day as this. Behind him, on the man's horse, were burlap sacks, lumpy and uncomfortable. His horse was pissy, stomping and huffing after he dismounted, but sullenly agreeing to stay put as the man untied the burlap sacks.

Inside were some kind of plant Tree did not know, big grey-green thick pads, kind of egg shaped in outline. There were many dots on the plants from which an array of spiky thorns grew. As the man handled the plants, he expressed himself loudly and Tree surmised that this animal was in pain as a result of this plant. But rather than slinking away and trying to wrest the thorns from his flesh like any other animal would, he kept on with his self-appointed job. He unlashed a half-sized shovel from the back of the horse's saddle and found a prominent place along the trail that came in across the eastern ridge, and he dug a series of holes along it, stabbing the resistant mountain with the shovel, standing on it in his boots and jumping on it until the rock crumbled with the strain. He made seven of these little shallow pits. Then he rode his mare up and down the hill a few times, loading up two *botas* with creek water and dumping this in each dent he had made in the mountain ridge. Then he took the cacti out of the sacks and broke his first prize into four main sections, each of which he planted into the ground. Then he kicked the rocks around the base. He unwrapped his second burlap sack and broke this plant into three sections that he also planted.

At this point, despite his leather gear, he was fairly miserable from thorns, but he was done. He surveyed his cacti with the satisfaction of a mountain lion that has marked territory with scat and urine, eked out to seventeen stops around the perimeter of his terrain, to his mind a job well done. He talked to his new grove of prickly pear before he remounted, "*Buena suerte mis tunas.*"

NEW GREEN

Half way down the ridge, a solitary century plant reached dramatically to blue sky, unconcerned with anything but sunshine.

The center of the meadow nodded with thousands of oats, foxtail, red brome, with an undercoat of annual bluegrass. Tree continued to be startled at how few purple needlegrass e could find and felt an ache for the loss of the grass community of yore. Less than the year before and less than the year before that.

E did not even see one Mexican sprangle grass this year.

Mustard flowers turned big curls of the whole vista yellow like marble swirled stone and purple and white radish flowers dotted it with white and purple like a festive granite. Hemlock came in, with pale violet dots on its green stems, a dainty pattern evoking death.

Rock spoke up. C-h-a-n-g-e---i-s---l-l-l-i-f-f-e.

CHOLERA

The second to oldest daughter of the *ranchero* was so ashamed. María Marta was a big girl, nearly a woman – she would be fifteen the next summer. But she was so sick she could not get out of bed to go the outhouse, not even to use the pot under her bed. So when she had to go, her mother and one of the *criadas* hoisted her out and lifted her nightgown and held her trembling over the pot. And what came out of her was disgusting – a thin fluid mass of brown and ocher, liquid and lumpy, hot and fast. To make matters worse, she was still throwing up. The doctor had said the throwing up usually stopped after the first two days. She knew she had ruined her clothes, her nightsheets, that the whole room smelt, probably the whole house…how could she ever look at the maids again? Her mama still loved her, of course, she knew that, as incomprehensible as it seemed after this, but she felt awkward about everyone else who was stuck caring for her. Still, she was too weak to make them leave her alone. Her hair stuck to her forehead and down her back in slimy tendrils. Her cheeks were hot with fever, scarlet. Her eyes dark pools of light in the shadowy room, she prayed for it to be over, one way or another. And then she moaned, because the revolting pain was slicing her gut. She had had to go so much that now it felt like she was being scalded from the inside every time she went. She felt her eyes prick as if she was going to cry, but she was too dehydrated to cry.

María Marta's mother Alma watched her oldest, her pride and joy, wracked with pain. As soon as she lifted her María Marta up and pulled up the skirts, the old Indian woman in the corner – now called María – jumped up to help unbidden. Alma wished she were helping her girl birth a baby instead of wrangling with her death. But, all she could do was be there. Take warm water and wipe off her pale thighs and her pretty bottom. Keep her skirts clean and put her back into bed. The old woman rushed outside with the nastiness, both women anxious to cling to civility and cleanliness in the face of sickness, dumping everything into a cauldron to wash later.

Alma knew how humiliated her child felt, but she didn't care. She just wanted her well. She prayed to God to spare her child, promising that if He wanted a life, she would give her own in exchange for that of her own angel. But spare her beauty, her heart, the sweetness of her life. She leaned over to kiss the hot, dry forehead and the liquid gaze of her daughter, long past fright, wrenched at her.

She murmured the sweet things that mothers say to babies at her nearly grown daughter and felt María Marta relax, almost smile. She asked the maid, when she came back, to get *champurrado*, the wonderful hot drink from rice and cinnamon, smooth and unctuous, hearty as a bowl of oatmeal. Her daughter's favorite. Now María Marta shook her head no. Too rich. Too much like food. "*Manzanilla?*" her mother asked. María Marta agreed to a cup of tea from chamomile flowers. Hot or cold, it sounded wonderful to be soothed by flowers.

Alone in the kitchen, María added from her own teas into the *manzanilla*, coffee berry and dried green bark from California live oak. She had a dozen other dried plants in baskets in a shelf by her bed that could help but thought she'd start with the most reliable.

Alma propped her daughter up on pillows and gave her sips of tea, teasing her that this was like when she was a baby, telling her she'd be better in a few days, that her father was still going to have to spend a fortune on her *quinceañera* next summer, teasing her that he was afraid already about all the boys who would ride up, and dismount with fast beating hearts, begging to see her, hoping to marry her. No longer teasing, she told her about the beautiful cloth she had purchased for her wedding gown, about the lace she had purchased, sight unseen, in Portugal, from the same family that had provided the lace she wore at her wedding to Papá. The familiar plans soothed María Marta and the tea tasted of the love with which she'd grown up.

Exhausted, she slumped down on her pillow. Asleep.

Crying, Alma prayed again. "Protect my girl. Take me, if you must. Don't take my María Marta. PleaseohpleaseohpleasemiSeñor."

Then, feeling like a rotten mother for obsessing over one child when she knew there were three others who craved her attention and care, and seeing herself as a neglectful wife to the husband riding back to her from the other side of the valley back for dinner tonight after days of accounting for the huge herds that made up their wealth and livelihood, she turned towards the kitchen to make dinner. She rinsed her hands in cold well water and wiped them clean. She even changed to a clean blouse and put on a fresh apron, tired of the smell of the sickroom. Then she walked into the kitchen with a smile on her face.

Something within her told her that the tide had turned for María Marta. Her staff brightened to see her expression. Maybe the *hija* of the house would survive.

Alma would be happy and when she was happy she was generous. Don Antonio was coming in tonight. All would be well.

* * *

It was quite late at night when the family sat down to dinner. Alma had fed the little one bits of this and that to keep them from crying but had finally had to sit down to the big dinner she had made without her husband, when Oso, who ran the stables in her husband's absence came in to mention that the *vaquero*s returning after a long day had mentioned seeing a campfire in the far distance. Maybe it was Antonio. She thanked him and had a plate made for him and sent him off. All the children loved the piles of fruit she'd cut up for treats and had to be prodded through the piles of beef, rice, beans – which they loved, of course – everything was always of the best in their home – in their anticipation of soft dried figs, the first new pomegranates, the carefully tended offspring of mango and papaya trees, clearly craving the tropical weather and moisture of their antecedents' homelands. Distraught not to have her Antonio back after three days away, she caved in quickly and agreed to have the mass of kids in her bed. Thus they were all together when the wrenching pain hit her in her lower belly at about two in the morning. She saw that Marisol and Clarabella were sick, too. Tomás seemed frightened, but still well.

She called María for help, herself too sick to do much more than clamber onto her hands and knees. Usually sluggish, especially at night, María came at a run.

Thank God for María. Alma knew all of María's children and both husbands had died working for the missionaries. María's devotion to Alma's family was unfathomable. Alma could not imagine the kind of grief the old woman had weathered and imagined that she herself would die from it. Instead, María had agreed to come to work for Alma and her husband, functioning as maid, nanny, confidante, wading through the enormous gap of understanding between herself and her mistress every day, aided only by her limited Spanish vocabulary and good intentions.

Now no language was necessary. Two daughters and one mother

were struck with the same sickness that had nearly wiped out María Marta. The first thing was to get the boy to safety. María went out and called for Oso. Nicknamed "bear" for obvious reasons, Oso lumbered in, ducking under the low doorframe into the bedroom, feeling uncomfortable at seeing the mistress in her nightclothes. But he agreed to take the boy out to the stable and to his own room. Away from the sickness. To care for him. And to hope for the others.

María called some of the other, endlessly rotating staff of displaced Indians and impoverished Spanish Mexicans, to come and help her. They dragged the girl's beds into the same room as the mother to make caring for the trio easier.

Alma wanted to keep them close but María explained that it would be easier to keep them each clean if they had their own bedclothes and nightgown. Already too sick to care too much, Alma agreed. Then Alma saw red and black in waves before her eyes, and she threw up and threw up into the bowl someone kind was holding in front of her and she passed out.

* * *

María Marta woke up feeling ravenous. Her belly felt empty, clean and light. Her limbs were shaky, but she got out of bed, stood up and stretched and thanked God for the morning. She cleaned herself up, did her hair in a neat braid, put on a clean shirt and apron over her skirt and splashed water on her face a second time. Life was amazing. How could she feel so marvelous after so much illness? She walked into the kitchen, expecting her mother to be up to her elbows in chilis or some such and saw how everyone's eyes darted away from hers. Horrified, she ran into her mother's room, where she saw her sisters, her mother and María herself stretched out at the foot of Alma and Antonio's bed. Her first thought was for her brother. "Where is Tomásito?"

Alma grunted "Oso. Not sick." Relieved to find that at least one of her siblings was healthy, she looked around the room and got piles of clean sheets, brought in a pitcher with water and cups, clean chamber pots. Shaky, she pushed her hair out of her eyes. Her mother saw that she was there to take care of all of them and grunted out a command, "Eat. Go eat."

Marta hesitated, but it was obvious she would need to eat first. She ran back into the empty kitchen and ate cold beans and rice on stiff cold tortillas. The fruit had been sitting out too long to look appetizing. She heaped up the fire in the cast iron stove under a pot of water because she believed that the right kinds of teas could cure anything and then washed her hands in cold water and splashed her forehead and the back of the neck for energy.

Later she would look back on the next two days and remember fragments – Clarabella throwing up into the bowl she held while Marisol threw up on the floor. Trying to mop up vomit with old rags. Trying to make her mother, delirious now, to drink something, her mother slapping her. Crying when María died. Falling asleep in exhaustion on Sunday morning and waking to find her mother and Marisol, dead. Somehow her mother must have gotten up to hold the girl, because they were in the same bed, now. She could not separate her mother's arms from the girl so the mother and her middle daughter would wind up buried together. The increasing fragility of Clarabella, the youngest sister, like an injured bunny, doomed by lunchtime, yet taking another long afternoon and most of the evening to relinquish her sweet young life.

She could not piece it together, though she had fed and mopped and taken damp cloths to heads and brushed back hair and prayed and said sweet things and tossed vomit and worse into a washing tub because the privy was too far.

Whatever she had done it had not been enough.

She had fallen asleep clutching her last sister, after. When she woke up, hours later, there were flies and she had run shrieking from the room. Oso had caught her like he would an hysterical mare running amok and then taken her by her shoulders and made her sit. He wedged her in a sunny corner between him and the barn wall, petting her hair until she calmed down. Then she broke down weeping and he stayed with her, not saying anything, not doing anything, just sitting.

Her father rode up to find his oldest daughter weeping and the hair stood up along both forearms, along his back and up his neck into the hairline. He looked at her face and then ran inside. When he came back out, he leapt to his horse and took off for two hours.

By the time he came back, he was composed and so was his María Marta. Oso had gone for the priest. Tomásito was sitting quietly at his daughter's feet.

The little boy ran up to his father and his dad came off the big horse to hug his son close. María Marta said "The servants have run off. No one wants to die. I must clean the kitchen."

Her father told her, "You did your best. I know you did your best."
Bitterly she admitted it, "Yes."

She returned to throw out the beans, the rice, the beef, the fruit.
She ripped apart the kitchen scrubbing pots with sand, flinging boiling
water on the floor and dishes to dislodge every scrap of scum she could.
Her rage boiled and the room shone.

Her father heard her banging and told her to go to bed.

She wanted to dress the dead but he knew exhaustion from years
of watching the herds and the men who herded them. She was past the
point of rationality and was grateful to have him to tell her she must
find a way to escape this unending day. She fell asleep immediately and
did not dream.

That night, Tomásito slept in his father's bed and it would be hard
to say who needed whom more. When they woke, Tomásito's small
fingers had left imprints on his father's arms where he had clutched
him all night.

The next day the women and men who lived and worked on
the ranch drifted back. Oso, who had taken on animal care chores
extending past his own stable, feeding chickens, throwing jerky to the
dogs and cats, dragging water to the horses in corrals, said not a word
to those who had fled their customary roles. He retired to his room and
without a word being said, his own daily tasks for the riding horses,
were, for once, miraculously done for him.

Everyone was quiet, feeling the watching of the bodies in the best
room in the house. The living watched those they had loved and most
everyone believed the dead were watching them back.

The funeral was well-attended, the Doña and her pretty girls had
been popular, María respected. Everyone knew the Indian woman was
rejoining her own dead children at long last and so mingled a bit of
hope in with their grief; God willing they were together now. A few
ranch-hands, servants and farmers knew the old stories and spared a
thought that her soul might yearn for the Western Gate, Šimilaqša and
people gone before, but they were silent as others awaiting the service
reassured themselves that as a Christian convert, María would even
now be seated with the Lord.

The Don, his tall girl and the slender boy stood together stalwart,
not crying in public. They walked into the church and sat upright for
the whole service.

Everyone admired their bravery and grace and prayed from the heart for the dead.

For María Marta, the well-wishing and the feel of the lace of her mother's old black dress on her own skin; the somber stomping horses who rode them there and back. The untouched heaped plates of food. More blur. She had survived the funeral. They would survive the grief. She would run the house. She would raise her brother and see him married. Maybe her father would remarry. They were still standing somehow.

But that night, her brother cried out from her father's bed, "María Marta!" and she knew he wanted his mother. She came running in time to see him lean over the side of the bed and throw up. Aghast, she caught her father's eyes. They sent for a doctor, who really had nothing to offer and the father held the son in his arms the whole of the course of the sickness. Asleep, awake, throwing up, over the chamber pot, while his sister tried to get water, tea, broth, bread, anything into him. He got that limp look and she knew what was coming and she shrieked at him to fight back, to resist, to choose to live, but he looked at her with his doll-blue eyes and she could see that whatever had him was holding him so deeply that she had only his fingertips in her hands to pull him back from the precipice. She could not figure out how to grab hold of that last little piece of him that was alive to hold it back from the edge of forever. She felt him falling and it was as if she was going with him but she felt her father's warm hand on her shoulder and his voice, used to commanding horse and man, telling her, "Let him go." So she did. It felt like something in her just tore that shouldn't be torn; like she was one of those ladies who died after the baby got ripped out of them.

Her father grabbed her, a hand on each side of her temple, and looked into her eyes. Disoriented, she could read nothing in his face. Could feel nothing. No thought no word no faith no no no. He spoke and she heard, "You must live."

He left the room and she acted like a woman automatically: closing the eyes and mouth of her brother, arranging him, washing him, changing his clothes. As she worked, she reflected on how strange it was that he was still the sweetest, dearest little thing, though dead. How could he be such a delicious little morsel of brother when he was no longer inside himself? Yet what was left was so evocative.

The priest came and she left.

The second funeral was awful. Her father just broke down.

Ultimately, he had to be carried out of the cemetery. Everyone, woman and man, identified with his grief and he was nearly drownt by kindness.

Little children held his hand and caressed his cheeks.

María Marta rode her horse in the middle of this entourage and slowed to a stop. The entourage passed her in a slow stream of people, horses, carriages. She pulled aside a little and then rode off the trail. She slipped into a grove of trees and disappeared within ten yards.

The quiet eased her. So many voices. So many hearts.

Too much. She let her horse have her head and the mare picked the way. They wandered through trees and across a long valley. The mare picked up the pace and the girl let her go into the ground-eating lope that cowboys use for travel. When they hit the foothills, she let her pick her way up and she found they were in Topanga. The mare found the headwaters of the Old Topanga Creek and then crossed the confluence of Topanga Creek, meandering back north.

She went up through some tree-spiked grazing lands and down into another watershed where they came across a still valley with a huge California live oak standing in the middle by itself.

Tired with her jaunt, the mare stopped to graze and the girl slipped off, landing on the soft dry grass, which crunched – like the papers with face powder her mother used to get from Spain – when she walked across them. The shade of the tree was inviting in the heat of the day. She stretched out on the cool damp ground before the tree.

Full length and cool at last, she loosened her bodice so she could breath. Privately, she realized that she was supposed to be crying her eyes out in public with family and friends. Or crying her eyes out here, all by herself.

But she felt – nothing.

The more she tried to drum up sentiment by remembering her mother, her brother, her sisters, the more she could not feel. Even her memories stalled out – she could not seem to remember anything much.

She lay still on the grass and finally fell asleep.

Tree noticed the human stretched out on the crunchy leaves over e's roots. E observed she was female, more of a sapling than a tree, and appeared to be dormant.

María Marta's grief drained into the ground as she slept and Tree's roots caught a dissolved portion of it; enough to stop photosynthesizing and listen. Inside her core was a bleakness like some harrowing astronomical conceit: black, airless, featureless. It was the truest thing in all the meadow and surrounding hills.

Tree felt a bit tender of this human because it was the first time e had identified a big feeling coming off a human, confirming e's suspicion that perhaps animals were not so far from plants after all.

She lay as if she might not wake again, not moving, barely breathing. More and more of her feelings from the funeral crept up into Tree, radiating off her skin like heat from a rock, being captured by e's leaves and lowest branches.

The afternoon wore on and as the sun began to cozy up to the western hills, a chill breeze slid over the meadow, raising tiny hairs on the girl's arms. She shivered, hugging herself without waking. Tree felt coldness on the tips of e's bark and a feeling like new leaves being pulled off e's branches. Odd.

From the creek, the new crop of Pacific treefrogs, more or less the size of a *real*, started in on the tenth chorus of the day in little two syllable couplets. Tree heard them – and so did the girl – for her eyes glinted open at the sound and Tree saw the underside of a California live oak through a meadow of miniscule black lines; dry branches and dead leaves and higher up, more vibrant branches and thousands of deep green leaves. A gall or two; a squirrel zipping around a branch and out of sight. Was it eself?

The girl sat up and looked towards the creek, where the noises were coming from and Tree felt a crush of emptiness in e's core – and realized it was her core, not e's. Her loss, not e's. Some little sprout had loved those frogs and now their exuberant noise was pulling her to pieces while she sat still. E felt the prickle of dead leaves through e's roots. E's dead leaves, her legs, Tree guessed. Her unspoken shout for her brother's death played loud in e's core.

Tree went into eself and collected the care e had received from 50,000 days of hot/light. Affection from a rock. Patience. Faith. Hope. And Tree let this accrued warmth come up into e's trunk, into e's curving branches, down into e's gnarled roots. There was so much in e, so much to give and to share.

The girl's eyes popped open, startled. She turned to look at Tree and e knew the hot/light was in her now.

Her dark eyes slowly filled up like the trout pool in the dry creekbed during an unseasonable drizzle.

Tree poured more of e's core into this flesh and blood creature, this animal who walked and talked and ate and shat. She took it like a seed taking in water. Whilst Tree gave light to her, her eyes leaked water, surely a strange thing to do in such a dry world. She reached out and put her hands onto Tree's old trunk and from her hands Tree felt light coming back at eself, something small and fragile but as unctuous as spring. She pressed her lips onto e's bark and Tree could not help but recoil. She felt it and pulled back. She spoke "*No quiero comerte; solò quiero dar gracias à mi amigo.*" Tree understood her as easily as Univervia and looked into e's core for words that a human could understand. There was a long gap. Tree felt stultifying – a space came up between them. As if, impossible as it might seem, e were moving away from her.

E rushed to connect again.

"Uh…" said Tree, struggling to move forward into a common language.

María Marta leaned in close, embracing Tree as once she had her kin. "You don't have to talk," María Marta thought, slipping into the middle terrain between them. "I hear your feelings. You have given me kindness. And love. And this" – she gave back Tree a serving of what e had poured into her – "this is light?" she asked.

"*Luz.*" Tree agreed.

Once again Tree could feel the best within e's core moving into the core of this young human. E could not help it, e wanted to give her anything, everything, to drown her grief in the largeness of e's own life. It was too much for any one person to take on, yet María Marta held on to Tree.

"Don't leave me." María Marta said in their silent space of two. "Please don't leave me." Tree answered truthfully, not knowing how to lie. "I will try to stay."

She didn't say anything while the hot/light went down and the moon rose, clinging to Tree though e could feel that she was growing cold as a snake in a winter-burrow.

At last her horse, patiently submitting to the illusion of being ground-tied for so many hours, meandered over, carefully dragging the reins to one side and walking as if the ground were strewn with thorns and holes, imagining the jerk on the bit when the reins caught on the fictive pole to which they once had been tied in her imagination during training so many years ago. The horse was a big old mare, her mother's horse, gentle enough to have toddlers or babies riding double with an adult. She pushed her nose into María Marta's hair, now with a few leaves in the fuzzy braid, leaving a damp spot on the girl's neck. She looked reproachfully at her rider when the girl turned her head: she wanted other horses, dinner, the luxury of a warm barn. Enough of standing in the woods like some cowpony.

María Marta spoke aloud to the horse like young women throughout millenia, just assuming that there was some degree of understanding. "I'm sorry, *Dulce*. I know you want to go home. And Papí will want me back. And I'm cold."

She stood up, unfurling her legs from the heap in which she had been sitting. Blood rushed into her feet, giving her prickles as the circulation returned. What do you say to someone who has been in your heart?

María Marta leant forward and kissed the bark atop the ancient tree. She could feel Tree simultaneously recoiling from *frisson* at the close contact with a mouth used every day for eating plants and warming up to the love she was giving. She half-smiled at Tree, "*You'll get used to it.*"

She gathered up the reins and vaulted onto the long-necked deer, as Tree still considered this new species, and cantered off. As they went down the trail across the meadow and up onto the west side of the valley, heading for the road in the next valley which Tree could not have even imagined, Tree sent out another wave of stored hot/light after her and could feel the balm it was to her core.

Later that night, Tree spent a long time playing with the Spanish words between them, wondering at how easy it had been to leap into her thoughts, how difficult to pick up more than a handful of words from all the other generations of humans who had been in e's presence.

What was the difference between them and her?

BIG AND BIGGER

Toying with memories and the engaging sensation of growth, Tree's reveries were interrupted again by the feisty saplings, who referred to each other, accurately, as "Big" and "Bigger." They were now a big two feet and three feet tall, respectively and felt themselves quite the champions of the meadow. Each of them leaned towards the southeast, focusing growth on the side of the meadow furthest from Tree's shade. When e stilled, e could feel their sap moving as if in eself, could feel the twin taproots reaching and struggling towards the groundwater they were just above, could feel Big's struggle to get around a rock in e's path. A crow landed on Bigger and the tree wavered with the weight and the bird, irritated by the insecurity, pushed off, flying away, leaving his perch relieved.

"I am Bigger and I am growing," said Bigger, shrugging off the fear of losing a limb just a few seconds earlier.

"I am Big and I am growing more!" said the other Tree.

Tree just smiled. They had no need of e's reassurance. Childlike vanity would fuel them just fine.

SIESTAS

María Martá came back the next day and sat under Tree for two hours, doing nothing. Soon this became their habit in the afternoons in the time after lunch and before dinner, that she would come and sit. At first she just sat grinding her teeth as the Pacific treefrogs peeped, teary eyed and silent. Tree let her be. E waited, curious and grew leaves and did other tree-things.

Sometimes she brought food and sat eating under e and e could catch a whiff of the feeling of eating, which was interesting and quite different than the sensation of being eaten, but clearly related much as a mouth feels the cheek which it kisses while the cheek feels the mouth.

She had long black leaves, tiny like the skinniest grasses ever, which came off her head and down her back.

At first Tree had thought the shiny black part fit on her head neatly like fur on a fox, but then one day she had taken small sticks out of it and it had come down in a long mass all plaited together. She used her *dedos*, tiny branches which moved at her will attached to her main upright branches, and undid the thick black grass so that the tiny pieces of it fell all around her trunk.

The wind caught them up and Tree was reminded of the look of a field of grass in the wind. She sighed and ran her fingers through her hair and Tree could feel how soft the strands were. As if catching e in the act of eavesdropping into her feelings, she smiled up at the Tree and ran her hand down e's trunk with a handful of hair in between the palm of her hand and the rough bark.

This was delightful to Tree. One hair got caught on a snag and when she pulled away it stayed snared. Tree felt decorated by a piece of the girl, which was rather nice.

GANADO

Two months after the death of his son, Mariá Marta's father started to let her run with the cattle; he figured she would inherit the ranch eventually and he wanted her to know everything. Besides, he felt the best solace for a broken heart was riding a horse running under the open sky. It seemed to ease him. There were usually three or four groups of cattle being rotated throughout the *rancho* to keep the grass fresh, so she was usually with the older *vaqueros*, which seemed right to her father. The men were fond of her and looked out for her, often without her realizing that another rider was leading her horse out of a wash, for example.

One afternoon, she was feeling edgy and she told the men they had to corral all the cattle. Unused to her taking command, everyone nevertheless hustled and pushed to get the cattle penned up by late afternoon. She told them to watch the animals that night and rode home, worried about the household for reasons she could not articulate.

QUAKING

Around 2:20 in the morning, María Marta fell out of bed on to her hands and knees and clung to the tile floor as it tilted and bucked, the hard earth floor in her bedroom cracking open in places for 14 long seconds, the earth a horse no man could ride. Adobe walls cracked and floor tiles in other rooms split and buckled upon themselves.

Two watersheds over, Tree felt the earth drop and roll and jerk up in a series of spasms. For a horrible moment, Tree wondered if e had been turned into an animal through some magic shock. When the earth came back down with a loud smacking noise, one of e's main roots that ran parallel to the creek and out for a few dozen yards severed near e's trunk. It was startling to feel the pain and then the disconnect. When the earth pushed up on the north, it stayed pushed up and this shove from beneath put Tree, always growing at a regal exact perpendicular to the ground, at a quirky 15 degree tilt towards the ocean in the southwest. E's limbs and trunk took the shift and saw the sky, the horizon, the ground differently. And e felt the weight of gravity pulling different parts of e downwards while limbs once out at right angles thrust skyward, shy leaves suddenly thrust to the best place for photosynthesis.

Moving was so unsettling, so alien, that Tree stopped talking to other plants while the hot/light came and went and came and went again. E felt the memory of the major severed root as if it were still there. E was relieved to hear e's friend come riding into the valley. E telegraphed e's fear and discomfort at her as soon as she came down the pass, the whole time she traversed the trail towards so that by the time she arrived and slithered off her horse to get to Tree, she had had full doses of e's unhappiness with such a new emotion. She put her arms around Tree.

"You don't like being made to move, do you?" she asked the obvious.

Tree gave an arboreal grunt of consent.

"You look nice, like this, in this new position." She tried to give the big plant a compliment for comfort. Tree shared with her the discomfort and pain of roots being jolted and jumbled, e's trunk fractured, the weirdness of having to see things from a different spot. She stopped trying to tell Tree it was not really a big thing, recognizing the chasm between their species. So she sat, back against the Tree's trunk and just tried to offer moral support as the Tree earnestly tried to grow e's roots into a more stable hold on their new terrain, even as everything shifted. Just as Tree was starting to relax and recognize that things would be fine, a days late aftershock came and e could feel the softer dirt shifting up and down, the rocks moving sickeningly downward by an inch and a half.

The girl laughed and told Tree, "The earth will settle down again, I promise."

Rock spoke up from deep under them, "U-n-t-i-l-l-l-l-l i-t----d-o-e-s-n'-t." Tree sighed. María Marta looked around for the new voice.

Tree grunted, "Rock." María Marta's eyes snapped and sparkled. Another spirit. The mysteries of the world she would have said she knew continued to unfurl. An earthquake was nothing compared to the shaking realization that even rocks could speak and everything, everything was alive. She caressed Tree's trunk and called her horse without words, she could not have said how, and jumped on, full of exuberant need to find a way to celebrate the aliveness she felt. She didn't understand what she wanted, for what she was searching, but felt the need to ride and move.

Sprouts become trees.

STILL

In the wide valleys to the east, the herd María Marta's father had been tracking had bolted and run off the edge of a hillside during the night of the earthquake, leading to many animals injured and killed. The third herd had also scattered, creating days of work to gather up the fractured herd. It was then that Antonio hired Aurelio, the son of his rival to the north, who had been publicly disinherited at church two Sundays before. Antonio knew the boy was a good tracker and figured he would earn his keep – and he felt sorry for the young man whose own father had treated him so badly. That man had always been all bluster and shout, had indulged himself in lawsuits, two against Antonio, and death threats and card games that devolved into gunplay. All the other *rancheros* felt sorry for his wife, his children, his workers and livestock. Antonio surely would never have done such a thing to any of his children.

As soon as the herds were coherent, Antonio brought them all down in to harvest the hides and tallow he sold every year to the Yankee ships. During the fiesta of work and branding and *matanza* and games of horsemanship and feasting and more work, Antonio introduced Aurelio to his daughter as he would with any new *vaquero* and was too caught up in thoughts of cattle and water to recognize human alchemy in action; young adults photosynthesize love out of air, by the light of a smile or the spark of an eye.

REGENERATION

Winter rains brought María Marta the same emotions they did the plants – the heartening first course of what seems an eternal meal; a taste of promises kept, of life recurrent, growth triumphant. She left the house at dawn and rode until dusk and some nights, she slept under the stars, a dog or two at her side. Every field went from grey and brown with a lattice of dead shadowy dark stalks from standing mustard and falling apart dead thistles, to a light green undergrowth that went from spiky sprouts to knee high proper grasses, before a second Sunday had crossed the calendar. She didn't mind riding with her hair plastered to her head in the wet, her leather jacket shedding water onto her horse's back, all the animals' hooves making splocky sounds as they pulled legs out of mud step after step after stride at run, walk or pause. Her face wet for hours at a time, her nose and fingers cold, the amusing discomfort when a tree branch caught under her elbow, bowed and then popped free, dumping icy water down the back of one boot, leaving her with one wet foot for the rest of the day, it was good. She could feel the pastures leaping to life and she, she spent every waking moment hoping that her herds would cross the one that Aurelio was working. It had only happened a few times, and the first two times, she felt his eyes on her back from a distance before she heard the animals or saw them and turned back to gaze at him.

Then one afternoon, after she had been out riding for days and for nights, she had an instinct to go back to check on the ranch, to sleep in her own bed, to bathe, to get the household ready for a proper Sunday the day after next and she bid her *vaqueros* adieu and headed homeward right before sunset and somehow, he too, had taken off time from the unending work and was riding on the same trail ahead of her. She wondered if she had known he would be there and it had called her to him.

She kicked her horse to come loping up to him, her braids in shambles, her clothing decorated with dried mud and the patina of sweat, hers, her horse's, that of the cattle, and her tanned face as bright and clean as the sun in the sky. He smiled the instant he saw her and she forgot the clever things she had been rehearsing that she might say to him and it didn't matter. They rode silently together, almost touching, but not quite.

She took them deliberately through Tree's valley; Aurelio knew this was a detour, but he would have followed her wherever she rode without question, just to be near. She paused near Tree and so he did too; she circled her antsy horse around his, her normally calm mare picking up on something electric in her rider's mood. Tree picked up on her mood too and wondered at it; it was like water running too fast to track visually, a rush of white, a torrent of sound hidden in the hush of day's end. The young man looked up at the main trunk that bifurcated into two stems about ten feet up, the huge limbs, six of them, the dozens of branches that were thigh and arm sized, the smaller, younger branches coming off of them, the thousands and thousands of green-black dark leaves, the new burnished maroon infant leaves coming out at their tips. His friend's lips were parted and he felt her sense that this was a holy place, so he expressed his understanding with his eyes and then she smiled again.

From up in Tree's branches, a courting mockingbird warbled trilling songs complex enough, long and involved enough, to inspire the suspicion that the notes were words and the songs speeches, letters, proclamations of territory, love, *joie de vivre*. Human, human and tree heard the bird catch, repeat and vary the song like a musician showing off and any mockingbird's bravura performance from now and into the future would repeat for the each of them the pending magick of this evening.

Aurelio's restive horse stepped side to side and he heard the wet sound of the leaf litter crushing underneath their animals. María Marta wheeled her horse near to him, but just out of range and the pair turned again and rode through the wild roses at the edge of the Tree's canopy and Aurelio imagined them bursting into bloom simply because of this girl's presence, like the roses that fell out of the rolled canvas that turned out to contain the miraculous image of *La Virgen de Guadalupe* when the Indian Juan Diego was gifted by God on a roadside in México. María Marta rode away and he followed again; they moved up the eastern hill towards the watershed on the other side of the ridge where her father had built his house, twice, once again after the earthquake in 1812 took out his first effort. They rode through ceanothus, all of it bursting into flower, white and then later on blue, and the smell, like musty honey and the French *millefleur* soap that his mother used to use, made him smile. She turned her horse to look over her shoulder at him and behind him, she could feel the grand presence of Tree filling the valley. Happiness snuck up on the unsuspecting bereaved, an echoing surprise. From the distance, Tree could feel this, though e could not know how many layers of words it would take to fertilize this mutually recited spell. E would grow and stretch and be, not waiting for her return, but enjoying it as an eventual inevitability, like the hot/light but not as predictable.

NOVIO

Long days of heat and light drove plant and animal and human alike into an open-hearted summer, fresh, new.

Months of conversations and notes and eye glances had passed between her father's newest *vaquero* and María Marta. They had arranged to go riding together on a Thursday afternoon, with no particular plans.

A decade earlier, her parents would have mandated a *dueña* for a young woman out for a ride with a young man, but given her status helping her father run the ranch, she had the run of ranch. Her father hadn't quite seen that his child was a beautiful young woman.

They headed out for a gallop through the grasslands and then went lumbering up into the foothills.

Aurelio grabbed a frond of pampas grass as he cantered past it and shoved it into his hat, making him look like an eighteenth century French nobleman instead of an impoverished Mexican cowboy. She liked the look.

Now he began to chase her through the twisty trail up the back side of the eastern ridge near Tree's valley, as she lead him closer and closer to Tree. Narrow young coastal live oaks reached up to intertwine and kiss over the trail, so they rode in and out of shadow. Both of them had to duck periodically to avoid being rammed into low overhanging branches. The horses' hooves made soft thuds as they hit the damp sandy ground beneath.

She was lighter and her horse was fresher so as she popped her heels into her mare, the horse struggled gamely to canter up to the top of the hill, far outpacing the larger stallion behind her. Her *novio* lashed the stallion. Given the intensity of the request, the big horse grasped the bit in his teeth and took off at a gallop, taking hunching, short powerful strides to catch up to the smaller mare. The mare slipped up the final tilt of the slope and barely contained herself as María Marta reined her in to a full stop. The horse reared slightly, irritated not to get the reward of cantering down the easy slope ahead of her.

María Marta shouted back down the hill, "You have to dismount at the top. Papá says we have to rest this valley from all grazing for a season or two." Aurelio rolled his eyes. How much damage could a pair of blown out horses do to a big field in an afternoon? As his horse leapt up the final portion of the path, he reined him into a showy spinning stop.

María Marta laughed at him, "I grew on a *rancho*. I've seen it all. Can't impress me with your horsemanship." Flinging his right leg over his horse's neck he leapt down gracefully beside her. Privately she conceded that he was easily the best rider she'd ever seen, including Papá and Oso's son, now off to sea, the idiot. He leaned towards her, reaching for her hands and she leaned in took his hands in hers, then leaned back. His fingers were hot, his skin, rough and soft together, like *piloncillo*, right at that point when the little castles of crunchy brown sugar transformed and melted into smooth. She wanted to taste his fingers, but instead, she slipped her hands out of his and backed away.

There were wild things in the air and she figured she needed to keep her distance from this man. He took the pampas grass he'd shoved into his hat and tapped her on the head with it. She laughed as the little seedlets, each attached to a strand of blonde plant-hair fell around her like confetti. Then she saw them clinging to her new dark green dress. The laundrywoman would kill her if she came back covered in grass – worse she'd talk bad about her.

María Marta pushed Aurelio away. "*¡Basta ya!*" Then she ran down the path towards the tree. He dropped his reins next to the mare, already grazing placidly. These were both cow horses and wouldn't go far when they were ground-tied. He chased after her. When he got close, he slapped the pampas grass against her back, soft as a cat playing with a kitten.

But she could see the little pieces of it showering all over her fancy dress. "*¡Aurelio, no!*" she laughed, as she turned away, already picking at her dress. For answer, he grabbed her hand and traced the pampas frond around the curve of the back of her neck, from one ear, to the nape and back to the other ear.

Torn between propriety and delight, she held still and then jerked away, running off quickly down the path. He followed, holding back, then sneaking in close to catch her with a wave of pampas grass, showering with seedlets on the green cotton dress. By this time, she was laughing like a child, completely breathless, dignity forgotten in the game, ducking and twirling to escape the shimmering seeds. He was laughing too, a boy on a schoolyard, not a grown man with a father who had disinherited him, nothing but a horse to make him a gentleman. She looked more and more like a kid on a farm and less and less like the lady she was supposed to have become.

She shouted over her shoulder, "When we get to Tree, it is safe. No more with the pampas grass."

"Only if you get there!" he agreed. He reached out and caught a piece of her skirt and yanked him to her. He turned her around to face him and his face was suddenly a half an inch from hers. He could feel her breath hot and grassy sweet on his lips as she looked into his eyes. He knew this was the moment. He should kiss her. This is what young men do. But looking into her eyes this close was like falling into another world – he suddenly noticed little strips of green and sparks of gold, hiding in the even dark brown. Her pupils seemed huge. He couldn't look away. Her arms snuck around his waist and her fingers jammed into the muscles on either side of his spine. The effect was like a spark to flame. His back arched and his head threw back. So she reached up and laced her fingers in his glossy dark hair and pulled his head back towards her own, his lips bumped into hers. He pressed his lips into hers and moaned. *"Mi vida."*

"Not yours yet. Have to catch me." Breaking the moment, she extricated from him, turned and ran again. She got to Tree and yelled, *"¡La base!"* both hands pressed up against it. He came up behind her and turned her around.

"A salvo," he agreed.

Nearly somnolent, Tree had been reaching e's roots further into rock, cell by cell. Enjoying the crickling crackling give of the rock, basking in the sun. When the youngsters came running up, the familiar swelling happiness of having María Marta around brought Tree's thoughts back out of resting. E could see she was completely engaged with this boy – when she pressed her back into e, e could feel that she wanted e's support, e's affection as she escalated this thing between her and her man – but not e's participation. E held back from thinking a bit, polite, cautious. Yet watchful.

The girl could only see dazzles of sunlight, pieces of green and blue sky in the background. Her foreground was all Aurelio. She knew Tree was there, after all, she had lead her Aurelio there for the security of being in the most beautiful place in the world, to have the strength of a friend as grand as good behind her. But if Tree had spoken to her that moment, she wouldn't have heard. All she could see was gold skin, curls of dark muddy colored hair, those black eyes. His bright lips.

"Oh María Marta," Aurelio whispered. "What a mess your dress is." He put a hand on either side of her face, his fingers pressing into Tree's adamantine bark and then he leaned in close to kiss her. Later, he would say this was their first kiss. She knew better. He knew that she knew (he was there, after all) but appreciated her support of his vision of things. They had to have some dignity, of course. He reached into her hair and pulled out a flutter of pampas grass seeds.

"This will never do." Aurelio reached to her sleeve. "Another. And another."

María Marta looked up at him, "There are hundreds. How can I go back, looking like this? Papá will not be happy."

Aurelio smiled at her. "I have all afternoon. I will take every single one off of you." She reached down to pluck one off her breast and he took it gently from her fingers. She stopped breathing. He took another one off her breast. Two, three. And he rubbed her breast, looking into her eyes. She couldn't talk.

He smiled at her, "*Inhala*, María Marta." She took a big gulp of air and looked down and saw his hands were shaking. In fact, she realized he was as nervous as she was. Maybe more.

She took his hand in hers, "You're shaking."

"No, never," he joked. "I can ride my horse off a cliff and into an oncoming stampede of cattle in a thunderstorm. Why would I be scared?"

"You tell me," said María Marta. For answer, he put both hands on her cheeks and pushed his fingers into her hair. He kissed her for a long time, until her mouth opened and his opened and he thought he'd faint with the rising feeling of wanting her.

"I think I'll die if I do not have you," he whispered.

She whispered back, "Will we get married?"

He answered, "If your father will let me."

She laughed quietly, "I am my father's only living child. Don't worry about my Papá." And she was kissing him again. Trying to slow things down he reached to her waist to pull off more of those blessed little seeds of grass.

"I think there at least a thousand. I've pulled off about ten. That means I have only 990 to go."

Her voice had somehow dropped an octave – he had never heard her speak like this – she had never heard herself speak like this. "I don't care about the grass. I don't care."

Somehow they slid down Tree – later he would see the tree had left red ridges on the light gold of her pale skin – and onto the grass.

The grass beneath them was crushed, releasing a wave of smell, the scent of summer, of joy, a scent that only satiated horses, cows and maidens and youths can completely taste. He was on top of her and she limp for a moment, eyes boring into his.

In a strangled voice, he asked, "Shall I go catch the horses?" But in a moment of transcendent clarity, she knew this was the moment that would make her life and she told him: "Don't leave me."

Being *caballero*, he could only answer "Never – " but realized as soon as he had said that he had bound himself, bound himself for life. At that moment, he could no more have left her than a mastodon might exit tar. The sticky sweetness of the love was growing between them binding them as tightly as a mother and child, a tree and roots, a sun and e's sky. Giving in to the moment, he shifted awkwardly and asked her if he was crushing her but her smile gave him the answer. He thought of horses mating and was suddenly hard. Her eyes startled and he realized she felt it too.

They smiled shyly at one another, cognizant through the haze of their mutual innocence that something was happening between them. She pushed her hips up into his and he cried out.

Beneath them, strand after stand of grass was crushed, ripped bruised by their weight. The dirt sifted around, feeling the ancient weight of life trying to dominate non-life. A battle forever in abeyance. As each grass released into the destruction, a piece of soul went out with the scent into the air. Grass exists to grow towards the sun, proud and alive for a season, full of offspring each meant to wave in joy for a summer only to die and be reborn again. Of all plants and creatures, perhaps it is grass that is best at accepting mortality, because each new year, a new crop asserts immortality. And because grass' chief value to the world is pure deliciousness. How many animals yearn only for grass, all day long? The process of being eaten, being slept on, died on, made love on, has to be a process of shared bliss for grass or the continuance of existence would come into question. So grass gives into the weight of bodies in joy. Is it pain or pleasure? Who can tell? It is just destiny and destiny must be embraced.

María Marta looked at Aurelio through the tiny fence of her eyelashes as they rolled around trying to get closer and closer. His hand crept down to her ankle. Up a calf. And on to her thigh, underneath her green dress, underneath acres of white frilly things. And he saw she did not want him to stop. Thinking of unwed mothers and children with no fathers he said, "We must get married soon. This month." And he put his hand on her.

Fragments of the boy's thoughts, of María Marta's thoughts drifted around in the air like a haze. The pure hunger. María Marta was telling her lover, "Give me a baby."

"Not yet, *mi corazon*," he answered, thinking about the future, about the years ahead. María Marta had always this grief for the babies. Her sisters. Her brother. Her own mother. And for María of the mangled Spanish, who cared for them all. She wanted something new, something fresh.

Something that meant her family was alive and powerful and moving forward in time. And she wanted it now. She could not have articulated this but it was this that was driving her kisses, her appreciation of the extreme beauty of the man on top of her.

Thus Tree was granted the insight that human passion was at its depths, about babies. He was giving her a seed and she was going to grow it. Tree's sap ran thin and fluid at the realization: they were animals – not trees – and it took two of them to make another animal. It was completely different. Tree had both pollen and flowers and made acorns every year, self-contained, a family of one. These two were unable to breed each without the other and, given the enormous social constraints of being Catholic, being Mexican, being rich and poor, being, above all, from rival families, were nearly torn apart by the tension between desire and the realities of their humanity. But nature wins. And there they were, intertwining above e's roots, underneath e's branches. Tree released all the love within eself and felt it scatter into the air like a benediction

Like a wedding.

PROPER NAMES

Aurelio had asked to meet with her father after Sunday dinner next after he'd picked off all the seeds. She'd ridden in hot and flushed to her home, unsaddled the horse and given the mare to Oso and met her father for dinner.

After dinner, she brought him a glass of port and asked him to sit on the front porch, where it was finally cooling down.

She didn't remember the rest of her conversation with her *novio* because she'd answered him mechanically, obsessing over ever detail in his face – his girl-smooth skin, the toyon-berry colored lips. His eyes. His hair. Amused, he'd given up trying to talk to her and just stared back until they both had to concede that the sun was setting and that she should return. But he had listened to her rote answers, when he'd asked about her mother, her father, her siblings, the long dinners, the piano, the port, the fireplace. Family *historia*.

And then – after the sun had set – Aurelio had gone to his old piano teacher's home, knocked on the door late at night, and had begged. Begged. A tough German Jewish widow, Doña Blumenthal would have been happy to help him for free, but when she saw how desperate he was, she could not resist an impulsive idea. She'd gotten him to agree to teach her only grandchild, a girl of three, how to ride the next year. Secretly, she was happy to have an excuse to have him underfoot, he had been one of her very favorite students. She would not have minded if her daughter married him, even though he was a Christian. And was only moderately talented on the piano. But such a lovely boy. However, her daughter had found a nice American who was also a Jew, which had surprised Doña Blumenthal, but she was pleased as he was a doctor and a *mensch*, even if his lack of knowledge about their traditions was appalling. She digressed, even in her own thoughts. Her granddaughter might even end up with a free horse out of it, if she knew her former student. They discussed new Mendelssohnn and Verdi, her playing examples on her square grand piano, but settled on Mozart. She gave Aurelio the sheet music he needed and when he said he had only three days to learn it off and no piano of his own, she told him he could practice at night and then took a look at his earnest face and offered to let him stay over for the duration. And Aurelio began doing scales to warm up his fingers and then, heart trembling, took on the big task of learning music under duress. She wandered in and out, giving advice, but letting him gut it out. At dawn he was surprised when his teacher showed up with some corn tamales wrapped in a towel and *té de hierbabuena*. He offered to leave so that her students would not find him disheveled in her living room. She laughed at him; now that she lived in the countryside she had few students. On Friday she only had one student coming by and she was too old to worry about her reputation. Besides, the day after was a Saturday – who would expect an old Jewish lady to work on her holy day? Flustered, he stammered that he would leave but she smiled and told him about *mitzvahs* and spent thirty minutes listening to his efforts, gave him some suggestions for fingering and pacing and put him to bed in the guest bedroom for a two-hour nap before he tried again.

She didn't know his *novia* but she remembered the girl's mother because she'd heard her play Bach on the Serafina, a small parlor organ, at the De la Guerra house outside the Presidio in Santa Barbara, one Christmas Eve in happier times. She had the abrupt insight, halfway through Friday morning that he might be in deep trouble trying to elicit music from a piano whose chief owner had been dead for four years. She hoped that if she reached them they could get to the ranch and get the work done within the day. It would take a miracle. So she sent out for the American couple who did the best work, in her opinion, tuning, of anyone in *Alta California*. Probably in *Baja California*, too, she would guess, but since she had left Germany two decades before, she had not gone farther than fifty miles from her new home. She'd often wondered who amongst the *gente de razon* might be *Marranos* but had never had a hint. Maybe none of them. The piano tuner and his wife did not come all day Friday. She put her hopes that they would arrive the next day and kept working with Aurelio until late in the night. The next morning, the tuner arrived with his wife and Doña Blumenthal smiled as she always did to see them. He was a handsome man pushing sixty, with white hair in sharp contrast to his dark skin, tall and stately. He played Mozart, Bach, Telemann and everything else, even though he could not read a note of music. He was blind, like so many tuners. And so Doña Blumenthal's smile was for the eyes of his wife, twenty-five years his junior. The old woman found the younger woman's utter devotion to her blind husband completely endearing.

Apologizing, Doña Blumenthal explained the rush. They were charmed to be a part of the surprise and agreed that this was clearly what she called a *mitzvah*. She gave the pair of them directions to the *rancho*, Aurelio changed out their tired horses for the grey mares in Doña Blumenthal's field. She bit her lip and paid them; she never knew how many years of teaching she had left in her, so she hated to be extravagant. She told herself this was a wedding gift.

When they arrived at the house, María Marta was laying out the *sala* for the visit from her *novio* that she knew was coming the next day. She was a bit startled to see a blind man and a woman riding horses she didn't know in front of their door, however when they announced their mission, she just stood still for a minute. No one had touched the piano since the string of deaths which she and her father no longer discussed. Would the sound of the instrument be more than he could bear? More than she could bear? Seeing her distress, the woman came up to her and sat her down on the steps and asked her why she looked so sad. María Marta told her about her mother. About her sisters and brother. About the music lessons she'd escaped after a riding accident damaged one pinky so that she could no longer reach an octave. About silence. The silent piano. Silent graves.

Finally the guest spoke, "We don't have to tune your piano. We can give the money back to Doña Blumenthal."

Her husband spoke. "*Mija*. Life is full of sad stories. God put us here to be happy. It takes courage to be happy. Your young man has been working day and night since he left you to be ready for today. He had to offer to teach Doña Blumenthal's granddaughter to ride a pony in order to borrow her piano to practice – he doesn't even have his own instrument anymore. Let us fix your piano."

When she thought about Aurelio sitting for hours at someone else's borrowed piano, she had to smile. María spoke. "I have no manners. I have told you everything about my family and I don't even know your names."

"I am Betsy Moses and this my husband, John Moses," she said.

"I am María Marta Leticia de Gonzales."

Everyone muttered "*Mucho gusto*." And then they were in front of the piano. John did a quick series of scales, bottom to top, wincing at the sound. Then his wife easily moved the heavy top of the piano and they set to work. She anticipated his needs and fluttered from back to front to tool to underneath whilst the steady drone of notes going from sour to sour to better to sweet went from bottom to top of the keyboard. While they worked, the three of them talked. The guests' Spanish was perfect but the accent sounded like warm honey, every vowel wide, the cadence slow – and the way each of them spoke, matched, which made María smile.

When María asked them where they were from, they didn't say "America," they said "Georgia." So then Betsy had to explain where Georgia was and soon one question lead to the next until she felt compelled to launch into the story of how she came to be with John, beginning with slavery, her childhood and the house she grew up in. It was not a story Betsy told often, but both she and her husband felt that telling people about Georgia, about slavery, was the only way they could express caring for everyone they had left behind. So, when someone asked, they would tell the truth.

Betsy explained that ownership of her person had been given to the daughter of the house, the same age as herself, at birth. Their childhood might have had some charm as seen from the outside: they had played together, ridden ponies together, even, at one summer picnic, been dressed in similar fluffy white dresses where the white neighbors found the two of them together endearing. Waiting for that moment when her only child would run smack into the wall that divided the girls, Betsy's mother seethed with unspoken rage.

At seven they both got a sickness which left them bedridden for months, while Betsy's mother ran up and down the stairs to care for them; the white girl in her tall bed, Betsy in a little roll-away on the floor next to her. But by fall, a much thinner Betsy was finally up and walking, whilst her mistress lay still and pale in her lacy clean sheets. Betsy took over the care of her playmate and then the plantation owners sold Betsy's mother.

A black note sounded painfully off and then John worked it and worked and worked and it sounded pure.

And Betsy continued her story, as if there had been no pause. There were other children in the house, the girl had had three older brothers. Gradually they went from cute rambunctious youngsters into arrogant young almost men. My girl died, Betsy continued. The boy's father made the boys play piano, read Latin, go to church, but he let them hunt and drink and.

And.

Her husband cut in, "Be unchristian to my Betsy." Maria heard the magnitude of the understatement, all that the word covered. He stopped tuning the piano and put a hand on his wife's back. María found herself hand on mouth, unable to find anything to say.

John jumped the story away from the three brothers: "I lived with an old couple who made their money off of me. Since I was a boy, I was good at music. They must have spent a pretty penny getting me taught to know so much. I had no value as a blind slave, unless I could do something no one else could do. So like so many blind men before me, I learned music and I learned to tune pianos. And I got driven up and down and all around Georgia. And other people paid my people top dollar for my work. I never got anything."

"Until me." Said Betsy and both of them smiled.

John continued, "When I heard Betsy's voice the first time, I knew she was the girl for me. Because I played music, so many women have been kind to me. But I could hear her troubles within the tones of voices of the people in the house who talked to her and how they said things and it just tore me up. And though we'd just met, I decided to put my faith in her. Because I might never come back to the house where she lived, and there was no way we could find one another that I could imagine. So that night, after everyone else was asleep, I crept about until I found her. I told her we had to run away. That I would follow her and do whatever she might say and that once we got far enough away, I would marry her and support her with the tuning and that we would have a life of joy."

Betsy spoke softly. "And I believed him. He told me about California and told me we'd learn to speak Spanish and that we'd never be turned back."

"¿Como se fue?" asked María Marta, on the edge of her seat.

John laughed. "That's a story for another day, my dear, we have a piano to tune before your father gets home." Betsy laughed, a quintet of notes from the final octave of the piano. "Let's just say that the trip out West involved many of the seven deadly sins, but we figured just about nothing was as sinful as slavery." María Marta laughed and didn't really notice when they changed the subject over to Aurelio, because of course she was at a stage of life when anyone appearing interested in the story of her new love story was just fine by her. Later, she guessed that they almost never told anyone about the escape because it was an ugly story and they liked to live in beauty. This was true enough. What she missed, was why they had had to tell her some pieces of it at all, why every now and then they would delve into their lives before California, from that time before, with each other, with friends, even with strangers. For each of them, talking about the people, their own people, all those people, left behind living in slavery felt like the only gift that they could give to them – husband and wife both believed that to tell the truth about that world was to honor those trapped in it. But to think about those times too much was to risk sliding back into the actual hell that they had endured – so they would abruptly leap out of their histories in self-defense.

María Marta noticed that Betsy was nearly constantly touching John when they weren't actually working. Her fingers were in his hair, over his arm, tickling the skin underneath a fingernail, brushing the hair on his arms lightly. Both of them were nearly always smiling. They had found each other, obtained their freedom, built a life together, in a society categorically opposed to any of these things happening. Now, sitting anywhere at any time in the country of México, they were in heaven on earth. She imagined how much her mother would have liked them and experienced this as a happy thought.

John pushed Betsy away. "Let's finish up, woman, we have to be out of here before her *Papí* gets back." Betsy pushed him back. "You get distracted just as easily as I do." Soon he was bouncing notes into order in the highest part of the register. Then he sat down and did some scales, working every key on the board. He smiled in the direction where he thought María Marta was sitting, but she had moved since last she spoke. Both Betsy and María Marta noticed that he was off by about thirty degrees and smiled at each other ruefully. María Marta got up and moved over so that she was in range of where John thought she was.

John spoke "Well child, this piano is as good as good can be. I'd love to play on it, but I'm going to leave the first music to be for your *novio's* hands. Any time you need to get a tuning, just contact Doña Blumenthal. We stay in touch with her."

Soon she had them back on their friend's grey horses, off at a slow jog-trot. It had only taken a few hours. Her father came home and, with uncharacteristic restraint, she said nothing but nothing about the piano or the tuners through the whole of dinner.

For just this once, she stayed home from mass and started cooking as soon as her father left the house. She thought things were well underway but when he returned, she rushed into the kitchen where the meat had burned badly on one side. Using words that would have embarrassed Oso, she shaved off the burnt side and tossed it to the dogs outside. She knew the women who worked in the kitchen would come back from church within half an hour or so and then she'd have piles of cut up fruit, fresh tortillas, *aguas frescas*. The beans and rice appeared spot on. It would be acceptable. She tried to regain her equilibrium.

She went into her room where each of her sisters' dolls and her brother's broken toy *carreta* sat on a high shelf and splashed cool water on her face. She toweled off and put some French ointment onto her face that her mother had told her to use every day. Her father moaned at the cost and said it was gilding the lily, but never let her run out either. Then she disrobed and put rosewater in the damp at the back of her hairline, under her arms, over her breasts and belly. She put on clean cotton underthings and pulled out her favorite skirt, the very blue of the Virgin's veil and then she ground her teeth at the awkward thought – she was no longer a virgin. Still. Grown women wore this color all the time. No sin in blue on a lady. She put on a white blouse exuberant with lace, clean white stockings, soft black leather shoes with tiny mother-of-pearl buttons. The shawl she had was black with hundreds of flowers and butterflies and hummingbirds and had taken over a year to embroider. It was such a riot of color that anything she wore it with, matched, automatically. She looked at her cheeks, pink verging on scarlet and wished that her nervousness was not so evident.

Why be nervous? Papí had not said no.

He had not said yes.

He had agreed to meet with Aurelio. That was a good thing, no?

When she came back out into the *sala*, it was only minutes before Aurelio was due to arrive. She clasped her hands and looked up at her Papí and she could feel kindness coming off her father like heat from sandstone in summer sun. She sighed in relief.

TUNAS

Aurelio rode up to the house. He had been in front of the barn a hundred times; he'd even been in the house on occasion. It felt different before a momentous occasion. His horse was groomed within an inch of its life, he was wearing the best clothes he could put together, his hair still damp from his attempt to civilize it post church.

As he gave his horse to Oso, he looked up at the house. Outside one of the windows of the east wing of the house was an impressive array of *tunas*, cactus pear. That was were the girls would have slept, where his own beloved must sleep every night. Fathers across California planted *tunas* outside the bedrooms of their daughters to keep the likes of him outside. With considerable chagrin, he choked back a small smile – so much for the virtue-keeping efficacy of the *tunas*. She had asked him to love her, she had asked him. How could he have said no?

He walked towards the house, his heart beat slow and strong, his steps measured. This mattered. This mattered.

The door opened and he saw her father standing there. The two men made eye contact.

LUNA DE MIEL

She dreamt he was whispering, so softly, in her ear, whilst she slept, "*Esposa, esposaa – e-s-p-o-saaa--*" and when she stirred and woke, it was true. The light of dawn swept in through the window and she could see clearly what had been shadows last night: him, golden and pale with brown-black hairs waving along his shins and curling like fragile corkscrews on his chest. The mass and size and drape of him. She was embarrassed to stare at him naked like that but she could no more have pulled her eyes away then left a colt being birthed: he just fascinated her. And when she looked up at his face, through her own eyelashes and a hefty blush, she saw he was smiling at her. His eyes felt like sunlight on her and she smiled back. He was lying on her black hair, all strewn across the white sheets, trapping her, and he put a hand on her waist to roll her in close to him and she knew she would always say yes to him, no matter what. He started kissing her and they pressed into each other and he put a hand to her leg and there they were again, being married.

Afterwards when she was filled with his sweetness and he was lazily kissing her mouth, still unable to let go of her somehow, she pulled her head back to put her hair up over the edge of the bed. The morning had grown hot and for a moment all she wanted was to cool off for a bit. But then he whispered in her ear, "There. Do you feel it?"

Like a little kid buying into a fairy tale, she whispered back, "Feel what?"

"The bed. It is lifting."

"Yes?" she asked, not sure.

"There. We are levitating. Not very much. Maybe a foot. Or two." And then, weirdly enough, she felt it too. The bed was raising. And they were rising up above it. Maybe only a few inches. But such was their bliss they were, for a time, free from gravity. Not flying like birds, who must earn the transport. More like spirits floating up to God.

Faces glowing with sweat and joy they looked into each other's eyes, the dark lit from the inside. She felt afraid. Could such a beautiful thing last in this world? Didn't saints end up being burnt or flayed for their private happiness?

There was a clatter as the bed shifted and she felt all her weight return and she sank into the soft bed, feeling his weight come back down beside her. His eyes were wet.

He kissed her.

And then there was a knock at the door.

He laughed, *"Asi es la vida."*

"Un momentito," said the bride, looking for clothing and blankets and modesty the day after.

"Un gran momentito," said her husband, kissing her.

The knock came again and she knew they had to go back to the rest of the house.

She told her man, *"Esta noche."* And slipped out of bed.

BREAK

After lunch, María Marta found an excuse to ride out and snuck off to Tree, looking to regain her serenity. So much sugary passion left her overwhelmed; she was drowning in oceanic bliss wherein she herself, her separate soul, was obliterated by honey.

She rode crisply to the site, not wanting to stay long enough to be missed. Her horse stopped to graze, seeing lounging in this meadow as her right by now. María Marta heard mourning doves cooing and realized there was a mated pair, nesting just out of sight. Incorrigibly curious, she looked for the hidden nest. She had never climbed Tree before but found herself heaping up some fallen branches and rocks to get purchase and skinning up the trunk and onto a branch and looking eye to eye at tiny little eggs. She sighed, happy and maybe a little envious. She was startled to hear Aurelio's voice below her.

"*Hola.*"

María Marta was a little embarrassed, to have been caught climbing a tree like a child, to not be at home as she imagined a new bride should be, to see him in the open air after everything was changed between them. He, however, was more at ease with her than he had ever been before and she found his emotional comfort contagious. Relaxing. So she smiled at him. Aurelio told her he knew he would find her there and offered her help to come down. When she got down, she told him about the eggs and they held hands and kissed and whispered and waited for the parent birds to return. The mother returned first and when she settled into her soft repetitions of "Coo, coo, cooooo…," Aurelio's facial expression softened further.

"What is it?" queried María Marta. He pulled her in and nestled his face into the crook between her neck and shoulder and told her that when he was a toddler, a baby boy, he remembered walking towards his favorite Tía, over at their house for *café* with his mother. In his memories, his dark eyed aunt offered him a sip of milky sweet coffee off the edge of her saucer. At that exact same moment, mourning doves cooed outside the open window in the courtyard across from the kitchen. Within the sound, he recognized that he was hearing, tasting, feeling, thinking. Himself, living in such a world. Sentient. Separate and unique.

Mourning doves cooing was his earliest memory, the moment of awareness of being, the sweetness of recognizing his own self in such a world. And now here they were, hearing time beginning, together, in their together beginning. She twined around him and mimicked the birds cooing at him and he tasted sweetness in his mouth. For e's part, Tree felt birds and eggs and humans, horses, grass, dirt, groundwater, sunlight and skies stretching to other worlds. And heard birds cooing.

HEART RACING

A little boy on a tall horse came trotting up to the front door, his feet pointing downward as if he stretched hard enough, he might have a chance at getting his feet in the stirrups. María sent Ana Julietta to get the *sandia* she'd said she'd squeezed and greeted the boy before he'd even dismounted. He rushed the niceties, too.

"There's a ship in the harbor. Your husband's horse is on it. You must come get it."

This was the first she had heard of it. She invited the boy in for dinner, but he didn't even get off his horse. He had other *chisme* to share throughout the mountains, so he said he would go. He drank the watermelon juice without getting off his horse.

Dinner was entertaining when she pinned her *esposo* like a butterfly in front of her father. He squirmed and admitted this had been a purchase before he'd fought with his father, a racehorse, from the Barbary Coast that he'd read about in the three months out of date French paper – the fastest horse in the desert, the writer had stated. He'd bought her, sight unseen, for an amount that made her father's jaw drop and her husband, now modest with his expenditures, blush. Then her father surprised them by laughing and punching his son-in-law in the arm. He said they should stage a race in six weeks time, make a *fiesta* of the whole thing, he would provide the hospitality.

Perhaps they could beat Diego's new stud with the big bottom.

Guessing at the stamina of a desert-bred mare, he suggested that a long course would allow them to crush him, or rather, them.

María had thought they would ride out in the morning but found herself, stuffed with dinner and sleepy, out at night on horse-back, with blankets rolled behind the saddle and her father chattering at them like a schoolboy on the way home after term. A full moon came up on the horizon, distorted to Biblical proportions by the horizon's illusion, as soft and luscious as a white peach and about the same color. María drifted into reverie and only started when her horse slowed to stop and graze, leaving the other two to wander ahead. By the time she caught up with them, both wits and horse collected, she looked back into the sky to see the oversized children's ball turned a kind of fluorescent cantalope. María's eyes drifted further to the stars, Ursa Minor forever looking for a bullbaiting with the constellation of Taurus and no way to bring on the drama.

Her mind drifted and she found her head snapping back up as she came out of sleep and into some kind of barely real sentience. Her dad and her husband were still talking, planning some project for the barns, discussing ideas about refurbishing the house. Her husband wanted a father to approve of him and her poor father, any kind of son at all would do. Sometimes she felt left out and other times she just felt so happy that they were friends.

Such a thing was not a given, of course.

When they got to the shore, they could see the ship's watch, tiny as matchbox dolls in a boat made out of a distant baby's slipper, with a drawer of miniature doll's handkerchiefs as the neatly rolled up sails. María felt some strange, ill-defined longing and recognized this total surface-of-her-skin yearning as travel-lust. So tired that when she slithered off the horse, she fell in the sand, she was relieved when her father suggested that they wait until morning to pick up the animal.

"One more night aboard won't kill it," he asserted philosophically. She thought about a fire and tea and about grooming horses and taking off her shoes, but before she could formulate any kind of reasonable next act, her dad had all three horses ground-tied and was unsaddling them and taking off bridles and one of the saddles was put under her head and she found herself stretched out on a blanket that she had not laid out and two more atop her and then her husband with an arm around her and she was fast asleep before she could think how odd it was to have them care for her as if she were a tiny child, unable to care for herself. But as a motherless girl, she had not been watching her monthly cycles and wouldn't have put it together what it signified had she noticed their disappearance. But both men came from large families and ranchs and knew the signs. The nausea, the mood-swings, the completely disproportionate exhaustion. Her father lay near them, smiling at his son-in-law's face over his daughter's shoulder. They hadn't needed to exchange a word, they knew that the other man knew and each man figured the other man's happiness, if anything, only exceeded his own. Soon the dainty woman was snoring and they tried to jolt her out of the raucous noise without actually waking her up. It was hopeless. They settled in, the horses grazing near by.

In the morning, they found a number of the local men piled up nearby, waiting for the racehorse. María's father told them about the great invitation-only tournament in six weeks time. Word travels fast in a small community and everyone liked horses and speed and contests. Everyone wanted to see the newest horse in California.

But when the ship was unloaded, she was pathetic, more than anything. The mare had to be lifted and dropped into a boat. They missed and she struggled in the water. Aurelio had to swim out and coax the skinny, dull-eyed mare to shore. Once she arrived, she lay down like a colt in the sun, uninterested in anything further until a half effectual nap was out of the way. The city men scoffed and ran back to their world of glossy horses and narrowed horizons; the *rancheros* and their *vaqueros* rolled their eyes. This was a horse?

Both men looked at the bathetic mare hunched over the sand and started to laugh. María Marta shut them up. She told them once a champion, always a champion and then she woke the horse, crouched down and talked her into standing. She could only get her to follow when she walked initially, until the mare made friends with María's mother's old horse. Then they walked nose to throatlatch all the way home.

When they got there, María released the quivering mare into her own boxstall with an attached corral and shut her in. She unsaddled her own horse and was compelled to go inside and to take a nap. It was just too much. Marriage, new livestock, old plans, money and …this tiredness.

Before dinner, María met her husband and her father standing dejectedly in the barn. Her father was trying to explain how hard a trip across the Atlantic and around Argentina and up Chile was for man and even more so for beast. Imagine lying in bed for two months, only the bed is heaving, the food is terrible, the water stale, no light, no companionship. María quietly slipped out and nabbed the mare she'd been riding the day before by the forelock and brought her up to the stall. The men agreed with the wisdom of this and pulled open the door to let the older horse in with their prize. The younger horse banged at the smaller mare and scuffed the wood of the wall, but the older mare nipped her expertly behind the ears on the neck and the younger mare stopped quarreling. Neither had really meant it, just that it was a small stall for two full grown horses. The men talked desultorily about what to feed her, her coat, the condition of her hooves (a bit thrushy, actually.) Six weeks wasn't enough time, they were both ruefully conceding, but María remembered getting over cholera. She reminded her father of the long walks they had taken, morning and night, beginning just to the water trough and back in the front then back up the stairs, taking fifteen minutes for what should have been a bouncing half a dozen strides. But in a month she'd walked to church and back. So the family haltered the two mares and went for a stroll in the afternoon heat, pausing under the shade of the oaks along the way, letting the horses graze for minutes at a time here and there. By the time the sun set, the horses were grazing amongst the tombstones and family crypts at the little church the family had helped to build.

"Good girl," said Aurelio fondly.

"Yes," said María, petting the new horse.

"No, I meant you," he said. She punched him in the arm not hard enough to hurt, but enough to set him back a step.

He laughed, "I would have let her sit in the stall for however long it took for her to fatten up and look a bit steadier on her feet. But she might as well wobble down the road as wobble in her own room."

"Morning, noon and night," said the patriarch. The young man smiled. He could see that his ordinary duties had been erased. Everything for the new mare.

A few walks later, they ran into a trio of young guys, *borrachos*, out riding their horses at a gallop. One of the kids yelled out, "Is that going to be a walking race?" Mean laughter spilled over the bleached wild oats in the field and the evening smell of damp dry grass. They whipped their horses and galloped off. Aurelio looked over at wife and father-in-law and shrugged. "*A palabras necias, oídos sordos.*"

The family walked back in a daze of laziness in the warm evening, crickets in the fields and frogs in the creeks, the moon slightly waning in the velvety sky.

Overjoyed by his deep sense that he had done right by his daughter by letting her marry this penniless cowboy, the son of the man he most loathed, enjoying their evident happiness, holding hands, the two horses companionably keeping pace with the people, the old mare jamming her head between the lovers to be a part of their herd, the new mare crowding in for her space, it felt so cozy, so familial, so evocative of his own long-ago marital happiness, that he burst into song. From the fullness of his heart, he rewrote the lyrics to the old melodies to talk about horses belonging to desert kings, about impoverished cowboys winning the hand of the maiden of the house, about old men pining for grandchildren, about girls with dark eyes and shining hair, about moons and stars and the noises of the night (which he emulated in the chorus) and he was just starting to think about singing about his dead wife when they were abruptly back in front of the house, the horses leaning down to slurp from the trough, Oso coming to take them in, the smell of hot food coming in from the kitchen and the spell was broken and he fell silent. But his little girl, taller than her mother had been by now, leaned over and kissed him on the cheek, "Wasn't she beautiful?" she reminisced and then she turned and ran up the steps in a swirl of skirts.

WALKING

Walking their Barbary Coast prize in the morning before it was too hot stretched into longer and longer meanders; up on ridges with coastal scrub, hot as Hades.

A roadrunner burst into their way, dashing into the bright and downy sandstone dust. Down grassy hillsides yellow with mustard and nodding oats, into little tree-lined arroyos, where the younger oaks stood the height of four men, boughs reaching across the path to make contact with their companions, looking like soldiers crossing swords for an honorary stroll out from church doors.

Even the chamise, lemonadeberry, toyon, ceanothus and manzanita in these hidden crevasses grew tall enough for Aurelio and María Marta to walk in shade.

The couple chatted their way through each other's infancy and childhood, debating the merits of relatives on both sides of their family, discussing favorite songs and poems and dances, the few books they had read cover to cover, over and over, envious of the trunk of books they knew was rotating with some *ranchero* families in the north of Alta California, planning their future with the verbal building blocks that are the architecture of young love, lasting castles of hopefulness. Groundwork for babies and clean sheets and new barns and all the things a new family might need. The horse's stride lengthened as she strengthened and relaxed and the strong young people didn't realize how powerful they themselves had become; few visitors from a city could have kept up with them on their lazy jaunts. The ease of the day blew up when María Marta screeched and jumped backwards; Aurelio's fight or fight reflex kicked in; it took a moment for her to calm him down. The marauder was neither man nor beast, but poison oak. As someone who had no response to the plant, this was only a theoretical disaster to him. So she spelled it out: Mariá Marta had gotten poison oak a number of times as a child and a young woman – big raised pink splotches that oozed white, clear and yellow fluid and for the weeks that she had it, made her resemble a Biblical leper.

But then her Maria had taught her how to ward off the poison oak and she would rub her bare skin with mugwort whenever she rode by some, just to be on the safe side.

And equally wondrous, the old Chumash woman told her that the youths and maidens of her village used to make pillows of the fresh or dried leaves and then fall into dreams that told the truth of their futures. With her nanny's encouragement, María Marta tried it once, when she was ten, but after claimed she'd had a terrible nightmare sent by the devil and refused to discuss the details. Now she wondered if that had been about the cholera. To her surprise, her nana made her lie down on the blasted pillow again and this time she dreamt of a man with brown-black hair and dark eyes and her heart sang and the old Indian lady was smug – this was more like it. When she told her mother of the whole experience, the younger woman was mad at her child's ancient caregiver – she had no doubt that the mugwort worked, she just did not believe in exposing children to soothsaying of any kind. The future was as apt to be ugly as to be beautiful and how could one bear life if the story were to be foretold? Better to face the future in a haze of cautious optimism, fueled by prayer, music, dancing, poetry, good food and plenty of time out of doors.

At the least it was good to pass the time enjoyably.

EN CASA

With each turning of the earth, after long days of working the new horse, while still running the house and tracking the herds, the young couple would come home and late or early, eventually find themselves behind closed doors.

Inchoate erotica.

SECRETO

Late at night, when his bride had fallen into a deep sleep, because he could not resist, Aurelio started to sneak out to ride his new horse – just to see what she could do. It was not that he did not believe in his wife's all walking recovery regime. He did. It was working, obviously. It was just that he could feel the mare's past triumphs skimming over golden hot sands and he knew the horse had started to yearn for the feeling of letting her power fly through her. He would slip on her bareback with a hackamore and let her pick her path and her pace and her gallop felt like glory and fire.

Hours later, he would slip back into bed and nestle into his wife's warm back.

He could not wait to race his shining horse.

PICNICS

Aurelio and María Marta came by to see Tree on a Sunday after church, on yet another of their interminable walkings. Her father went off to see neighbors, but they were young and wanted to be together without an audience. He lay a blanket down over the duff and they settled onto the crunchy bed of leaves. The girl's conscious and unconscious thinkings drifted into the light breeze like a dried chrysanthemum flower struck by boiling water in fancy Yankee-imported Chinese tea, opening up from a dried husk into an entire floating world. Tree could feel her happiness fizzing in little blips of emotion like carbonated water popping at contact with the air. She directed some of her joy at Tree intentionally and e was astonished; e realized it was the first time since Univervia that anyone had deliberately given happiness away to e.

E loved her for her generosity as if she were the hot/light herself. E radiated appreciation back at her and she clutched her husband's hands in her small fists.

"What?" he said, feeling the edges of this thing.

"Do you feel it – do you hear it?" she asked. She tried to explain, feeling clumsy. "The tree, the tree is happy." She stood up, feeling she could better translate with her body than with words and began to dance the way she felt for Tree, Tree for her, the feeling of light on leaves, the joy of their baby in her stomach. And he understood, more or less, as there was a reason it was he who was her man. He smiled, feeling nearly exactly the same thing Tree did. She was just profligate with happiness and he, for his part, was happy to just sit and be showered by it. When he couldn't stand it anymore he grabbed her skirts when she swayed too near and yanked her down into his lap, where she laughed at him. He put a hand out on the trunk of the Tree and then made eye contact with her, wanting her to feel that he was including her feelings and visions in their doings. If she were a saint, he'd bow to her god whether he saw it or not, because he saw her and believed in her. And while Tree could not read this man, he understood this human gesture of inclusion and tried to express dignity, admiration, affection in loud echoes of Tree voice.

Crickets whirring and dozens of lesser birds warning each other of the advent of a falcon, María Marta rolled off her honey's lap and back onto their blanket, gazing up at the spreading boughs and the thousands upon thousands of leaves. She could feel the power generated as leaf after leaf after leaf calmly photosynthesized, roots took in water, trunks and branches grew and the sky covered them all. The ennui and weight of her pregnancy caught up to her and she felt dizzy and tired and heard her honey whispering in her ear, sleep, *niña*, sleep and she dreamed of saplings and infants and milk and sex and happiness, curled up in her lover's arms in summerlight.

TEST

They had had to put off the race twice due to other people's problems with *their* horses; their little Barbarian mare had made it up to ten miles of walking a day by that point and, now that María Marta was in on it, was secretly being run at night for a full gallop at 6 miles a shot, up and down hills.

The horse was skinny like a whippet and not an easy ride, but the whole family had come to like her. The day before the race, the family rode into Los Angeles, their racehorse trotting behind them, and stayed with the Avila family. The course was set at four miles and though there were twenty horses in the race, everyone soon saw that it was between Aurelio's mare and a big black gelding belonging to a Pico cousin, a famous horseman and gambler.

The bay and the black horse took the lead from the moment the starting shot rang out. Most of the four miles of the course unspooled out of sight while María Marta clutched her father's hand and most everyone around them bet on the black horse. Oso put down his savings on their mare, to the shared horror of both María Marta and her father. It was hot and dusty and the wait for the racehorses' return felt elongated. She could feel her heart speeding as if she herself were riding at a gallop for a long run.

Abruptly the two prize horses came pounding down the main street and María Marta could feel her father's fingernails digging into her arms as he clutched her. Most everyone had bet for their family's own horses or for the black gelding except the three of them and Oso; there were huge huge amounts of money at play. To say nothing of pride.

She could see her lover ask his mare for her all and she could feel the small horse gather up fire from some internal wellspring and it was like an oasis bursting into bloom, like fire leaping in a cold grate, she just took off and was one lead, two leads, three, four, five, twenty ahead of the other horse. Everyone was standing, shrieking and yelling as horse and rider tore through the finish line.

Laughing, yelling, cussing, hilarity and wroth burst out from everyone in the crowd. Even people who lost money had to admit that the little horse was exceptional. Maria Marta jumped away from her father and ran in the sandy street towards the sweaty horse and her laughing man. The gelding came running through, a definite second place. His rider leapt off and Aurelio gracefully kicked off his stirrups, flung his leg over the withers of his horse and landed on his feet like a fencer ready to dance. But there were no swords, only a derringer that he didn't expect, pulled out from his rival's vest. The noise of the two shots were lost in the sounds of the whole crowd and it took a moment for everyone to see the hero of the day sinking to his knees and pitching forward, his wife running to lift him from the dirt, blood in the sand, on her shirt and skirt and his face and out of his pretty lips, in his hair, his shirt. It was a nightmare and women wept and covered their children's eyes and men leapt over chairs and dogs and pushed each other aside in their eagerness to grab the murderer. The killer's own family members pushed aside the vigilantes and he was shoved onto a fresh horse and half the town took off after him and María Marta did not care whether they caught him or not, it was her heart that was bleeding on to the dusty road, her heart pumping the blood of her own life. Her lover's eyes met her own and told her how very sorry he was to be leaving, how he did not want to forswear himself, how he wanted life, his own, their own, their child's. She wept and in her heart begged God, María, anyone at all, the lost gods of the Indians, for mercy. The sun shone down on Los Angeles and her man died.

HEART'S BLOOD

María Marta woke up at home, on the sofa, her head in her father's lap, a crick in her neck. It looked like he had not slept. She looked down at her hands – though someone had washed them, she could see blood under her fingernails. She looked up at her father's face and the years dropped away. That was the look he had had after Tomásito. His fingers were knotted into her hair as if she might get away somehow if he didn't tie her to him, physically. She shifted and she could feel that the crinkle of dried blood on the front of her dress. It had soaked through to her skin, so it felt like a bandage that had dried on, stuck to her from some wound on her own self. Heaven is not a place constructed above the clouds, but the places inhabited by the breath of those one loves; remove the breath and all the miracles fell to delicate meaningless fragments like a house, a love letter, burning to ash. She wanted to give up, to let her life dissipate, to spill the rest of her blood. She noticed her father's legs were so much skinnier than she remembered. How had that happened? When did he become old? She looked up into his eyes and knew what he was thinking. Don't. Leave. Me. Having an accurate sense of what each breath was going to cost her, of how incredibly slowly her life was going to pass as a widow, she still bore a childlike devotion to her father. He had been so good to her, to her siblings, to her mother. To her husband. He put a hand on her belly. She brushed it off. Too much of the father in the baby for her to take that on right now. But she would tell him what he needed to hear to be able to sneak off to sleep, "I will stay with you."

She pulled his hand out of her hair and sat up awkwardly, ridiculously big. "*Tengo que bañar –*" she said and she walked out of the room. She walked into the kitchen to put water on to boil and saw someone already had pots on simmering for this purpose. An almost grown maid gestured towards a chair in the corner with her chin and so María Marta sat down while the girl and her father together grunted several big pots out towards the bathroom.

When the water was gone, María Marta followed it, heading

towards the trail of steam. When she got into the room, the new girl was waiting to help strip her, but she sent the young woman out of the room.

She pulled off the velvet skirt and the jacket made a tearing sound as she separated it from the chemise. The chemise itself was stuck to her like a scab. She peeled off her stockings and stepped into the hot-hot water, gently removing the pieces of cloth like sunburnt skin. The water swirled brown and red from the blood and as she rubbed her skin clean it felt like this was the last time she could make love to her husband in flesh and blood. She knew she would remember everything he had ever done to her, but this was swimming in his life force, his baby in her, him on her. Wanting him so very much she touched herself intimately, imagining what he would do, were he in this tub with her, were he in this world.

No one was surprised when late that night, she went into labor; it was a month early or right on time, if you thought about the exit of the child's father. The fifteen year old who María Marta had snubbed earlier in the day was compassionate anyway. The shock of witnessing her first birth begin had brought out the best in her and she sent María Marta's father out for a midwife, who was attending a birth only five miles away. The older woman wouldn't leave one dicey birth to go off to the next, and María Marta's father was unwilling to settle for the new midwife when the woman he considered the best was telling him, hour after hour, to just wait a little longer. So Celestina was the one to stand in for sister, mother, midwife, doctor, even god, in María Marta's eyes, the one who yelled at her to keep trying when the contractions weakened, who made her sugary lemonade to drink, who knelt on her belly when it seemed no progress had been made, who got lard from the kitchen and tried to stretch the surface of her poor vagina to ease out the head, who bit her own lip when she saw a small tear as the head crowned, who cradled the half-in, half-out baby until the next contraction pushed him out, who wept big fat tears of joy as the afterbirth slithered out and she realized that, thanks to God, the baby was breathing, the mother was breathing and in this house of death, a new life was shimmering. She kissed María Marta's forehead, her cheeks, her lips and embraced her, the little boy crushed happily between them. Celestina accepted congratulations from the old midwife, who showed up in time to make sure that María was not bleeding too much and got the baby latched on to the nipples that seemed too large for such a tiny mouth. The old woman told María Marta that she had attended her own mother's birth, which made María Marta cry. It wasn't actually true, but it was a story to bring joy into the room and so María Marta's father, who knew the midwife would have been two years old when his wife was born, let it sit there like a fairytale. When they handed him his grandson he knew that he wanted happily ever after.

MELINA SEMPILL WATTS

HUMAN SPROUT

María Marta walked down the path to Tree, beaming.

Tree had understood enough of her private thoughts over the last few months to understand completely how perilous an undertaking human childbirth could be.

Though e had never been there, instantly e could picture the gravestones of two of her friends, could see the fancy dresses like upside-down full-blown roses which the girls had worn at their weddings, could see one in white, with a sweet tiny baby in white lace nested to her chest, in a black coffin, could picture the other, pregnant forever now, and alone, skin ashen, looking like one big kiss from a storybook prince would bring back the pink and gold to her grey cheeks and the sparkle into the eyes hidden under long-lashed smooth shut lids.

Pulled from such a reverie, Tree felt such happiness at seeing María Marta leap down the hillside like a rainfed spring brook that it felt like a bright light shining from e's core.

She was more exuberant than e, though.

Personal survival was trivial compared to what was in her arms: a son. Black-eyed and brown-haired, fairer than she in complexion, all laced up tight in her *rebozo*.

"*¡Mira!*" her voice rang out clear and solid. "*¡Mira mi hijo!*"

She jumped over the trickle of creek and ran panting up to under the canopy of Tree's branches. "Do you see?" her heart cried out. "Can you see him as I see him?"

Tree understood with a start that this person the size of a large cat was the center of the universe to her.

For Tree, eself had been the center. E had come to understand that for others e had loved – each grass – even Rock – each self had been the center for which the, experience of being sprang. As Tree grew more complex, e theorized that the hot/globe was perhaps the true center of everything. But María Marta's whole being indicated her new understanding: the sun rose and set for the furtherance of this little being's life.

So Tree whispered to the infant boy "*Hola.*" Tried Tree song. Tried just putting out friendly puffs of energy at the mite, as e would to new sprouts of grass, but it was clear this infant heard no hint of Treespeak.

María Marta was kind, "Human babies take years to learn human speech. And I myself did not hear you until I was fourteen years of age."

Tree muttered, "Your husband never heard me –" regretting mentioning the dead on such a sunny day.

But nothing could gloom up the new-mother euphoria she trailed like gold pollen glintering in the wind. "Oh Tree," she smiled. "– when he was with me, he could not see or hear anything but me. He was so *enamorado* –" and Tree understood that as much as e had once loved grass, e now loved this black-haired girl with two wet spots on her thin white cotton shirt and sparks in her eyes.

"*Yo tambien.*" Tree said. Impulsively, she reached around Tree's broad trunk – her open arms encircling less than a third of e's mature full girth and she kissed e's hard bark. "I love you too." she whispered aloud. Tree was glad, though the baby cried to be caught between the soft mother-body and the hard Tree.

"Silly boy." she murmured, settling down to nurse him into contentment, dropping her *rebozo* over herself and her boy.

Tree observed the feeling of love in her core translating into fluid and pouring into her breasts and into the child's hungry mouth. "That's how it feels when my roots drink water from the Earth." Tree observed.

"Then everything loves everyone and every thing is one and we are all one –" she exclaimed.

For today, it was true.

The baby nursed.

Tree watched.

EXPROPRIATION

The *carreta* was filled with all the household gear she could assemble in a rushed morning; a bed, bedding, the big piece from the living room with the mirror, several candelabras, her mother's silver, her own jewels hidden in her son's clothes, her clothes, the boy's clothes, her saddle, bridle and some horse gear, her mother's music, her own books, sewing things, knives, scissors, a comb, just a jumble of thoughts, the family bible. Beside her was her fifteen year old mare, inherited from her mother, still pretty and sleek, her boy atop, and tied behind them was her husband's horse, about whom she remained ambivalent.

Had not his love for this animal killed him? But all the horse had done was to excel, she had run when she was asked to run and she had won her races with pride and flair. She hoped the American's ignorance of Spanish prevented them from knowing who this animal was. Maybe they were too stupid to tell her worth by looking.

She thought of how beautiful her father's family had been and how small it now was and she clung to her interior vow: whatever it took, she would save herself and save her boy. And she would not cry before thieves. She got into the *carreta* without a word and lashed the lame ox they had left for her.

One of them said to the other, "I want the Arabian horse." And with that, he leaned over and cut the rope tying the horse to the back of the *carreta*. She slapped her thigh so that the horse would come running to her as her husband had taught the horse to do five years ago. She jerked on the rope trying to return to the safety of her presence, but the lead was already wrapped several times around the horn of the American's saddle. The power of the racing horse jerked both horse and rider after her. Something in María Marta snapped and she saw red, a phrase she had thought was metaphorical until it happened to her. The next thing she saw clearly, she was standing at the back of the *carreta* and she had withdrawn from its scabbard her father's old Spanish sword and in one furious slash, she had cut the rope again. She jumped atop the cart and called over the mare and she, skittish at the swordplay, came jittering over. María Marta jumped astride her husband's horse and then faced off before the two armed men. Now it occurred to her that they could kill her and her son and keep everything and that no one would be the wiser.

"We let you keep your household goods," said the quiet one. "We didn't have to do that."

"We let you live," said the meaner one.

"Now Johnson," said the first man, "Don't scare her." He rode between the woman and his partner, seeing the man's hand reaching for his gun. "I'll make you two a deal," he said, playing, as always the good guy in their constant game of quasi-legal chicanery, "Lady, choose. The horse you sit on or all your household goods." She hesitated and looked over to her son, frightened, on the placid horse he'd known his whole life. She asked him in Spanish whether he'd rather have Papi's horse or all their furniture. The grandson of two *rancheros*, to him there was no question as to the answer. Shaking to lose yet more of things that they would need to survive, she swooped over the cart and picked up the heavy family bible in one hand and a silver candelabra in the other.

"Fine. Take it all," she said. "*Vaya conmigo, mijo.*" She kicked her heels in her horse's sides and the mare took off like a shot. It was awkward clutching book, sword and candelabra, riding the smooth horse bareback with no bridle or saddle, in a slippery silk skirt with layers of undergarments in the way of her grip, but she held on through pride and fear and she heard her son cantering after them. She prayed quietly that they would live to the turn of the road. As soon as they made the curve, she turned to smile at her son, "We have each other. We are alive. *Gracias à Dios.*" He looked at her and a little of the strain left his tight face.

"*Gracias à Dios.* Where are we going Mamí?" he asked.

"*No sé,*" she responded. Indeed, she had no idea. People who spoke Spanish felt like a good thing, so she told him, "Let's go to Los Angeles and find a room."

Two weeks after that bleak day, she saddled up their older mare and rode double after church to Tree, the first of many Sundays spent in this fashion. When they got to the valley, María Marta spread out a blanket and laid out the treats she had packed up. Mother and son ate *tamales*, fresh fruit, drank *orchata* and *nopales* wrapped in tortillas and then her boy went down to the creek to try to catch frogs, and, after a few minutes of begging, gave up on engaging his mother in his play. She sat, back against the trunk, numb. Tree's presence gradually entered her own and she relaxed.

She didn't even know tears were rolling down her face She let her thoughts unroll, knowing they were pouring into Tree without her effort. Tree saw images of her handing over the imported Arabian mare to her in-laws, for a handful of coins. Her son, dressed in a white ruffled shirt, neat pants and soft cinnamon colored leather boots, reaching up to kiss his *abuela* and she, turning her cheek. Without understanding, Tree felt the sting of this in his friend.

While her child played and birds sang, she pulled out a christening gown and, Sunday though it was, continued sewing on it, stitch after tiny stitch, concentrating until she heard her son fall in the muddy water with a yelp. She put the tiny dress aside and ran down to the creek, pulling him out. He was unhurt, but covered in mud, so she stripped him down to underclothes and rinsed the mud off his finery.

Appearances were all she had; she wouldn't have his clothes ruined.

When he cried, cold, she dried him off then wrapped him up in her *rebozo* to snuggle him up. As she caressed his hair and sang old songs to him, he relaxed, but he only slept when she closed her eyes and pretended to sleep with him. Then the trick worked on her, and she, too fell asleep in the grass, her work cast aside. The luxury of an afternoon nap was intoxicating to a tired single mother – and she dreamt inside Tree. Everything slowed down and she felt the rich warmth of sun pushing into her skin cells, feeding her, felt the slow pulse of water and soil coming up her veins; the parallel slow pulse as sap moved through lazy arteries running down her trunk and limbs. Her toes stretched unconsciously digging into the soil, the delicious stretch of roots growing slowly sweetening. Tree's big personality just steamrollered over her loneliness and all the void in her heart was filled with the largeness of oakness. She turned, human that she was, in her sleep, and stretched one arm away from her child and around the ground and roots, as if she could capture this feeling like a lover in an embrace. Her little boy squirmed in closer, still asleep and her lips parted, breathing in the warm air, the smell of dry duff, soil, strands of sage and chaparral interrupted by a wisp of mulefat scent coming in a cool vent up from the creek. She could feel the nests being built against her throat, in her hair, the imaginary insects and blue skink on her bare skin, the voices of other plants, the emotional undertone of rock's silent existence. Thanks to Tree, it was a familiar orchestra of life and her troubles floated off down the babbling creek and disappeared. Tree's intense dedication to growth and magnificence translated into a knowingness when she woke that she was loved, that she would grow and thrive. That there would always be sunlight and water for her and hers.

Her son woke up and cried fitfully, having difficulty transitioning out of sleep into waking, but he was soon distracted by the effort to pack up food and horse and people and when they were mounted, he in front of her, gear behind her, they circled underneath Tree, María Marta telling her child to tell Tree good-bye, to tell it they will come again. He was so young he thought of Tree like a relative, an uncle or something.

He kept expecting the Tree to actually talk, like an animal in a fairytale and wasn't disappointed when it didn't because he was so certain that someday it *would* talk to him. He thought to himself that the plant was holding out on him until he convinced Tree of his worthiness.

COINS

With every stitch, she hoped that the people for whom she was sewing would be happy wearing these clothes. That was why she never took on military uniforms or police gear...she worried about the potential for spilt blood on the cloth.

Instead, she specialized in elaborate christening gowns for boys and girls, in dreamy wedding dresses, in *quinceañeras*, or, the daily bread work of letting out pants and sleeves on little boys' school uniforms, adding a bit of fabric to someone's husband's old suit, so that he wouldn't have to buy new clothes to fit his increasing girth. She liked to pretend she wasn't being paid, that this was all for love. It made her happier to sew for friends than for clients. Sometimes she'd do things for free, unable to control her charitable impulses. She had a soft spot for orphans.

Stitch. Pull. Stitch. Pull. Fabric turned. Stitch.

María Marta's mind wandered to the open spaces of her childhood, the rhythm of a cantering horse fueling her daydreams, Tree's branches spreading inside her head, dissolving the cramped ceiling of the rooms that they rented into the majesty of open land and infinite sky. All the beauty of her youth stored up in her head, an endless supply of fresh air.

GROVE

In the forest of black walnuts, new trees had come to maturity, two young sycamore came into balance the mix. The black walnuts stood tall, mature, a limb fallen in a storm, some leaves in the undergrowth dead, but essentially confident. Just above them to the northwest, the stands of ceanothus outgrew their customary sizes and became cathedrals of bushes, arch after arch of branches touching, creating a walkway down the paths they overhung, wherein they talked amongst themselves, creating private magic for themselves and those who passed between their trunks.

Edging the meadow, the elderberries were covered with light greenish-white flowers.

In the creekbed, the willows had fuzzy green or furry white evidence of their gender, depending.

All the trees in all the meandering groves of the valley, even the self-centered younger oak pair at Tree's canopy, talked amongst themselves in the soft breezy afternoon, blowing past anything but the simple joys of growth and light with damp root bases.

HUMAN SAPLING

Antonito could remember a time with full tables and servants, a
corral full of cattle and horses, polished silver, lace dresses. Or at least
he thought he could. Mostly, he saw his mother aging as she sewed
from breakfast until dinner, and then again after dinner, day after day
excepting Sundays, his inadequacy as a boy to make things as they
should be. She tried to communicate her sense of the wheel of fate, a
kind of Catholic version of karma, that once upon a time perchance
they had had…too much…that the Indians had been robbed and now
so had they and some day, the white people too would be robbed. That
only God himself owned property. But thinking in centuries did not
mesh with his pre-adolescent hormonery, with his outraged young
manhood that a lady such as his mother should have to work so hard,
that someone of his breeding should have an implication of struggle
ahead…

He remembered his father's imported mare, the story of the race
and murder, the glamour of it running brighter than his mother's grief,
which tarnished her shine.

So, somehow from even before he was as tall as his mother, when
schoolyard card games started and coins flashed, he loved the early
wins and the feeling of jingle in his pocket. He hid what he was doing
from his mother with care – she was disparaging about cards and ill-
gotten gains, would rather drink water from the *zanja* than wine from
the devil's coin – and she saw only the signs of his father in him, only
the sunlight. Her schoolboy had the tongue of a poet and could ease
her heart. Indeed, for him it was an honest pleasure to see the strain go
from her face and her eyes light up when he spoke to her like a half-
grown *caballero*. His teachers enjoyed and castigated him at a ratio of
two to one and she could live with that. Both of them hoped that his
obvious intelligence would provide him with some kind of ill-defined
future brilliant career. He thought about law to get back their land and
the land of others and she was dismissive; she advocated for some kind
of relationship with commerce that would result in accruing capital.

Both of them thought about public service for the chance at being a Robin Hood, a Moses or even just a pillar of their community. He wanted to win enough to buy them a house, to pay for their lives, to purchase respectability, but such things are not won in a single card game, or at least not won by ordinary people at local venues. Instead, even with moments of dazzle, what he was losing was the faith that work could and would save them from hardship, that a penny saved was a penny earned, that frugality and savings could lead to an education, a career, stability, a reconnection to some kind of bourgeouis/aristocratic life of security and abundance. He was teaching himself to risk and risk and risk. To hunt. To get, as the Japanese say, "dead fish eyes."

She, however, saved with ferocity and dedication and learned English and chitchatted with her richest clients and learned where they sent their lanky boys off to school and surprised her son with interviews to lofty East Coast boarding schools and it was she who talked their way into a trio of possible scholarships, playing up her role as widow, as dispossessed, as the last remnant of *Californio* culture, charming the staid Yankee men in grey suits into wishing that maybe maybe she would consider coming to a land of snow and monolinguistic regularity. Her son did his part and so one summer she put him on a ship with some young marrieds, former clients, who promised to look out for him as if he were their own son, to go to the other side of the continent and both of them wept and then she was reduced to writing letters, carefully across the horizontal with the second page cross the vertical so that you had to tilt the page 90 degrees to find out what happened next. Legibility required absolute regularity in letter definition and size, and a tiny nib on the pen, so that the spidery words of one thought did not overshout the ideas of the other half of the letter. But it saved on postage and allowed her room to tell him of her adoration, her interest, her concern, her loneliness, her happiness on his behalf. It ripped her up to send him off, but she was as proud of his achievement as of anything she had ever done in her life and she sent him small dollops of cash so that he was not shamed before the rich boys. He was excited about jumping into the center of American culture and was reasonably diligent about the work, excepting higher math, which was far more alien to him than any language of which he had ever heard. The other boys were fascinating and it took him no time to figure out the stature of their families. He played up the concept of his being a Don, and failed to mention the loss of all their lands. It was too dreary. So it was easy to have his peers advance him cash that first semester for late at night games of poker and whist.

At Christmas, it was traditional to pay off all debts. It was a very bleak time. Notes were sent to his mother. Her savings were depleted. His scholarship was not renewed. His mother asked him to come home. He took a trip to New York and did not tell her where he was until almost May.

Her black hair shot through with silver during those days and weeks of silence. When he sent her a check for all the amount she had had to wrest out of her hard-earned sums, she was saddened. By now she understand whence the sudden generosity. She cashed it anyway. She asked him to come home. He refused. She looked at his books and school uniforms and wondered if there was anything she could yet do. Prayer seemed constructive.

STORMY

Clouds loomed at the edge of the western ridge like an angry parent preparing to take over the rest of the afternoon. Every being in the valley braced itself as the white condensed into grey and nearly black. Soon the fury of water separated from its self, spilled over the whole of the sky, a wet blanket. Clouds of different density heaped into gaps in the main and the whole writhed like *orchata* boiling on the pot. Tree's littler branches felt stiff and uncomfortable, like they might move or crack with the tension. A mountain lion came, ears flattened, down the trail, tail low and looked up at Tree's large limbs. In one leap, he bounced off the main trunk, the next limb up and two further up. Ensconced half way up Tree, he curled up in a spot where three limbs commenced. There was an oppressive quality to the air and the animals felt it as a desire to move or flee but the front was too big to outrun.

Everyone waited for something. At the first crack of thunder, Tree felt relief. Lightning. Of course.

The owl mother opened her wings and felt her chicks pull in close to her breast, and then she tightened her limbs around her brood, holding them close. She twisted her head, one eye upwards to watch the progress of the storm. Once upon a time, she might have flown out into the wet, looking for prey, for a male owl, for the flash of light that convinced any who saw it of the value of their own life.

But she hunkered down this time, looking out for those too little to fly. Another crack of noise with simultaneous white light and a patch of the meadow smoldered and blackened and then went dark and damp. Too wet for fire.

Two more cracks of distant lightening, a cry from a young coyote wishing to howl away the discomfiting feeling of being at the mercy of – and the next crack hit Tree like an assault. Tree felt every tube of phloem from root to trunk to limb to branch to leaf simultaneously, each drop of sap electrically alive. E wanted to stretch each cell, each limb, each branch like a dancer to reach the sky. Was this what it meant to be a star? Was every moment of sun-ness this euphoric shout? E wanted to yell a cry of joy and did not realize that every plant throughout meadow, creek, both ridges and multiple parallel watersheds heard e's passion and felt a reflective empathetic jolt. E reached deeper into e's core to answer back the sky and e's pleasure inverted into searing pain. The sparks had rubbed into the core of Tree, dry, into a weak spot between the topmost major limbs and caught fire. Fire hurt. And there was nowhere to go to escape something in e so centrally.

It was not like fire along e's bark from which one might retreat internally. This was a tearing pain, not just flame. This was the branch itself torn half way to center, bending, ripping like muscle torn from a bone, shrieking, cracking and the whole thing falling off, taking a big piece off the trunk along the way, like a cuticle ripping into the flesh. Tree screamed then realized e had an audience and tried to contain eself. More dry wood open, the fire spread and Tree wondered if this could kill e. But the rain dumping in buckets from the sky was coming down full blast and the fire went out and Tree's fire-pain abated. E could feel sap rising up to the surface to try to seal the open wood; the water softening the intensity of the tear, the empathy of a bunny family, underground, hearing e's pain. E had not noticed the mountain lion skittering down e's trunk and fleeing out of the valley to escape madness.

The limb itself lay dead, half within e's crown, half without, branches and leaves open to the pounding rain on the outside half, under e's protection in the inner half. Tree knew this was just minutes ago part of eself but now e experienced this branch with the same reflective disinterest e did fallen leaves. In the torrential rain and southwesterly wind, e felt eself shift inches at a time at an angle inclined in a southerly direction. The world seemed different from this perspective. Tree experienced this tilt and twist as if e were a human child moved from one home to another, just the next neighborhood over. Everything was similar, but not the same. The sky, the rainfall, looked different from this angle. E's roots, long wedded to their places in the rock, moved and shifted, like finding out whole new vistas in a life partner. Tree sighed and e's trunk moved a whole foot. This would be e's new position, once the storm abated. For now, e felt the cracks opened up by root-shifting filling with water. Despite the loss of a major limb, this would be a richly rewarding rainstorm. So much to capture and keep. For her part, owl threw her weight to the far left of her nest as the Tree sank southerly, and the whole nest shifted deeper into the crossing point of two branches that had created her home. As wind and rain hit this precarious nest, she dug her claws into the base of the nest and spread her wings, moving in response to each gust and twist, like a surfer on an all-night wave. Her heart hurt with that one twelve inch lurch, but at dawn, exhausted, wet, sore and afraid, she found all her chicks still huddled close. She had not lost a one. She fell asleep curling her feathers in tight over her children, a mother triumphant. Tree was aware of the bird's success and despite the ache of the lost limb and the open tear along e's trunk, felt glad for the chicks and their mother and father.

HONEY

The portion of Tree's trunk with the big limbs that had fallen off after the storm transformed quickly without water and sap and photosynthesis to keep them vibrant.

Insects broke down the structure of the wood; bacteria dug in on the underside where it was moist, and lichen had a field day on the crumbling bark. Within the center was a void, however, a bare space that invited in an adventuresome queen – a matriarch bee. And her workers followed her. Hexagon by hexagon they built a castle of wax and sugar and she retreated to her inner sanctum. Her lovers and workers and children flew in and out all day long from dawn to dusk, gathering pollen from every species of flower and bush, and translating these into honey inside. Tree smelt the sages strongest in this new translated form and came to hear the daily drone of the bees in the morning as a sign that the sun was shining and all was well. Inch by inch the hive grew from the size of a baseball to something weighing four stone; the size of a large school child, but hidden in crevasses, deep in the crumbly wood left to open air after the storm. A bear came by and tore into it, eating much of the work of the generations of bees in an afternoon. But even he unwittingly helped the queen's domain – for he tore apart pieces of the old trunk as he fought into the heart of hives, providing them with more hidden tunnels to build their fortress. And the worker bees made good their life sacrifices, stinging the bear over and over until at last he wandered off to roll in the mud in the creek and amble off, licking his paws and his pride, biting at his stings, paying the price for his wonderful excess.

SOLITAIRE

Sometimes María Marta thought about when the men took the house from them and she had to choose between the cart of worldly goods and her husband's horse. On the days she found time to ride and Sundays when she rode out to Tree, she could feel the animal dancing between her legs; some years ago she had bought her husband's mare back from his awful relatives with some of the cash her son sent her; even if it was ill-gotten gains, it seemed right to her that the animal, now past breeding age, live out her days in her hands. She never regretted having selected a living breathing being over stuff. It was the last thing near to him. The horse had been an expense when she kept it in town, but as she grew older, she put it to pasture with clients, who took a christening gown, sewn with love, in exchange for permanent care for the aging horse. She adjusted blouses and shirts and repaired tears as a matter of course. Feeling lonely, she would pay for a ride out to their home and walk directly to the pasture. The horse would always come up to greet her. She liked to visit her after church on Sundays and if she put a saddle on her, the horse always knew where to go. So rain or shine, hot or cold, María Marta would find herself under the limbs of her oldest living friend. And she wondered at the strangeness of being a human being, so driven to talk, to communicate, to earn, to self-educate, to dress oneself in prose and fine clothes and possessions and the finery of accrued culture and history, when all one really needed was wind rustling through grass and the *veritas* of sap moving slowly in a tree. The wavy many grass-strands of her hair changed from black and silver to white like rainclouds and her sandstone colored skin, while still soft, grew a visual texture as complex as that of bark. Tree liked how she changed as she matured, now she moved and spoke more slowly, which made her seem slightly more tree-like, a good thing. She stopped bringing work to do and would just come and sit, like when had done when she was one day to inherit a *rancho*. Her memories of her little boy were enshrined quiet in the deepest corners of her heart, like Univervia in Tree's core. They never spoke of these others, existing in the present of each day, unique and still achingly familiar. She would listen to e grow and e could feel her empathy for e's vital mission infuse her human form and when she left at dusk, mounting her horse and riding off, she sat stately, tall, refreshed by rain and dirt and sky, ennobled by stillness. Tree felt her go and knew her return before it happened, and her departure, and return and depart, her love regular like a very elongated heartbeat or sped up seasons and years.

PRODIGAL SON

Antonito patted the bay's neck and let her jerk the reins out of his hands so that she could stretch her neck long and low as she ambled down the road towards the livery where food, water, a groom and her equine friends awaited her. He patted her neck, taking comfort from her sturdy body. A good mare. She stopped at the barn and stood still as he dismounted. A final pat, an exchange of coins and she walked towards the cross-ties. She shivered with pleasure as the cinch was undone and the saddle dragged off her damp back. Her simple pleasure dinted Antonito's grim feelings. She deserved to be groomed and fed and loved.

As he walked away in the twilight gloom, dust rising in the street, he reflected as he had since childhood that his mother had been wrong to pin every hope on him. It was she who should have been doctor, professor, writer, intellectual. He fingered a handkerchief she had sent him just two months back, every stitch a message that it was not too late – that his life had value and meaning to her.

He thought bitterly that the word for to hope and to wait in Spanish is the same: *esperar*. And her hope had been waiting, either never fulfilled. God. The key to the bank burned in his pocket like a silver dagger in the heart of a vampire. He would not, would fucking not, gamble a dime of it. What could he do? He could teach Mexican children English. He could teach American children Spanish. He might be able to wangle a job writing for a paper. He had done that here and there before. He could invest that money in opening a publishing house. He could. He could. He could. He could give that money to an orphanage or a school so that he could never touch it and the fruit of her spirit would bear more fruit.

Fifty-two. Fifty-two. Fifty-two. People lived to a 100. His *abuelos* on his father's side had lived until their nineties His mother's people were said to be very long-lived, at least until cholera and the Americans. Had she been happy? She swore she had. One true love. One son. One church. What must have been millions of stitches enrobing the hopes of every client she had ever had, her immaculate clothing pride made tangible.

A tree for a best friend. She had been unique. He wished he had seen her alive, again. He was sure she was beautiful until the end, those eyes of dark sparking thought. At last he felt it – he missed her soul. Remembered her from his earliest childhood. Remembered when she chose his father's horse over all they owned. And a smile cracked his face. What a feisty young woman she had then been – it was completely the kind of thing he would have done. He felt their kinship, the restraint of her work, of her ladylikeness, remembered that his father had once been seen as an enemy of her family and felt her life bright in his chest. She had raised him without a moment of want – god knows how – on the best food, in the best clothes, with piles of books – in a two room apartment above her *tienda*. It had been for him. She had loved him, he felt it now, the warmth of her bed on a stormy night, black hair like lace around him, her warm body and cool hands and her promises that lightning might fork down from God himself but that it would not strike her boy, not while he was under her protection. And he missed her.

One of her bachelor tailoring clients had paid to have her body kept in an ice house until Antonio could make it down from San Francisco. Antonio wondered why he had never come sooner. So much time between them lost. But he had been and was so ashamed – he was nothing like the man she had hoped he would be. Seeing the body of the woman who had been the world to him as a little boy was not as he expected. Her hair was white and silver, with a few strips of black.

Though she was old, her cold skin was so soft – as he had remembered from boyhood. The color of her skin was pale and yellowy and the flesh seemed waxy, yet she looked beautiful still and he was relieved; seeing her old or mean or destitute would have been too awful. Her fingers were curved as if she was reaching to hold a hand and he held onto her still fingers, feeling her deadness. God, what he wouldn't give to hear her talk about anything. He tried to tell himself that he had protected her from the truth of him but he knew she had missed him and missed him and that he had been a fool. He figured, correctly, that such a one as she had made plenty of friends. But still. The fellow who had taken care of the body and written him the note to come south stopped by to tell him that he had also arranged for a priest, a funeral, a spot in a crypt with some other old *Californio* family, but Antonio had not heard of these people, did not remember them. He flashed back to Sunday picnics with her tree, when he was young and felt worthy.

He smiled and the other man looked at him like a smile at this time proved all his basest suspicions about her boy. Not a boy but a man of fifty-two, Antonio asserted himself as next of kin. "Thank you, but no. I know where she would wish to be buried." The other fellow did not take it well, so Antonio agreed to the public service two days later at 10:00 a.m. and asked for the body to be turned over to him afterwards.

The next day Antonio rode out with a quartet of guys he had found looking for work, God bless them, just after dawn. They rode out to the coast and then inland to the mountain's center, mist hanging heavy over the hills and rain falling sporadically. Everything looked pale grey in the damp but he could see the plants starting to spark into green. The men dug out the grave, rushed down the hill and Antonio went off to the hotel bar.

The next morning, Antonio slipped back into his nice clothes and was at the church by ten after ten. It was surprisingly full, though he only recognized the very old piano tuner and his white-haired wife as mementoes from his childhood. After the mass, the priest took him by the arm and assured him that everything was paid for, that she would want to have been buried in a churchyard like a good woman from Los Angeles and Antonio shrugged off his arm. Though he was sure they had to have heard about his plans for his mother's body, the funeral guests looked aghast when he got on his horse and told the driver of the hearse to follow him out of town. He figured they'd come with him to honor her wherever she lay but he found himself alone with the matching black horses plodding behind him, the hearse jolting over the irregularities in the road. The other man stopped him, cursing, sometime around lunch, but Antonio gave him two gold coins and won silence for the rest of the day. It was the middle of the afternoon when they got to the crest above the valley where Tree resided. The road down through the creek that ran past the meadow with Tree was narrower than he had observed and much narrower than he remembered. The driver asserted it was undrivable – he would not take out his axles on this whim, even for two gold coins. Antonio got him to agree to walk the coffin down but it was way too heavy for two men. The sun was moving toward the back side of the hill and Antonio had a horror of smelling his mother's death – seeing her and touching her was plenty bad enough. The driver suggested they go find more men to help, but Antonio felt a strong urge to do the right thing here and be done with it.

Though the other man tried to command him not to do so, he opened the coffin and lifted her body out of it. She weighed the same as a sack of grain; difficult to manage but not impossible. She did not flex over his shoulder like a living woman would but stood erect like a statue of *Santa Mónica* or *La Virgen*. The hearse driver, angry at this breach of all human decency, drove off in a clatter. No longer having an audience, Antonito lay her down on the path she had ridden so many times. He talked to her as he had long wished to; apologized for the gambling, explained that he was not as clever and talented as she had hoped, said that perhaps he had become invested in being a scoundrel and could not imagine how to fit himself into being a good man anymore. She listened, her expression unchanging and kind. It reminded him of church except that he loved her more than the fragile stories upon which everyone else seemed to pin their hopes. He felt better, the longer he went on. He apologized, only half-joking, for keeping her up late, and then he picked her up again, facing him this time. Her ribs felt familiar from childhood hugs, while stiff and resistant in death. He walked down to Tree and the open grave. Now that he was here, and completely committed, putting her down on the dirt felt wrong somehow. He lay her in the grass and wildflowers and she looked pretty. He unwound the braid pinned to the back of her hair and saw that the bottom half was mostly black, the top half mostly white. He knew she wouldn't mind, so he took a pocket knife and cut off half her braid. He put the hair in his shirt pocket and sighed. He sat down and held her hand again. He wished there were more time. He leaned back against Tree and spoke to the plant the way she used to do. "I am not sure if you can hear me or understand me, but this is my mother. She said she was your friend. Please take care of her." Then he stood up, prepared to do what he must. As the grass waved around her form, he realized he did not have to put her on to bare soil, not at all. He harvested big armloads of wild oats and lay it down six inches deep at the bottom of the grave. Then he picked flowers of every color and variety he could find and lay them out with the heads facing the perimeter of the grave.

When he picked her up and her gently on the pile of plants, she looked like the painting of *La Virgen de Guadalupe*, with her radiant lines of gold paint indicating her spirit emanating goodness, hot pink valerian, neon yellow mustard flowers, deep purple lupine, pinky-white wild rose, pale blue-violet ceanothus that had required his pocket knife to trim, orange sticky monkey flower, pale violet and cream mariposa lily and brodaiae, blue-eyed grass, red Indian paintbrush, pink and purple Chinese pagodas, creamy clover and local buckwheat, white mallow, bold yellow coreopsis, happy canyon sunflowers, multicolored vetch like confetti on stems and dusty yellow fiddlesticks bursting around the edges of this multi-colored flower bouquet, bright as a celestial being. He wished there were a way to capture this image, for seeing her in her final resting place, bestrewn with flowers like a bride made him happy even as he was sad. He felt like his heart was getting pulled out of his chest. He had missed her so. Would she have loved him if he had explained how he was failing at that expensive school, that he could not write English well enough, that his math skills were years behind his peers, that it had felt like a hurdle too big to jump?

God. He had felt so far away. A habit of failure.

But today was not about him, it was about her. And doing honor to her. He got into the grave and kissed her eyelids, her cheeks, her cold lips, held her close. It was unsatisfying, she had never once not hugged him back. And he missed her warmth and soft strength. He pulled himself back onto the meadow and steeled himself to finish. He grabbed more handfuls of *nussella*, purple needlegrass, mustard, radish, California fescue, melica – everything that the meadow bore in indiscriminate profusion. In a rush, he filled up armload after armload until he looked down and could no longer see her. "*Ah, mamacita,*" he said to himself and to her and then he realized the damn undertaker had driven off with the shovels. So he pushed the dirt he had pulled up the day before in piles into the grave, using his arms to sweep it in. He kept going until there was a lumpy mound on soil, underneath which she lay.

He did not feel very good. He gathered armfuls of leaves from the duff and scattered them next so that it looked more natural. The sun was getting low but he wanted to make it nicer, so he went down the gently rolling incline to the creek and brought up as many stones as he could manage in a trip, repeating the process over and over, not thinking about it until he had seventy-two stones. He made a cairn out of fifty-two of them and then took the other twenty to outline her grave. The evening star came up over the western hills. He realized the sun was done. He lay down next to the grave as if he was holding her. He watched the moon come up over the eastern hills and sang romantic songs from his childhood and the ones that she had repeated from her childhood.

He lay back and looked up at the branches of the Tree and individual leaves, the outline clear in the moonlight. He could see the little points under the leaves closest to him, the same points digging into him where he lay in the duff. Without words he sent a prayer towards Tree as if the plant were a pagan god, asking this deity to protect the body of his mother, to love it for Tree's long life. The man knew the Tree would live many generations past him and every human now on the earth. He hoped his mother was with her husband, her brother, sisters, mother and father. In a place with room to gallop on horseback and laugh in meadows. He jerked to his feet, bowed at Tree and his mother's grave and turned to the hills and walked out.

Tree thought about María Marta and their friendship and her life now complete and e's own life still going. E thought if e grew roots interlaced with her bones, perhaps pieces of her would leach into the water that e drank and become a part of e. E could feel the weight and shape of her body in the earth atop e's roots. While she would neither talk nor emote again, she was here to stay, like a plant or rock and this seemed right to Tree. E wanted her wit into eself, e's leaves and branches and acorns new. E wondered if dead humans were different than dead plants; e had never heard from Univervia after e's death, but maybe María Marta's skull might speak to e someday like Rock did every ten decades or so. Gently, e sent love to the still corpse, just in case.

HOW TO SING

Antonio had caught a ride with a driver with a cart full of vegetables coming in the night before for the early morning market and then got out and kept walking past his hotel and up to a bridge that overlooked the Los Angeles River. He wondered if each plant in the riverbed was as complicated and majestic as she swore her tree was. He could smell the creeky smell of willow and mulefat and unfortunate human and animal additions. He wanted her back. And she was dead. He wanted the years back to spend differently. Why had he spent so much time being angry? No father? No money? No land? No *gran éxito*? Who needed more than he had had?

He cussed in French like a schoolboy and walked up the stream until the city turned into countryside and walked back under a quarter moon, deep orange with a cloud-sticky surface looking like a hard candy partly eaten by a child and left on a dark blue night table.

Footsore, he walked into the lobby of the National Hotel, which was the Pico House when he saw it last.

Night pushing dawn, his intention was to go up to bed, to wash his face and hands and disrobe and search oblivion in hard sleeping. Then he heard it – a voice that spoke of solitude and grief, and hunger for love and pride in the face of prejudice. Although the voice sang in Spanish, something about it reminded him of the music of New Orleans in the way it clearly rose up from despair, vanguished, overrode and ran roughshod into the heavens in triumph. A woman with a contralto. He stood listening while the concierge asked him if he wanted his key. The second time the concierge asked and was ignored, the other man smiled and sat down. He had seen this before.

Antonio felt his heart being squeezed like a dish towel, every drop of feeling splattering all over the room, leaving him light, refreshed. How was it possible some stranger could read his sorry life like a book and turn it into a promise of spring? He was too old to be susceptible to music, he swore to himself. But after desultory applause, a new song came out. These were the songs of his childhood – old México. He was compelled to walk into the bar. Two men played guitar, riveted by a singer who had come up from their audience and asked to sing… for no reason. He saw her slight form, her hair tucked up in a bun at her neck, her 1900 prairie-cut dress made from a navy fabric with pale polka dots shouting Seville or at least México, in the middle of Los Angeles. He walked around the bar so that he could see her face. He watched her, not knowing that she could see him too. What he saw: an *India*, a young woman made newly adult by the fire in her heart, dark eyes, lips of pomegranate, a short wide nose, a square jaw, a slender body that spoke of not quite enough while growing up, wavy black hair, a wide brow, long eyebrows and eyes that did the thing to him her voice did – that grabbed his loneliness, mirrored it and somehow shrugged it off with a voice so big and bright that she could sing anyway. He wanted to live in that anyway. He with four broken engagements to East Coast American girls with relieved parents and all sorts of complicated relationships with other men's wives, he was just taken by this young woman slouching on a stool in the candlelight.

And he thought with uncomfortable honesty: he was too old. Too poor. Too East Coast. All he could be was an adoring person in the audience.

What he did not know was that she saw him too – he was only ten feet away from her. He looked distinguished, well off, responsible – all the things he had not yet been.

And the funeral, the emotions about his mother, his life, his walk – it was all on his face. Every thought he had been having about his mother was on his face. It made his eyes look beautiful. Young. True. The silver in his hair caught the light and she found him attractive rather than old. She finished her song and said something graceful to the guitarists, bowed her head at them and prepared to go back to her seat. Her new admirer asked her for "*una mas*." So she sat back down. And sang. And then went back to her chair.

He was not going to talk to her – he figured her trio of songs was just one of those magical gifts the universe will sometimes give you on a terrible day. But another man approached her about ten minutes later under the assumption that if offered her enough money she would go upstairs with him. When she declined in a way that impugned his honor, he grabbed her by the forearm and Antonio could not help himself, he wrenched the other man's hand off her arm, hoisted it up behind the other man's shoulder and then shoved him completely out of the bar in less than a minute. It was an automatic response. He faced the other man who took one look and saw that this was a live or die fight and shrugged and turned and walked away.

When he came back into the bar alone, his songstress smiled at him and asked him to sit down. It took only minutes to determine that she was woefully uneducated, smarter than he was and as ambitious as his mother might have wished for him to be. She wanted to be a singer, but the world was, as she said her mother told her it would be, full of men who would mistake her singing for something else. But she'd be damned if she'd clean houses for white people her whole life.

She seemed to understand his spirit – her eyes had snapped and smiled as they talked late into the night.

She excused herself and promised to meet him in the morning. He spent the last few hours of the night in a combination of ecstasy and melancholia waiting for dawn.

The next morning he took her to see his mother's new grave under Tree. She kissed his cheek and missed and caught his mouth, then she jumped back and away from him. He didn't care if it was on purpose or not. Time enough to determine what would come next.

And then because her life was young and bright, he took her to Long Beach to catch a coach to get them down to Mexico City. *D.F.*

All he knew was that when they stopped next for dinner, he'd sit and let her grand voice wash over his ear and hope that her fire lit his own. And he knew he would never see this sad grave again. After the two of them had caught the boat headed towards México, he took the first coin he had ever won gambling, the one he had kept in his pocket during every win and loss for decades and threw it into the sea, thinking of his mother.

"*Te juro*," he said.

The girl looked up at him. "*¿De veras?*"

For any promise she wanted. "*Sí.*"

35 DEGREES SOUTH

Once upon a time, Tree had ignored Univervia's children: they were too evocative of e and too multitudinous and e's relationship with grief itself was too hot and new. Now e wondered ardently after María Marta's boy, wished him well. But the man had no way to send letters to another species, anyhow he suspected his mother's claims of intimacies with a plant to be *cuentas* invented to becharm a lonely little boy. On the other hand, his young wife believed the stories second hand and used to tell their children that they had to go visit their *'buela* and her *encina*. Or *roble*. She got them backwards. The family never left *D.F.*, though. He started a school, she sang, the children thrived and her music rolled through their life like wine heating up the early evening of a party.

PEACE OF DAYS

Days of peoplelessness stretched into seasons and years.

Tree relaxed and magnified. The dirt road that had been laid in by deer, then Chumash, then Mexicans and Spanish, had fallen into disuse. First in over the road crept what are called weeds – the hardy foreign species like mustard and oats, foxtails and scarlet pimpernel. After a few seasons, manzanitas edging the side of the road closed in deeper. Mugwort and mulefat and miner's lettuce, with white dots at the center of the jewel green heart shaped leaves, all coming in at the wet spots into which water drained and sat for half a season. The width of the trail shrank from cart-width, the same as used by the Roman empire, the Spanish settlers and the imagination of the West itself, to a space big enough for first two then one horse abreast, then just a deer or a very stubborn hiker.

Tree sat in the morning sunlight, a cyan blue skink looking like a fat snake with legs jotting up e's trunk, half welcome, half irritant like a wife flirting with her spouse's neck before the alarm clock goes off. E enjoyed the feeling of mass in e's limbs; limbs bigger than the trunk of any other single tree in the valley. And along these trunks, grew lichen on the north sides and the topsides, crumbly and grey-green like an English moor in a schoolbook, until rain hit; moss transformed from drab into regal emerald isles. Their languages were simple and rudimentary, like human babies just at the feed me, tend me stage. E was fond of these inhabitants. Their use of e's life force made e feel lordly, parental. The tenants of e's wood, roots, leaves and duff were ten times ten species, as diverse as a human megapolis.

GOOD BONES

Tree looked at the mound of dirt atop e's roots and had a sudden care for Univervia. Then Tree could remember a summer day, bronze-skinned Maria Martá walking towards eself, the wind rippling her skirts and tugging at her braid, lovely like grass dancing.

E pushed e's roots to interlace with what was left of María Marta, nestled under a pile of dirt, soft like tumbled blankets on a bed. E had no pretense of reconnecting; she was dead and e knew it. But e craved the feel of her bones and hair; the texture of the dark velvet dress she wore was familiar to e from past visits. What once had been a vibrant woman would become Tree. E felt she would have loved to be incorporated into eself; she would have regarded being part of e Treeness as an extension of her own life, a kind of semi-immortality. E would be proud to capture the shine of her hair, the power of her movements, the effervescent dust of her mind into eself. E imagined key roots weaving into her *carne y hueso* and understood it as what she had called a marriage; e would embrace her like a lover and keep her forever. A 152 year old California live oak tree, e was in no hurry. Love takes time. Every molecule of her being would eventually fall into the earth and some of it, some ineffable afterglow of her departed spirit, would be Tree.

Tree did not know that the two American men who had taken e's valley from María Marta's family had fallen into a mutually life-consuming argument over who owned what; human ownership of land remained so alien that the concept did not translate. A few sullen would-be heirs on each side. Lawsuits. Discussions of water rights. Finally a mean old woman won all, but she never once saw Tree or e her. By the time she had her paper kingdom, she was too close to leaving life to enjoy making use of her victory. Her depressed nephew inherited from her and his inertia bought a few more decades of semi-isolation and neglect to the valley.

O DAM

1944, 1945, 1946, 1947, 1948, 1949 and 1950 were drought years in Los Angeles and the humans in the Santa Monica Mountains took what they could.

The first winter rain of 1950 brought a raging torrent through the mountains, but when those waters went to sea, the fallen water that sank into the dense soil becoming perched groundwater, soon found itself pumped up pipes and homes and showers and two small backyard pools. Tree had no way of knowing or understanding that some of the water the grove and the meadow and all of them would have utilized was already being taken; no way of perceiving that on the back side of e's eastern mountains, a winding road, paved, had gone in. Northward, over on the low side of the rolling hills from whence Tree's creek flowed, houses had been constructed. And thus wells.

In the watershed on the other side of the northern hills, two young men, fathers with seven children between them, laughed out loud with happiness to see their creek, which had seemed an abandoned arroyo, gushing and flooding the local roads.

The two men conferred; after much hiking, they had found the optimal spot to construct their secret swimming hole, about a mile and a half north of Tree.

During the lull after the initial storm, the pair of men spent a weekend collecting rocks and lugging cement and putting in a dam across a narrow spot in the creek. They stepped on umbrella plants and crushed cattails alike; it was muddy, gritty, wet work and to men who sat inside offices all day, the sweat and muscularity of it was a holiday of sore muscles, scratches and bruises. As Saturday afternoon trailed into dusk, the two men sat with warm sodas as the sun went down, admiring their completed project.

On Sunday, the men let their dam dry. Over the course of the week, the creek ran as they hoped it would and filled the sealed crevasse, making a nice deep pool. It did not overtop. Come the next Saturday morning on a warm Indian summer fall day, they got all the kids and their wives into bathing suits and stripped down to cut off jeans and everyone made the trek out to the muddy pool. So much better than going to the Palisades to the YMCA!

Downstream, the creek stopped.

Later rains during the year of the dam made this aberration in the local system seem minor. It was during the next two years of resurgent drought that the effects became evident: such a thing as a small dam, a few working wells in adjacent watersheds, had the opposite of a ripple effect on the local groundwater, rippling having such a nice liquidy sound to it, it was a drying that pulled inward and upward. Tree's roots reached more and more earthward, finding older water to drink, but younger Trees aged, leaves browning, branches, then limbs cracking with the struggle.

Grasses did not make it to seed. The creek shrank fast in size and went to dry, with a few stagnant pools standing here and there. At the low point in the valley, the cattail population clung to the muddy perimeter of the one pool, which diminished in size daily. No steelhead had survived the incursions of the wells; and a trio of chub clung on to living, slithering in mucky pools and corners, hiding under the algae, waiting for the right time to move and breed, hiding and hoping.

ONE PHOTON, INFINITE

An Anna's hummingbird flitted across the meadow like a *dilettanti* visiting an antiquities museum for the first time, zigging and zagging from insect to flower to viewing the air from the sky and back to plant in jittery glee.

She returned to a hummingbird sage, super sweet scent hanging in the air like little girl perfume and then zipped back to the place her heart resided: a tiny nest affixed to a high branch of an arroyo leaf willow down at the edge of the creek, wherein her only son, a tiny hummingbird, the size of a marble, sat eager and waiting, beak open, the two tiny triangles making a perfect diamond, pleading for food, which she delivered, along with some swift-beating affection.

Then she was off again, frenetically looking for food for her for him for them, green feathers and red-topped head, iridescent in the sun.

Tree marveled at the glittery swift life of the bird completely oppositional to e's own.

Jarred to awareness by the sparkling bird, e noted movement on the eastern ridge.

Two humans had parked a well-worn pre-war blue truck with a horse van on the other side of the eastern ridge and walked in, a human father, daughter and sway-backed mare. The dapple grey had become partially lame in one foot and completely lame in another, walking in a syncopated gait.

The girl saw the creek and thought there was fresh water; the meadow looked inviting.

"Would there be enough forage?" she asked. Her father nodded.

"I'll check in on her once a week. If I have to, I'll get someone to bring in hay once a day." The horse stopped in the creek, enjoying the running water on her hooves and legs. The man slapped the mare's haunches and she jog-trotted into the meadow, flicking her tail in mild irritation. She walked around in the grass, grabbing a bite and pausing to stand in the sun. The man stood back and watched his daughter. She was angry at her good luck.

When you get into an Ivy League school, every one is thrilled on your behalf and the word no is nowhere in anyone's vocabulary. But she hated cold weather. She didn't like the self-referential pride that had drenched her during her initial tour of the school. But – it was opportunity. It was instant entrée into society. It was the best education money can buy. So they said. She looked at her horse's big dark eyes, a glaze of white growing on the surface. She walked close to the horse and wished her father were elsewhere. She wanted to say good-bye in some meaningful way but felt her once absolute faith in inter-species communication blocked. Would she come back to California or get sucked up by the East Coast as had most of her friends' older siblings?

Mostly oblivious to her owner's angst, the horse meandered away from the hot meadow and into the shade under Tree. The girl sat down cross-legged, trying to be companionable, her beat up saddle shoes tucked under her knees. The horse's eyes drifted to half-mast, one foot tilted up, her tail switching lazily to block flies.

They had done this before.

Tree felt the horse's mind – old and large and calm. Her acceptance of life as it was evoked Tree's own approach. The horse let out a sigh of contentment when it bumped into Tree's existence. Tree heard the horse's simple self-definition, "Horse."

The girl turned to look at the tree.

She couldn't hear this conversation, but she could feel the mass and age of this tree, sensed it as a protector, a benign local god.

Her father had wandered off to chuck rocks in the creek. She could hear the tap-tap-tap-kerplunck!, tap-tap-tap-tap-tap-splash! as he skipped rocks on the water's surface.

Sure that his back was turned, she embraced the tree and asked it without words to look over her horse; she told it that she was leaving Los Angeles, going a country away, that she mightn't be back, that she was doing a terrible but expected thing here.

When she turned her attention upon the horse, the animal thrust her head into her arms, rubbing her forehead on the girl's torso, leaving a white shadow of white and grey fur on the girl's dark shirt.

This was the first betrayal she had ever made; maybe it would help to lead to the meticulous G.P.A. to come; maybe it was making her learn to abandon those she loved that would teach her to focus on her career, to shelve her mammalian desires.

The horse looked at her like she just wanted another afternoon together, but the maid knew that a horse wants every afternoon together. A herd animal cannot understand twenty hours of studying on a weekend.

She ripped herself away from the companion of her youth and turned her back and walked wordlessly back towards the truck.

Her dad saw her and followed.

When they got two-thirds of the way up, the horse whickered and the girl dipped her head.

The young woman turned and called back to her horse in a poor facsimile of a neigh.

Her dad did not tease but put a hand on her back and gently pushed her to keep walking.

For a herd animal, being isolated day after day brings on existential despair.

Horse's loneliness grew in creeping inches like the desert in the Sahara until it was miles wide.

When it got big enough, her heart cracked and Tree heard her solitude.

Tree's life force swirled up slow and strong like tree sap and breathed compassion into Horse.

The animal took to leaning on Tree like the plant was another horse, companionable in the hot summer. Every day the horse would walk a bit around the meadow and it wasn't long before every grass, flower, weed and bush was grazed or stepped on. By September, the ground was down to dirt; even the duff under Tree had been ground up and distributed. Horse manure dried in the sunlight and fell into bits in the dust too. The top layer of Tree's roots were bruised and then hardened in resistance to the constant weight of the animal standing on e. Branches up to the height of the horse's stretched head were knocked off. But Tree was old enough, strong enough, to find these personal nuisances mostly insignificant. E believed that the grass would come back some day.

Memories of running, jumping, bucking, waiting in a stall, communing with a cat, grazing in fields in Central California, being groomed, talking to other horses percolated in and out of Tree's understanding. In winter, the field turned to muck. Someone had noted that there was now no forage at all and took to delivering hay daily; as a back up to the erratic creek, water was dumped in a beat up metal trough, though it quickly went green in the sun.

Horse's teeth were old and ground down; she tried to eat the hay but it took forever to get through just a few smallish mouthfuls.

Mistakenly thinking her less hungry, the feeder took to delivering less. And Horse's ribs showed more starkly by spring and more so by summer. She wondered about her human, who she could not know was in summer school in Boston, trying to pass economics after dropping out of the class part way through the second semester. On sunny days, the young woman would study lying on the grass in the quad, dreaming of California and her dapple grey. The fun of getting soaked in a Boston summer shower and running in to catch the mail where she found she had received a miracle A – was undercut that very evening by the phone call from her dad that he had put off making for weeks on end. Now her California was inaccessible.

FLOWERCHILD

Time elongated and seasons moved one to another and another and every year, as Tree tired of cold, warm came and as warm became obliterating heat the hush of cool returned. The Age of Aquarius came and went and María Marta's bones nestled within e's wood.

SANTA ANAS REDUX

Almost every year of e's life, summer stretched into fall in a hot pile up of days, until in October or November the winds hit. The winds were called the Santa Anas – though surely the mother of Mary was not prone to these raging fits; perhaps the Spanish had seen this as a wind from *Satana. Satán.* Satan. Or General Santa Anna, who, while the Victor of Tampico and Savior of the Motherland, might nonetheless be seen as *satana* by those at the receiving end of his military campaigns.

The daytime air temperature went up and up into a hundred degrees and more and the nights were not much better; the gusty temperamental air dried out already fragile plants to death and deepened cracks in the hard-packed soil. Animals were skittish and leaves and limbs and stems of plants blew around like flags waiting for battle in the false still before assault.

The winds came blasting in at maximum speed and their wildness built up a yearning for passion, or active violence and rage, or just stacked up fear. Tree was so big e could withstand the minutes long sequences that bent grown willows down towards the ground and fields grass flat to the dirt; e withdrew into e's core and put e's life force into e's roots, withstanding the drama with calm magnificence. E was an oak to stand strong.

When the air came in heavy with the smell of smoke, e cringed along with any other plants old enough to have gone through a fire and come back. But upon reflection, e figured e was large enough to retreat into e's core and meditate on stillness, to be like rock, oblivious to the cries of the damned, serene as flames came to lick e's bark, cool, calm and centered as e's outside bark burnt, sure that e would withstand and grow and thrive. E turned e's sensorium inside out and closed e's looking/hearing/smelling/feeling like falling into a coma.

E did not see the fire coming from the southeast, so sure was e that e could go into a trance and just be in the face of terror and pain. E did not watch the animals running in panic to the western ridge, shut eself off as plants gave up their lives in sparks and flames and smoke and grit. E found a steady note and droned upon it, a bass *om* to calm all in the chaos. Until the fire came leaping across the creek, through the meadow and up e's bark in a glazing scorch of energy. E was helpless in the face of this fiery *blitzkrieg* and the intensity of the heat seared into e's bark all the way into e's core, violating e's meditational sanctity like a broadsword cutting through armor. E's voice rose anguished to the sky, e's leaves sparked and flamed, e's branches caught and held flame, disappearing into ash, e's limbs caught and held and e thought of death as mercy to escape this but e was too big to die and the main front of the flame continued westward up the far side of the valley and e could hear the panicked yells as heat hit tree upon tree upon grass upon bush upon bunny upon lizard upon anxious dust. Still e burned.

Even after the flame had come and gone, e burnt inside in places under e's bark, into the night and smoldered in the dawn. E keened for what e had lost and the winds continued to torture every sensitive portion of e's bark for the rest of the next day, the next night until dawn when they dropped and silence fell upon the ashy landscape. And Tree did not understand how such a thing worked, but fog came down upon the landscape like a blanket of mercy and moist and e felt hope that rains would come and heal what remained and bring life back to the valley as e had seen it before.

With a cracked and sere voice, e told the valley of the renaissance from a fire e had withstood over a hundred years ago and every surviving plant listened with cautious hope, clinging to the fog.

NEW NEIGHBORS

Horse had been dead for ten summers, most of them dry ones. This had been a wet year and the yellow mustard, the bush mallow, beach morning glory, the pale green wild oats, and some feral sweet peas, cape ivy and nasturtium had all gone crazy with the rains. Here and there were familiar entities: spots of deep purple lupine, hot pink and fuschia colored valerian, spiky milkweed and dots of light orange sticky monkey flower.

Along the banks of the creek on both sides, were stands of a new plant, arundo donax, evoking bamboo minus the iconic poetry of a millennia of water colors in a dozen languages. The new plant grew densely, crowding out most of the once sturdy slopes of willow forest, the classic mélange of two kinds of willow growing in a harmonious riot with mulefat, coyotebrush, miner's lettuce, wild rose, native blackberry, poison oak and stately California rye. Instead of this ecosystem housing all the bugs and snakes and turtles and birds and mammals that Tree had come to know, there were acres solidly packed with thirsty arundo. The blue-line stream, briefly restored after the check dam partially collapsed in the winter of 1965, ran dry now for more than half each year. Patches of pools in the creek held on, habitat for tough little populations of chub and the macro invertebrates that fed them.

The central flat part of the meadow had been grown in by a large stand of star thistle, crowding out all other species once within their current footprint. The proliferating plants were about six feet high and had purple flowers and green spiky leaves striped with white. Ringing them were another new species, castor bean, leaves growing with five fingers like a mean-spirited image of marijuana, only tall. Their flowers turned into spiky balls that housed their seeds and their trunks, an inch or two around, had a white viscous milky sap that irritated and stung the hands of anyone foolish enough to try to pick these without gloves. Like their neighbors the thistle, the castor crowded out the other species used to sharing this space and like mustard, gave off a noxious taste in the soil, alienating would-be new growth. At their border, some fennel, smelling of green grass and fresh licorice, grew seeds of anise, asserting their own need for territory.

Further upstream were three huge eucalyptuses, planted by the landowner who had agreed to let Horse pasture on site. Now they were taller than the biggest sycamore – and their children came up in profusion under the heavy-scented duff beneath them, the beginnings of an alien forest. While the bees loved them, song birds would try to crack open their seeds and get hung up on the gooey substance they secreted, sometimes gluing their own beaks shut and starving. They, too, used more water than the denizens of the older riparian forest, contributing to the drying of the creekbed.

At first, Tree spoke to the new forest by scent. The varieties of eucalyptus had leaves variegated in scent. These smelled of cough drops and over-ripe pineapple and their evident happiness every hot summer and wet winter felt like a new era – new players, same emotions. At first, the new forest's sharp melodies of flutes and piccolos jarred with Tree's stately slow bass. Then Tree's size and age dominated and the newer trees music began to blend instead of clash. The arundo was another story – the brusque percussion of leaves evoked the discomfort of sandpaper on tender skin, the knocking of hollow limbs sounded like an angry timpani. In the center of the creek, still muddy and damp, cattail continued to dominate in key patches. Their whispery hushed tones suffused the new species' loud voices with the memories of the land's past, steady as a heartbeat.

A particularly vibrant California rye, tall as a third grader, was playing up to Tree, day after day. The grass had heard rumors from the meadow that once upon a time Tree had befriended a grass and the healthy new plant was intrigued and wanted to hear about life as Tree. For this plant, Tree's age was not the charm – it was the mystery of wood, the idea of height and depth and mass and density.

Tree greeted the new denizen with grace and retreated to growth. E knew that Univervia would not see a friendship like this as infidelity per se, but for Tree, every other species was easier than these plants that waved in the wind and grew and died with such panache. The younger plant's life force felt like powdered sugar kisses. Irresistible. Just when Tree was thinking of yielding into song-sharing, the California rye abruptly turned its attention to the other grass, to some cowboy sage and white sage, whose husky scent made them easily available to any interested plants. Bemused, Tree stood back and listened to them all. In a time with no rain, they still expressed such exuberance.

Blessed with taproots that reached into groundwater, beating all the newer species for access, Tree deepened e's reticence. E missed the willows' vain plainsong – only a few kept up the chant as they were outcompeted by the arundo and drunk into oblivion by the Australian newcomers.

One day, Tree jerked out of e's days and nights, months and years, of seamless meditation, alert. E observed a blond human woman in a cobalt skirt and blazer with padded shoulders came up the east ridge and began the descent down the path towards the creek. Her running shoes had a thick layer of mud in sharp contrast to her manicured nails and made up face. Behind her came an old man and two younger men, all with beards and jeans and boots and gear. She was shaking her head at the horizon, but the younger man said something and she nodded her head in agreement. At first Tree could not hear. They crossed the creek and the woman slipped in, up to a knee, jerking her skirt up to protect the material. What must have been a cussword echoed across the land and then she laughed and the men laughed with her. She took off the muddy running shoes and slithered out of a thin skin of nylons like a snake in transition. She stepped into the mud and exclaimed again and then the men smiled at her like she was a child. She pushed her carefully blown dry hair out of her face and her damp hands made a few tendrils of disorder. Her voice shifted and the men's smiles dropped. This was still a work-party, not a picnic.

Now that they were down near Tree, e started hearing patches. Enough to realize this was not Spanish. Tree could not could not quite push the words flowing out of her mouth into any kind of meaning but occasional things would feel nearly sensible. It was very frustrating. Trying to understand someone else's language was a bit like being a human baby, reaching to gain word by word, María Marta had said.

The young men put strings up along the west hill, where scrub oak and younger California live oaks were mixed with California black walnuts. Little red flags marked the string every twenty feet or so. The meadow in which Tree lived was bisected then trisected with more little strings, these marked with yellow flags. More strings came with blue flags, these in straight lines ending in the middle of the pretend boxes created by the strings marked with yellow flags. They tromped around in the grass all day, scaring up bunnies, but nothing larger.

The old man came across a rattlesnake, but withdrew quietly without alerting others.

No harm, no foul.

The whole of a day crept forward and at last they were tromping across the meadow, cussing at the stands of star thistle, with their pretty purple flowers and white striped leaves, rimmed with sharp spikes, and towards the creek.

The most handsome of the young men impulsively picked up the woman and flung her across his shoulder to cross the creek. Her outrage was not really very sincere, he was clearly more fun than anyone in her immediate personal world. She had spent so much time and money making herself unapproachable and this was all it took to be embraced by the working class? The other young man pulled her from his colleague's arms at the other side and told the woman in off-the-rack couture and bare feet that she should wear jeans next time and didn't understand the cold look he got. The skirt suit represented her incipient success to her. She had worked hard to get to this point and needed to underline her importance visually. If someone had explained to her that the truly powerful do not need the accoutrements of power she would have been mystified. Look at what the Reagans wore as they campaigned across America.

And how could one possibly be more incipiently successful than they?

The woman stalked ahead of the men on the hill, her muddy shoes and ruined stockings in one hand, tumbled blond hair down her back. The suit still perfect, somehow. What it was she wanted, what it was she was stalking towards she could not have said. But she wanted it terribly. And the men figured – another job, another boss, each with oddments of its own. They were happy to stand up in any court of law in the land to swear that the allotments of land were accurately drawn in dirt and on map. What more could anyone have asked from them?

Over the weekend, hikers pulled up some of the sticks and strings and ribbons. The men came back. It didn't matter yet, anyway.

New sticks and strings went down.

Tree thought about the woman in the suit the color of a true-bug, cobalt blue. The outfit disturbed e. Only tiny things like insects and new grass should be so bright. And something in her was shut, even to her, and this actively scared Tree.

While e could not read her thoughts or hear her words, e knew she was doing something big, something that e could feel would touch e to the core. Once Tree had seen a large rabbit in the meadow, a snake slithering towards him. The rabbit had caught the snake's eyes and was gazing in rapt horror, pleading. The snake came forward. Tree thought to eself, "You're an animal. Run!" The rabbit stayed locked to the spot and Tree watched the strike and swallow. The picture replayed more than once in e's core as the days went by.

Tree worked to enjoy the rich spring, but the woman had started showing up, always accompanied by one, two, sometimes three or four other people, equally inappropriately dressed for a romp in the wild.

CINEMATIC

To a boy who loved green, Virginia had been perfect when Enzo was small. Green most the year round, with a minor bout of snow in winter. Trees so tall that branches often reached across roads to intermingle. This tickled Enzo and he would always point out the "kissing trees" to his parents. Back then, his father and mother were still completely smitten with each other and thus found even the most repetitive and benign pronouncements of their offspring charming. However, his father was producing documentaries for *National Geographic* and while this sort of thing was a dream job to most of his peers, he pictured himself in L.A. Big. He pined for the mainstream the way a scholarship girl might crave entrée into the debutante clique. His glossy wife craved right beside him. They plotted and pulled even the most tenuous of strings, often finding the fragile strands of some possible relationship in shreds in their hands. No matter. They persisted.

The documentary gig had fallen into his lap, when he was a big twenty-two. He had just met his pretty wife months before in his fifth year as an undergrad at film school. The first time he saw her was after she had auditioned for a classmate's project, been rejected and he'd found her sitting crying in the hallway. He'd taken her out for early 80s Italian food and they'd spent every night together since that one. That was how she'd become pregnant and, impulsively, he'd married her the very day she blurted out her secret. It was the one impulsive act of his life – or of hers. But then they'd sussed each other up pretty good that first day in the hallway at USC and each had recognized in the other a pretty tight match. So the M word was there from the beginning. The other thing – from the beginning – unspoken but huge – was that he would be a producer. Huge. And she would be his wife. Thin. As the years went by, each felt that she had kept her part of their bargain. His inability to measure up to their shared vision of his future rankled.

Initially, they focused on the kid, though. Which was why he'd said yes to the *National Geographic* people for an unpaid internship all the way across the country, had worked like a dog and been hired then promoted three times in two years. Any job was good with a kid – and the culture in this community meant a kid underfoot was more welcome than he might have been in another world. But there were times when some filthy, literally, not metaphorically, French director and his Czech cinematographer and a string of assorted scientific-anthropologist-biologist-botanist-illiterate-quasi-visionary others would be sitting at their table, rhapsodizing in glee over being lost in the snow of the (fill in the obscure mountain range), or discovering some miserable broken-down one-time castle, or laughing about mosquitoes, bad food, brushes with Third World dictatorships and their eyes would meet and say to one another, "Who are these people and why are we having them to our house for dinner?"

But little Enzo, who stayed up as late as he wanted back then, would be sitting at the corner of the table nursing a soda with eyes as big as a tarsier, silent. And what he saw was passion – in different accents, with different obsessions – but ultimately the whole blur of it infected him as severely as a lonely kid bitten by Catholicism. He saw purity in the terror of ice-climbing, inhabited the past in the echoes within the castle and adventure in the hardships. He wanted to go everywhere and do everything that these people had done. But already his father had stopped doing hands-on production: he hired others to go off into the woods or under the polar cap or out to the observatory.

Enzo wanted to be these guys.

But at last one of the string-pullings resulted in an actual offer to work on a major motion picture and Enzo's dad went to France. Enzo loved the light blue sky and fluffy clouds and his lips plumped forward so that French words could roll out of his little boy mouth. His Parisian nanny adored him. His mom took exercise classes of various kinds, shopped and took some serious cooking courses. His dad wrestled fiercely with the transition until he found a bilingual secretary ten years older than he, but twice as well dressed. When it came to him actually wrestling with the bilingual secretary, his wife packed up and moved back to L.A., leaving Enzo in the care of the nanny. Enzo's father took a paycut to move home and it took six months to get his wife to move back in with him and she wasn't impressed with the apartment, the job or the second courtship, but she was back. It was enough.

Enzo cried for months for the nanny. He had felt that she understood him. She loved museums and old things and sympathized about his fascinations with various elements of the natural world. She took him to see her relatives who were kind to him and she quarreled with him like a big sister. She sent him a few notes at first, then a photo of her on vacation with a beau. And then she fell off the face of the map. Enzo stopped eating. Stopped talking. It was an embarrassing number of days before his parents noticed – or at least acknowledged – either of these two things.

Therapy with a child who won't talk is challenging and involved both his parents and therapists having long conversations with anyone who had been a caregiver to Enzo in the past, including one preschool teacher, whose favored memory was that he had been the only four year old boy she'd ever known who knew more flower names (she stopped counting at sixty) than car brand names (Mercedes and Volvo and only because his parents owned one of each.) So Enzo decided he was impressed that his parents cared enough to drag him through this circus and decided to start talking but somewhere along the way something terrible had happened. His dad had become successful. Two shows that he had nurtured, one with a fading old writer, the other from a pair of smarty-pants UCLA film school students, had both been picked up by the same network in Los Angeles. The pilots had done well; both shows were picked up. Then the shows had gotten decent ratings. And great reviews. And better word of mouth. And then the ratings zoomed. And now he was riding an impossible stroke of double luck. He was busy. He was rich. He was important. And his wife took this to mean an escalation in her own responsibilities. First, she rented them a big house in Laurel Canyon – close to the studios – then she put Enzo in a school with a uniform. Enzo had not really connected with the other children, but after some disasters with American softball, his teachers let him sit in on fourth grade history, two times a week, and that had been a highlight as stories about early California intrigued him. Next mother performed a makeover on herself with the best help from all across L.A. so that she looked like the wife of a producer and then she took a good hard look at the successful wives of successful producers and realized that the ones with staying power were the ones who supported their husband's careers by creating a secondary career for themselves as large-scale epic do-gooders. They hosted parties for children with cancer and funded homes for abandoned animals. Sometimes they got into very serious things like Presidential campaigns and often they asked the kind of scathing insightful questions that made the recipients of their generosity understand that this cash was meant to buy performance. And the wives enjoyed watching the things that their largesse purchased grow and move about and do things and sometimes they felt that the entities their charities created – medical institutions, scientific advances, political transformations, happier once-lost domestic animals – were more important and more beautiful than the filmed entertainment constructed by their spouses and the casts of thousands who supported them.

Who's to say.

However, Enzo himself felt abandoned. The blasted cop show and the night-time soap opera took up more than all the energy his father had and his mother was brittle and full of bursts of light and spite. He stayed out of both their ways. The people they brought home were always perfectly groomed. A few of them had stories of adventure and mayhem and some had good will and good intentions.

But…Enzo was lonely. Months passed. It seemed things would be this way for his lifetime, or at least his childhood.

But Enzo's parents had decided they needed to buy an even larger palatial home. One that reflected their true value. Perhaps something in the countryside. With a view.

But not too too far from the studios. And that lead Enzo's mother, dressed all in creams and taupes, in silk and linen, with cunning little kitten-heeled cream suede half-toed sandals, to be standing in the mud on the edge of the Topanga State Park, tromping up and down various paths, through the creek, around the meadow, past Tree eself.

"How much did you say it was?" said Enzo's mother. The real estate agent repeated the number calmly. Enzo's mother said, "Access to gas, water, electricity? Permits already in place?" The real estate agent nodded emphatically to it all. This was the ninety-seventh time for her with a potential buyer for all of this. Enzo's mother smiled like a cat. Wreathed in all that cream. "Yes," she said. The real estate agent's lips parted. Millions of dollars exchanged in one syllable. She could never get used to it. She said, "O.K." and knew from Enzo's mother's expression that that was that.

They went tromping back the muddy path to the real estate agent's SUV. "You're going to need one of these." The real estate agent blurted as they drove off in a splatter of brown and wet.

Tree and Rock stood still, wondering what had just happened.

CHANGE

It wasn't long after that the men with machines came. Tree was utterly horrified to watch the road being put in – trees and bushes and grass cleared, the surface scraped then mashed and hot sticky asphalt laid down. In a panic, Tree woke up Rock. "What is this, what is this?" Tree asked.

Rock, laconic, said, "Man-volcano." But there was more, for soon the creek itself had cement laid down from one side to another in a seasonally accessible road/bridge in what the men called an Arizona crossing. Except the man from Arizona, he called it a Texas crossing. After a few days, the cement dried and they brought in equipment.

First twelve trees were chopped down. Tree had seen trees die before, of old age, of insects, fungi and even fire. But never had he seen this method that made e's bark feel like it wanted to peel off e's trunk. The first tree to go had been a young willow, in the way of the cement-makers and the cement creek-crossing. E's shriek of death had been instantaneous and had wounded Tree so severely – and the other trees – that they had all shrieked simultaneously in response. This woke Rock. Rock felt e's best friend's pain and did what any Rock should do for another. E wrapped e's own core around Tree's core and pulled e underground into a world of slow-growing crystals and dripping water that e had seen a thousand million years ago.

Tree went into darkness and then began to see as a rock sees, without perception of dark or light. Underground, each rock glowed to all the others, sending out a slow signal of being. As the stalactites slowly let water peel away morsels of eself, the stone relinquished the tiny fragments within water to the waiting stalagmites below, who took them on as wanted children, the one growing from releasing, the other from accepting. Rock found the process infinitely entertaining and as Tree's core slowed down to understand this hidden world, for a time, e did too.

The rock memories padded Tree from experiencing the rest of the day but Rock could only sustain the visit for so long and finally e had to release Tree back into the world of growing things. The whimpering meadow stood before the hardening concrete wondering what was next and the men jumped on motorcycles and cars and raced up the road to who knows where for comforts no plant could ever fathom.

There was one stump that was a foot wide and another stump that was fifteen inches wide where the pair of California live oaks had once been saplings together. Big and Bigger.

Dawn came after a lonesome night and Tree found eself dreading the day for the first time in e's life.

Bulldozers arrived and the men shouted and jeered, and, as the men pushed aside every living thing on the meadow, putting it in a hump of dirt over the space where one of the yellow-scattered strings had been, the bulldozers retreated to cheers. A job done.

Tree stood shaken. This wasn't grazing, when roots could sprout back, or digested seeds could be shat out to grow more pre-fertilized grass. This wasn't fire, that laid down a rich layer of ash and encouraged hidden seeds to sprout.

This was something new. All the grass and chaparral had been uprooted and buried. Snakes had been cut in half and crushed by the bulldozers. The older bunnies had fled for the remaining chaparral while the younger ones, too little to flee had also been crushed. Enormous familial cities of insects. Gone.

The wind whipped across the bare dirt and dust rose up to clog Tree's stomates and choke man and beast alike.

But the next day, the men were prepared with damp bandanas across their mouths and down came with a truck carrying what looked like a giant's rolling pin – hard and metal and spiky. They attached it to the enormous machine which powered it with a great big man at the wheel. The purpose of this vehicle was to lay down the equivalent of a concrete foundation, something worth building a house on for all time. As the rolling pin was lowered, the men shouted.

They had noticed Rock – and Rock was not crushed.

They stopped with the rolling pin and got a winch and a crane to come over from a field out of visual range – and Tree guessed that other precious valleys were being destroyed on this bleak day – and the winch was attached to Rock and the crane, without leaving the far side of the creek, hoisted Rock up, and over and dumped e into a Truck, which drove away. By the time Tree and Rock figured out what was being done each was too far from the other to hear a good-bye.

Then the vehicle pushing the rolling pin (itself taller than a man) came across the creek and the driver lowered the pin – not only low enough to touch the ground, but enough to drive the ground twelve inches lower than it had been before.

All the air space between the dust and dirt, all the hidden places for insects to crawl and roots to burrow, was pushed out. The man pulled another lever and the rolling pin drove even deeper and the ground gave out first a sigh then a squeaky noise like a mouse with a tail being stepped on.

Concentrating, he began to follow the markings on the ground, to create the foundation for the house. As he moved forward, the rolling pin came over the first tips of Tree's roots, flattening them like road kill. Tree of course was still very much alive and the pain caused e to give a great bellow that echoed across the whole of the valley and poured over the rims of the mountains. Trees who had never known Tree in 100, 200 years, cringed in response. The compactor moved slowly forward and Tree tried not to inflict e's agony about the entire universe, but it was impossible not to yell. When the compactor had made a straight line, starting about fifty yards from the creek and heading back about 100 yards, he turned a right angle and headed straight towards Tree. Now the pain was escalated by pure terror. Was the machine going to knock Tree down or crush e's roots up to the trunk? Tree yelled so loudly that the oldest Tree in the forest, two and a half miles away as the red-tailed hawk flies, heard this moment of grief and terror and sent forth a love-prayer, quiet as a flick of air. It reached Tree like a mother's embrace and e clung to it as the compactor came closer and closer and then stopped a big three yards away, making another right turn and heading back to the creek.

The half a day this took was the longest day Tree could imagine existing in the universe, for underneath every portion of the smooth flattened dirt, now hard as concrete, lay miles of interlaced roots – both Tree's and those of other trees and the long grass roots of purple needlegrass. Dead now. More dead than e every imagined, for nothing else would be able to eat them up and incorporate them into some new life.

The other three-quarters of Tree's roots were shriveling and wiggling in the ground in terror.

The driver lifted the metallic rolling pin, backed up, turned around and headed up the hill. His colleagues congratulated him on the project. Swift and clean. Not a one of them had heard the shrieking, though one had a dog who was cowering under his master's old red Chevy, whimpering and moaning. The owner could not figure out why his dog had freaked out and finally cajoled him with a friend's half-finished hamburger out from underneath and into the front seat. When he got into his truck to drive away, he found the enormous German Shepherd perched in his lap and unwilling to move. So he drove home with his neck laced around the dog's head so he could see where the heck he was going. He knew his wife would be irritated that he smelled so thoroughly of dog, but what could he do? A man can't turn his back on a whimpering dog.

CRUSH

Tree tried to reach through the crushed roots, but of course it was impossible to revive them, they were dead. But in e's core they lived. So e had phantom pains as e tried to pull in water and nutrients, to store away for tough summer days. Tree feared e would topple backwards with so much of the roots on one side gone. The living roots, the undamaged ones, functioned erratically, suddenly frightened and neurotic. E did what any oak would do and began to utilize the moisture and nutrients long ago stored in e's core. Panicked, e dropped half e's leaves for no logical reason, further diminishing e's ability to eat and drink. With Rock gone, twelve younger trees killed, hundreds of thousands of grass destroyed and e's own younger sprouts demolished as well, any kind of positive emotion was completely out of the question.

The workers came and watered down the dirt to prevent the dust but this just washed away a beautiful layer of topsoil. Tree watched it go with a sense of imminent nostalgia.

The next thing the workers did was to install the girders of steel that would provide the bones of the frame of the house. Then they brought in lumber to build the frame.

Tree smelled the cut wood with curiosity. These were tree. And now were not. What would they become?

Apparently not duff, not food for fungi, bacteria and insects, but something humanized. Stacks of plywood came too, but the next step was laying in concrete over the compacted earth. No basement here, but a foundation that would lie immediately under the fancy flooring. As the concrete dried and coalesced it acquired one voice and it jarred Tree to hear echoes of Rock in the brand new concrete: like hearing a familiar classical theme in the midst of a lacerating punk rock concert. But the voice, though juvenile, was attempting the same claim, albeit not quite so slow, "I am…rock. I am…eternal. Hear me or not. I am."

Then the frame went up and Tree thought of the beautiful architecture of the top stories of the trees once in this meadow. Now there were right angles and 45-degree angles.

Plywood. An appearance of stucco, meant to evoke adobe. Roofing with blue tiles on an impulse of the wife.

Another series of pieces of large equipment. A spa was going in on the side.

Then a layer of dirt over the compacted soil.

Sprinklers. More dirt. Preparation for incoming sod. Impatiens and English roses and day lilies and calla lilies and daisies and every flower from another land one could think up. A table and chairs made of exotic hardwoods from hard-beset Brazil. Creamy paint on the walls that stung where it sunk into the soil and remained wedged in clumps underground wherever it sank, giving off an odor of industry.

Much work indoors. Paint and tile and wood floor and fixtures and glass and spit and polish and then a truck backed up and furniture and expensive Near Eastern carpets and suddenly it was done.

Throughout the whole thing, Tree slowly deflated like a balloon days after the party. E was drinking e's stored water and eating e's stored food. By the end, e had lost access to half e's old roots. The roots which had been crushed had sent some waves of fear and pain upwards which impacted the remaining roots, the whole tree, in ways that Tree could not foretell. E struggled to produce new leaves, but leaves took food up at onset and e needed food to live.

Tree felt as fragile as the very first time e had experienced a night and e had prayed in a panic for the hot/light's return. But now instead of the answering burst of light and the feeling that the future lay ahead, e retreated more and more into a survival mode and tried not to re-experience the echoes of the pain of the day of the pressing. But the memories revived in e's dreams and e often woke at night screaming into the hearts of plants miles away. And all the plants knew now that humans were to be dreaded and feared.

Dully, Tree wondered if anything worse could ever happen.

SOD

The sod came in on a beat up wooden pallet: big stacks of sliced off grass and dirt, piled up like fur coats on top of a bed at a winter dinner party. Tree heard a general moan from the stack – thousands of grass lives, cut off from half their roots, slivered away out of their natal dirt and then stacked in piles, some of them suffocating from the weight of peers and dirt. Then the sun came and baked the pile, which grew warm and then hot inside. Tree could hear the shrieks as individual grasses gave up to the heat. It was somewhat like eavesdropping to the sounds from a holding pen at a slaughterhouse.

The men came again and Tree sighed. Men in jeans and boots made e cringe by now. What would they do next? The men scuffed the hardened dirt and commented about the cement-like nature of compacted dirt. Conferring, they called in supplemental dirt to lay over the pipes they had scattered about like a tinker-toy set. Once pipes and dirt were laid out, they attached the whole of the pipes to the water main and turned it on and cheered as the water fizzed in spheres and arcs, mystifying Tree who had never seen rain coming up from the dirt, but only down upon it. Nor had e seen rain that flew out in repetitive circular patterns, pretty like a spider web. Tree watched, dazed by the show.

The boss looked at a clock. 2:00. He challenged his tired crew to attack the sod. A feisty one declined to earn the extra dough on behalf of himself and his colleagues but the boss told them the sod would die if it sat another 24 hours. He promised everyone dinner out. Half grumpy laughter rose from the men standing around on the mud, whilst the water trickled in tiny streams towards the dry creekbed. Tree watched it thirstily and wished e's roots in that vicinity had not been killed. The water in the mud looked like it felt good.

The men headed over to the moaning piles of half-dead grass and began to diminish the height of the pile, which began at a man's eye level, taking slides of grass from the top and slinging them over a shoulder and throwing them with casual grace to meet the growing pattern of a line of green snaking up one side of the dirt. They reversed the line and so widened the lawn. Up and down, up and down. The mens' boots grew heavy with mud and wet clay. For men working at such a pace doing such heavy tasks, they were precise and careful. Not a one stepped on the sod once it lay atop the mud. In a very short time the once desolate field was now filled with…well…grass, Tree would have to say. The men turned on the watering system, rinsed their boots, turned off the sprinklers and headed back to trucks and roadbikes, looking forward to the promised meal on the company dime.

Tree sent out a hoarse whisper from e's core. But not a one of these grass were able to hear even each other, much less an enormous distant Tree, core lofty and high above them.

Tree, however, could hear the whole of the herd as it moaned in mortal agony over all the truncated roots. But Tree knew the truth about grass: grass is tough.

And though stems were bent and mashed and crushed and twisted and spirits were bruised and frightened by the uprooting, the stacking, the transit, the heated, crushing wait, by the alien mud with rock-hard dirt beneath and the chlorine-y tasting water sprinkled down from above, Tree listened to the sound of growth. And slowly, surely, grass after grass was standing up straighter. Tiny halved roots were sending out timid new shoots. Old roots were uncoiling and trying to find a place. The groaning moaning sound became intermixed with tiny echoes of the sounds of growth.

The grass never noticed when the sun set or the moon rose or dawn broke it – the whole herd was attempting to survive the rude transition. And with respect, Tree realized that most of the herd would make it. Without Tree's support in any way.

And as the littler roots recovered and transformed and actually grew, Tree wondered quietly what e could do to heal and charm e's own roots into growth.

Sadly, e concluded that mature oak trees do not have the bounce of grass. E would have to endure the loss of these roots. This new grass spoke a language alien to Tree and e listened carefully waiting until the emotions behind the words revealed themselves and the meaning fell into e's hands like pomegranate seeds in profusion after the fruit is halved.

Before, any variety of grass had always a simple refrain, "We are grass." But this grass had a different phrase that popped up even more often, "We are thirsty." And the newly installed pipes began to spurt on water, several times a week.

At first Tree was elated: rain, all the time, even in the summer. Surrounded by this sea of grass, e could see new grass starting to sprout, feel the sod's little roots struggling to push into the ground on the side where e's roots were still vibrant, sympathize with the grass that hit the compacted dirt and sent roots curling back out and amongst e'selves. But then Tree started to feel ill.

Really ill. It took a while for Tree to track down what it was. Fungi, always picking at e's bark and roots, trying to find a toehold, was growing in the summer heat with the sudden wet to an extent Tree had never imagined possible.

And the fungi was eating Tree whilst Tree was still alive.

Tree tried to harden e's core, to protect e's heartwood, but e knew it was only a question of time now before the suddenly wildly prolific fungi found little entrances inward. And Tree knew e would die.

But how could e build up toughness between e's outside and e's core when e was struggling to find the energy to grow new leaves? When eself was eating e's own core? Tree's remaining roots struggled to feed, to grow, to continue, but the fungi interfered with all the good things and Tree felt individual roots go to mush like white bread with a bucket of water thrown on it.

IN THE BACKYARD

A car came down the road. There had been hardly any humans after the house was done. The movers. Then nothing.

Gardeners came by a few times a week to put on the sprinklers. Bougainvillea struggled up along the lowest portion of the tallest wall of the house. Some young calla lilies stocked up furled white little buds, waiting to reveal themselves in time for Easter Sunday, Passover, Vernal Equinox and more pagan interpretations of spring. Birds of paradise sat on tall, firm stalks, pointy and bright, flowers that didn't mind waiting days and days for an audience. Jasmine sat smugly at the front door, waiting to wow all comers with that scent that feels like kissing a big crush. Though crush is a word that Tree would have been unable to like, had e known English.

The car stopped. Both front doors opened. A man got out of the driver's seat with big dark glasses. On the other side, the woman stepped out with slightly smaller dark glasses. They paused to admire their new possession. Then they both turned around and opened the doors to the back seat to speak to their child. There was quite a bit of speaking. Irritated, the father slammed his side shut and walked up to the front door, using the key to move inside and be swallowed up by the big enclosure of house.

The mom hung in there a while further, then she left the door open but also abandoned the car and went in through the front door, exclaiming in delight as she did so. She left the front door open, as if to invite the child in.

Twenty minutes passed. Enough for an average sulk to fade. This was no average sulk. But the kid tired of the boredom of sitting in the rapidly warming car. He slithered out the back door on his mom's side. He paused to consider the house and then tromped around the backyard, still in a snit. He had not wanted to leave his friends, his school, his fragile life in Washington, D.C. He had been almost happy there and feared that in a new terrain he would altogether be overwhelmed and destroyed. He wasn't very good with his peers and

TREE

he was terrible with his parents and since he didn't really have actively engaged grandparents, that left him with…not a lot. The place off Laurel Canyon had been a rental. He had imagined he'd get to go home to D.C. in the near future. This new place meant that that had been a daydream, with no more reality than a promise to an auditioning actor.

The boy walked into the emerald green backyard. The grass was no different than that he'd seen on a hundred thousand other lawns he'd seen around and about America over the course of his eight years, so he thought no more about it. But the dry, sere wildness just past their property line made him anxious. It was almost like a desert in terms of the heat, the dryness, the parched, baked soil.

But yet when you looked at it, it was packed with bushes, various narrow trees, some wild flowers and grasses. In fact, it was a terrain completely new to him. He had neither the vocabulary nor the experience to imagine such a place.

While he sat thinking about it, he heard his parents laughing and talking and he knew they were kissing. Not for the first time, he thought that they really weren't terribly interested in him. In fact, they'd much rather be alone in the house kissing than have him with them. Or come out here to see him? Forget it. Maybe at dinnertime.

Suddenly exhausted by the emotions of being an alienated only child, he stretched out on the grass over some of Tree's dead roots. Tree remembered the feeling of Horse standing on e's roots, of other humans lying on e's roots and the absence of the actual physical sensation of the additional weight just grieved him. The child looked up at the tree. Almost as if.

The parents' voices now moved upstairs. More laughter.

The boy was old enough to have a clue as to what was going on and old enough to form the judgment that this was not appropriate. Shouldn't they be showing him his room and arguing over who would sit where in the new breakfast room? Setting up camp to have cold cereal and delivered pizza whilst each of them made sense of their boxes? Why had they had him? Why wasn't he at boarding school already? If only he had a younger sibling to love and boss and tease and cherish. A pet. A mom with a capacious lap and bosom. A dad who did lame carpentry projects. He wasn't picky. He wished for the boy at his old school in D.C. who had been his sometime friend and wished that they had been for always and that he was out here with him in the backyard to pick grass stems and try to turn them into

223

musical instruments like that old guy in Brazil at the park during the documentary last summer. He gave up on the irritations and the wishes and just let out a big sigh. Alone. Nothing new.

But somehow here felt more alone. He looked up at sky and out at 1960s bright grass, then he cast a curious eye up Tree's enormous trunk and thought to himself, "What a fabulous tree." But then the strain of moving caught up with him and the lack of real friends back home, the impossibility of new friends, the fear of an outbreak of his sometimes excruciating stutter, the whole thing.

Too much. He was alone in the world with only bright colors of blue and green to which to cling. And the colors were not enough to quell this wrenching –

Tree caught a wave of pure emotion. Loneliness. The intoxication of solitude. It had been e's way in with María Martá. Perhaps this child was to be a friend? Tree released e's own sorrow and tried to send a warmness out to the boy.

Startled, the child looked right up at the oak and his eyes caught and held Tree's core. For twenty long seconds, Tree thought each would understand the other and the barriers between species would again be broken. But nothing happened and the Spanish words Tree tried out on the child either were not something he could hear or were something he could not understand. Still, the boy started to get up to go inside to the den adjacent to the backyard. The boy opened the door and stepped back outwards. Just in case.

Male laughter came from above and then a woman's voice, "Enzo? Are you still in the car? Did you come in? Sweetie, are you in the backyard?"

The father's voice rumbled, "Come back here." But the mom was off and came down the art-tiled stairs and out the back yard. Somehow catching a whiff of the almost-moment, she murmured, "Pretty tree."

Enzo glanced up at Tree and said somberly, "Yes."

Tree knew the child would be back. E wasn't sure why, but it was important that this child understand e. So e sent such a fabulous wave of oakness and love and treedom at the boy's back that just as he was stepping over the threshold the child turned around to face Tree.

To some query of his mother's the child was quite clear, "No, no, I don't think I'll be…lonely…here."

Tree rustled as the door shut but still the child gazed through the glass at the magnificent tree. The child whispered a word that Tree understood immediately, straight inside, "Friend."

TREEGLISH

Enzo kept on heading out into the backyard, sitting under Tree. Gradually the boy began to wonder if he could sense the shape of something invisible between him and the plant and he tried to feel it, see it, by any means he could imagine.

At first, Enzo emoting at the plant for reasons that made no sense, the boy aimed to put pictures into Tree, pictures of himself in preschool, digging in the sand, pictures of Enzo last winter drinking hot chocolate in Paris while his parents flirted over his head over good-morning lattés and private jokes. When he shared a vision of himself walking in the forest in Brazil last summer, Tree caught sight of the rubber trees and snakes as long as dump trucks, Tree's own imagination sparked and jumped into the imagery. E shared a picture of a rattlesnake and Enzo burst into speech in his head.

"Is that a rattlesnake?" asked the boy, excited to be at the receiving end of a thought. Tree fumbled for the right word and sent back "*serpiente*" and Enzo rolled over to put a hand on Tree's trunk.

"You speak Spanish?" he asked incredulously.

Enzo knew that California had been a part of Spain, then Mexico, and he had already figured out that this was a very old tree.

"You had a human friend before!" Enzo guessed. Shyly, Tree sent over a picture of María Marta as e had first known her, young and in a long black dress. The idea of someone, anyone, even a tree knowing a lady from the olden days knocked Enzo out.

It was better than a movie or a book. He blurted out a string of questions, eager to see her entire life, chapter and verse, to know someone from the past in a way no other human being had ever before done. But Tree was tiring and tried to flash the feeling of crushed roots over at Enzo.

Something broke down in the flow of communications between them and Enzo was once again an ordinary kid with an imaginary friend, separate and other from plants.

Still, he had caught a feeling. He put a hand on Tree and patted the gnarled bark.

CALIFORNIA PARTY

"You are hurting. Not well. Poor Tree." Alone on the other side of his mother's first big party, in the damp grass planted all the way up to Tree's trunk, the child moved to sit next to the plant, leaning against the trunk like a tired toddler would a parent at the end of the day. "Poor Tree," Enzo repeated. Embracing the hard surface, the noise of the band playing "*The Girl from Ipanema*" to his mother's annoyance (long story) slowly lost relevance to him as he drifted into peace and sleep.

Tree's soft spot for sprouts undid e and in e's core he found more comfort from the sleeping child than even the boy had found from the Tree awake. The jarring music, the masses of people in insect-bright clothes, the lights, the complicated smells of party foods, the noise...e rose above it like a butterfly drifting to better climes, looking to enter into the child's floating universe, wheresoever it now was.

* * *

The party continued as the father paid out giant sum after sum to keep the band going for two and a half hours past their official stop point. Exhausted, they finally gave up and left, despite offers of further wads of cash. Then one of the young women in black brought out her new portable CD player from her old VW bug and introduced the older folk to the low-calorie joys of *Echo and the Bunnymen* and melodic British misery. Those still standing recognized the romance in the songs and kept dancing, those sitting fell into the melancholic aspects and drank more big red Italian wine.

But finally even the owner of the CD player tired – no matter her youth – she still had to be up to cater a brunch the next day so she left and with her went a string of guests in spurts like a leaky sprinkler until only husband and wife were facing a sad man who wished he had a tailored brunette waiting for him at home, too. But no amount of wishing would make it so, so finally he got into his clunky Porsche and drove off in puff of smog.

Husband looked at wife and the lack of noise made clear the

silence stretching between them. The husband thought to himself that perhaps if they slept together it would feel like she loved him again and she thought maybe if she slept with him she would feel something at all for an hour or so and then through the narrowness of their unfulfilled desires an outside idea popped in.

She suggested, "Let's go kiss Enzo goodnight."

But then Enzo was not in bed. Not in the kitchen. Not in their bed or either of the guest beds or under his father's desk where he liked to build Legos, not in the bathtub where he once slept when the air conditioning wasn't working and it had been so hot. Not in the garage with his *Mad* magazine collection. Not in the front porch. Not even behind the couch in the living room where his mother had seen him reading *The Joy of Sex* one time and had discreetly walked away to let him tiptoe through incipient adult feelings by himself.

Both parents were now electrifyingly sober. The detritus of the party seemed meaningless and tacky and their lives loomed behind them as if enormous puffed-up résumés, every single screen credit emblazoned in fool's gold, written on trash, because the one thing they both now knew is that they loved Enzo more even than each other and now he was gone.

Drops of liquid hanging poised on his lower eyelashes, the father stated the obvious, "We have to call the police." And she was dialing 911 before he had finished his sentence. As soon as she was off, clutching her husband's hand she asked him, "Did one of our friends take him?"

"Who would take him from us?" said his father, "He has run away. We have not paid enough attention to him."

"What do little boys want?" asked his mother.

Pulling his wife close to him, he asked bleakly, "What do any of us want?"

It felt like years before the police arrived, flashing patriotic blue and red lights, but it really was less than ten minutes as they had been breaking up a party a few streets away which had devolved into something considerably more Bacchanalian then their own relatively mild festivities. The police went through the house with geometric precision and then begin doing concentric rings around the house. Husband and wife joined in the search, mimicking the logical patternings.

In less than five minutes after they had moved the search outside, the younger policeman announced, "Found him."

Husband, wife and partner policeman ran to the sound of the young man's voice.

Sound asleep, the boy looked younger than his age.

Cherubic. The husband hugged and clutched the policemen, one in each arm and the wife sank down to the ground to embrace her son. The police were kind. These things happened. Better safe than sorry. Always good to call. Perhaps less wine at the next party? And they were off in a rattle of gravel and sand, red lights retreating down the curvy road on the other side of the creek.

The husband sank down on his knees beside his wife, reaching over to lift up their boy. But the woman had captured just a hint of the kid's connection to the tree and she shook her head. She spooned her son as he held the tree and her husband crawled over their supine bodies to spoon her himself. Husband and wife felt a kind of peace with each other they had never known. They would talk about this night when they were old, wondering how come it couldn't always have been so sweet.

Shortly before dawn all three humans woke up in a beat-beat-beat like a trio of dominoes clicking down, surprised by the cold and wet. The mother picked up the disoriented child and they went into the living room and fell on the enormous new suede sofas, to sleep in a jumble. The parents would be irritated to find they had stained the sofas with the dew from their clothes but later, all the boy noted, was that this was the first time he had ever slept with his parents all together and it had felt like eating pudding at his grandmother's house, like happy endings in fairy tales. Like maybe everything would be o.k.

* * *

The next morning both parents woke before Enzo and they smiled at each other over his limp body. The father had a crick in his neck, but he still couldn't remember being in such a good mood in ages. His wife looked younger than she had in years, as if her biggest care was what to wear for a church social rather than how to jump in to get two projects completed (old projects from her husband's pre-Hollywood days that she had agreed to take on in a moment of egoistic generosity, forgetting the tear of the daily grind) in less than a week's time when the editor had been coming in later and later due to a suspected cocaine habit which really had to do with the fact that they'd hired him in a manic phase and were now dealing with the Janus face of his depression.

Smiling back at her, her husband asked her what she wanted and only one thing came to mind, "Food."

So before long, the three of them were sitting in a restaurant in Marina del Rey, them over salmon Eggs Benedict with multiple cups of coffee with a side of sliced avocado just for fun, Enzo with a gigantic Belgian waffle nearly lost under a mountain of fluffy whipped cream with a glacial morass of sliced strawberries, boulder-sized. His mother was telling him about friends she had made last night, neighbors down the street with bigger boys who had suggested that Enzo might like CaliCamp off on Old Topanga Canyon Boulevard. Enzo was shy of other children these days (private school in the city had been painful,) but had read about the fun sorts of things kids did at camps in a book and was interested. Especially, once his mom began waxing on about go-carts and ponies, pools and bamboo forests with mysterious paths and picnic parties.

Dad said perhaps they should troll the neighborhood that evening for other kids and invite them over to play Monopoly and Twister and Enzo was surprised: having other children to their home was a brand new idea. Mom said she'd make burgers and buy watermelon and vanilla ice cream. Dad corrected her, they should get strawberry, Enzo's favorite.

Both, Mom suggested and Enzo sat under the onslaught of attention, himself happy as a waffle under a pile of whipped cream.

They stopped at the grocery store and bought the party foods. They even got Orange Crush when he asked. It was all feeling promising. They drove around a little and didn't actually see any kids, but they carefully noted two homes with boy-sized bikes and a third with a very impressive tree house that stretched between two oaks and a eucalyptus. Both parents told Enzo that the tree house was bigger than their first apartment and he thought that was hilarious, though they did point out that they weren't really kidding. Dad suggested that maybe he should go home to check the answering machine and Mom and Enzo could drive around the streets looking for kids some more, maybe go door-to-door at the houses that said "child" most loudly and knock. Enzo practically leapt out of the car when they got home but Mom made the fatal mistake of stopping for a Diet Pepsi while her husband checked messages. She heard the fuzzy tape loud and clear: the editor's agent had called. There had been an accident. He was in the hospital, alive, but in intensive care. There was no way he was going to finish the film…and the agent had no available editors. Husband and wife looked at each other. PBS wanted the final cut by Thursday. It was Sunday. There was no one but them to make it happen and he'd have to go back to his main project on Monday. So they gave Enzo permission to watch t.v. and they piled in the car to go back down to the little rooms with no windows and doors that sealed tightly shut so that each filmmaker was not subjected to the sounds of his/her colleagues working away, the film making flicking sounds as they wound and rewound spools deciding what to keep, what to shed, what to elongate, what to truncate and how to elicit feelings and more feelings from pictures.

Enzo watched a half an hour of cartoons, but by then it was 1:00 and the cartoons were done for the day. He hated the old movies and reruns so he took the Monopoly and the strawberry ice cream out to the backyard and as he played himself, tiny car against thimble, he felt something in his head that was not him and recognized companionship of another kind of intelligence and curiosity.

After an all nighter editing, Mom came home and dozed off on the sofa in the living room while her husband was still down at Panavision dropping off film. God, so close to done.

When she woke up, the light had shifted and the filmmaker's eye gravitated naturally to the primary light source in the room – a bubble sunroof. Outside, the sky was blue with patchy clouds and was letting loose with a scattering of raindrops that drummed on the curved glass, each drop hitting the surface and breaking into four to six miniature clumped drops on impact. As she looked up, it looked like a pile of jaguar kittens with wet toes had run all over the rooftop. She smiled at the image and before she had let that go the rain intensified just enough to make the surface look mottled like a jaguar coat. While she was wondering how patterns in nature repeat, the clouds cleared with a wind that brushed the wet off the sunroof and the imaginary cats went with them. Her conscience pricked and she imagined that she could feel her son's loneliness like an unfed housepet in the next room; she knew she should get up to see him, but she didn't know how to connect with him. His need felt chronic. Why couldn't he get excited about something, comic books, skateboarding, girls, Renaissance art, she didn't really care what, just something, instead of looking up at her all the time with those black-brown eyes.

Christ. She got up, tired, and went looking for him. To her surprise, he was nowhere in the house. When she found him, he was under the oak in the backyard, fairly wet, completely engrossed in something. She asked him what he was doing and he demurred. Pressed, he finally admitted that he had collected the detritus from the owls that lived in the tree and was in the process of breaking them apart and reassembling them. "Theoretically, mom, I should be able to assemble an entire mouse skeleton out of this." She laughed and ruffled his hair. "You wanna bring that inside? It is cold and wet out here."

He shook his head, he liked the company in the backyard. She walked inside thinking about ordering dinner from the Thai restaurant at the foot of the hill; if her husband had the wit to call her first. Not for the first time, she wondered how she had and her husband had raised a kid who thought building a mouse skeleton from scraps was a good time. Must have been all those nuts they knew when they were making the nature films for the Yellow Magazine. She smiled to herself. Surely, this was not a stupid kid. She turned on their new CD player, U2's new album drifting out over the backyard and surrounding hillsides. Their garden and the wildlands responded to the melodic passion. *"In the name of love, one man, in the name of love..."*

PLANTSLAYERS

The gardeners came twice a week and without fail, Tree tried to talk to them and did not succeed. Their Spanish tantalized Tree with the illusion that communication was possible. But for ideas to flow between tree and man requires something more elusive than shared vocabulary because each species' language is completely different.

These individuals did not have the contours of María Martá's mind, and that particular oceanic heart.

One morning the gardeners came in and put an *escalera* up under Tree and soon they were stringing vines with little rocks on them all over e. E felt like a young willow e had once seen overtaken by an onslaught of ivy. The ivy tendrils had stickers that clung on and affixed like barnacles, effectively gluing the vine to the plant beneath. As the ivy grew up towards the sunlight, the support tree lost access to light eself and perished. There was nothing the much larger tree could do to resist the murderous onslaught and the whole thing took place slowly over half a year as spring slid into summer.

This growth, however, as it was assisted by humans, took only until mid-morning. Once every major branch and the whole of e's trunk was engirdled by the vines, there was a brief hurtful feeling wherever the vine touched e and then sparks of heat wherever the little clear rocks were. Looking at this alien vine, Tree realized that for the moment, the rocks were sometimes little shards of light. All very odd. First e's bark began to warm up, then gradually e's core.

While Tree struggled to co-exist with the rock-budded vine, the gardeners mowed and trimmed and fertilized and watered. There was so much fertilizer that the lawn smelt like the waiting pen of a stockyard; the sprinklers ran so long the water quickly filled up the top layer of dirt and then pooled atop the compacted subsurface. As more water shimmered down in the noon light, the standing water poured off the lawn, brown with fertilizer. The whole stew streamed down into the creek and then sat in the pools, turning them from clear as glass with undertones of greens and greys and browns into a dirty brown soup.

Tree's roots had puffed up at the first hint of water. It had been pleasant. Now the roots were swimming in warm water. It was not a sensation e had ever known before. The men took a lunch break and turned off the water, sloshing through the temporary pond in the middle of the lawn formed by the lengthy episode of sprinklers. One of them said to the others that the lady of the house was coming back and the radio got turned off, sandwiches put away and mercifully, the lights were turned off on Tree.

But it wasn't over. They left, but soon, new men came with tables and chairs and white tablecloths. Another round of workers came with rented china and crystal. Then some skinny young women dressed in pink came, as chatty as a flock of flamingos. They brought enormous trays out of the car, paper sacks, tools, aprons. They didn't look strong enough to carry the loads they flung around. Soon from the kitchen came smells that Tree identified as typical of human foods. Burnt meat, ripped greens, the fruit of trees, the smell of oil and the incomprehensible transition of plants into many-tiered spicings. Something seductively sweet.

When the sun set, the women took off their work aprons and then opened the door for men in black and white with instruments. Soon music was flowing and a steady stream of cars and visitors came. Tree was admired, ogled, touched and caressed. The rock-light vines went on again. Tree was the focal point of the whole backyard – a dance floor was set atop e's roots. Tree wondered idly as e watched the humans piling up and gyrating with the music if this could possibly further crush e's roots. How could e care? E would clearly die sooner rather than later.

Whilst in the midst of this emotional wallow, e heard a thought clear and piping like a young grass speaking.

"Don't die yet – you are my only friend here." Looking for the voice, e saw the human child in the window of the house, looking down wistfully at all the adults larking around in a drunken haze.

Tree's outline stood roughly elegant against the horizon, drawn to the foreground by the addition of all the twinkly lights.

The boy continued, "Another party. They're treating you like a slaughtered Christmas tree and it is still only the middle of summer. Parents."

Tree wanted the vine-lights off desperately but could not figure out how to speak to the child. E's emotions came out in a blur. Having watched James Bond movies since infancy, the kid knew what to do. He headed down into the basement, found the breaker box and threw the switch.

Curses came from the kitchen, from the band, from high-strung guests. He pulled out his flashlight and proceeded to turn on every power source possessed by the house, pausing only at the second-to-last switch marked "Outside, back, right" and then he left it down.

There were sounds of happiness as the lights mostly came on and then the child slipped out very quietly so as not to get caught by babysitter or parent and then he sat on the side of the oak tree facing the parklands, the part which no partygoer had yet to visit. And the boy told the tree stories from his life. In pictures. Tree looked at every memory, absorbed every word and stood fascinated by one so different and so yet the same as e.

BLUE

Towards the end of third grade at Topanga Elementary School, Enzo had started to like school, primarily because of Kobalt, a true wild child, a big strapping boy of Swedish descent whose father was a mostly absent soccer coach and whose mother drank like a Prohibition era flapper. Kobalt liked books, skateboards, D & D, scroungy looking dogs and staying up late and when Enzo tried to tell him about a talking tree in his backyard, Kobalt said it was a great dream. Enzo told him it was really real and Kobalt said it was a "true dream" which Enzo took as partial belief, which was hugely better than mockery or disbelief. Sometimes at recess, the two of them would sneak into the wildlands which began at the edge of campus behind the auditorium and amidst the rocks and weeds and trees, blocked from teacherly observation by the trash dumpsters, Enzo would tell Kobalt long winding narratives about life with the manicured backyard and the huge old oak and the various animals and the bigger boy would sit gnawing on "sour grass" with its piquant yellow flowers or picking apart wild oats to pop in the soft hearts of their seeds, rapt. At different times, Enzo had watched Kobalt pick the locks of the cage down by the cul-de-sac and let the stray dogs go free at Topanga Elementary, saving them from likely death at the pound. Kobalt was nearly impervious to discipline; he just assumed the mantle of constant trouble as a side effect of being a boy. And Enzo never told anyone who let the dogs out, just faithfully brought half his lunch to feed the strays on these nerve-wracking forays into law-breaking.

Sometimes Enzo got his parents to let Kobalt come over for the weekend, and his ruffian pal convinced him to watch scary movies on t.v., play handball with a basketball on the side of the garage which was great until it went through his parents' bedroom window, catch lizards with leashes made from grass and hunt unsuccessfully for rattlesnakes.

One time Kobalt brought a horny toad with him as a gift to Enzo, not realizing that away from his mountaintop micro kingdom, the spiky amphibian would starve, but Enzo convinced Kobalt that his parents would have the gardeners kill such an impressively pugnacious looking animal, so Kobalt reluctantly packed it back in his pocket to drop off near his own house the next day.

One Saturday when the kitchen looked clean and the refrigerator empty, his parents drove into downtown Topanga to pick up a pizza and Enzo took Kobalt out into the dark to sit under Tree and he tried to introduce plant to kid and kid to plant but neither could hear the other, though they both tried. Enzo tried not to be crushed and Kobalt said it was like ghosts – it being a well-known fact of childhood that only some people saw spirits. When Enzo told him how the watering during the summer was killing Tree, fungi overrunning the old plant, Kobalt briefly considered the balance of the lives of thousands of grass versus the life of the oak and came down heartily on the side of the tree. Enzo explained that he had already explained to his parents the problem and they persisted with the gardeners and the glossy green yard, saying that having a nice home and garden was crucial for entertaining, and by extension for their career. They could see that there were less leaves on Tree, but they figured it was some other cause – old age, disease, temperament. Who knew. And if Enzo was right, they were immovable about the importance of having a green lawn to go with their fancy house. When he was seeing things darkly, it seemed to Enzo sometimes that everything they did was for how it looked. Sitting under the ailing Tree, Kobalt persisted in his line of questioning though and grew angry – had Enzo told them this was a special tree, had he asked them to stop watering, did they understand what they were doing? Enzo had. For him, asking more than once on the same topic was a big thing. He had. And had. Furrowing his brow, Kobalt contemplated the problem. Treating the Bermuda lawn like a field of weeds, he ripped at the turf, but could see he was only getting the stems, not the roots. Enzo grabbed him when he started chucking rocks at the house. How would that help, he asked. Nothing they could do could help.

"Fuck that," said the brazen third grader. Enzo looked up at him, startled. The other kid was working up into a full sized rant and he ran in a tear around the house, the yard, the garage and found a big shovel. Kobalt broke off the knobs that started and stopped the sprinklers; he stabbed the pipes that lead to the water and they leaked water like a movie hero gushing blood. Taking a pipe hidden a few inches under the loose soil of an artificially created hill along the side of the house.

Feeling his success, he got more and more out of control. Enzo was shaking, following him around on his rampage, asking him to stop, telling him they'd be in trouble. Finally he grabbed the bigger boy in his arms and tackled him to the ground. "You have to stop," yelled Enzo. "Why?" said the blond kid. Flummoxed, Enzo fell back on preschool logic, "Because."

When Enzo's mother came back from the grocery store and Saw. Her. Yard. She made both boys get in the car and drove straight to Kobalt's family house, where no parents were to be found. She left him there alone, with a note for his parents, which Kobalt destroyed, feeling justified because no one but he seemed to understand that a life was at stake here.

Enzo was sad that Kobalt was not allowed to visit ever again and was not surprised when the sprinklers were up and running a few days later. At school, he told an unrepentant Kobalt about the new sprinkler system.

Enzo's attempts to describe to his parents why his friend went on a rampage – without implicating himself – backfired. Understanding finally that Tree was sick, his father called an arborist, who took a sample of the soil and scraped off a bit of spongy bark, but told them that one look at the chicken fungi on the trunk told her all she needed to know. From her point of view, this was a mature oak veering into a sad old age. She foretold falling limbs, perhaps a split trunk, danger to the pool and even the roof below, a failure to thrive, a slow death. She suggested that they remove the tree and find another tree more suitable to the rest of their landscape. Silent during the first part of this appointment, Enzo found his voice and said they should find a landscape more suitable to the oak rather than a tree suitable to the landscape. Everyone laughed at him. The arborist told Enzo's parents that the tree might hold on another year or two but reiterated the danger of falling limbs, talked about the possibility, even likelihood, of *Phtophthora ramorum* spreading to other trees on site, talked about the eyesore factor and the parents agreed for her to come back with her crew to remove it.

At dinner, Enzo told his parents he had never once asked for a puppy or kitten, understanding the allergy-related asthma both parents suffered in proximity from fur and dander; "Could I have this oak for a pet?" he asked. They told him that even dogs and cats had to be put down sometimes. They tried to tell him this was for the Tree's own good but he ran out of the room, ignoring the offers of ice cream for dessert and a proffered video. They would have liked to occupy Enzo with treats until after the arborist had returned and taken care of the mess in their garden, but they let him go when he stormed out. "Early adolescence –" said the mother to the father.

Outside the wind rustled in Tree's limbs. Enzo sat down under his friend, his chest empty and cold inside. He could not even find words or images to warn Tree of what would come. He felt Tree as the human equivalent of maybe forty-five; a man or woman in prime; the universe owed this magnificent plant hundreds of years more of life. The wind sounded like some shy translator taking the contents of his heart and murmuring them into a foreign tongue that all the beings in the natural world could hear. The itchy Bermuda grass, the spongy petunias, the big-headed English roses with outsized spines and dark leaves, the mustard, radish, and wild oats fronted by fennel in the middle of the ice plant hillsides, the elderberry, toyon and eucalyptus just off the property owned by Enzo's family, the drying stands of arundo, the dust and sky all heard Enzo's unvoiced thought and Tree spoke softly into the child's center, "I know," e said.

Then brutal images of chainsaws, falling trees, clearcut forests, chunked logs came bursting into the child's consciousness and Tree took the quick cut images calmly. "Nothing lives forever."

The child sat silent, head in hands, grief filling in the silence as plants waved away and towards the human child. Tree took hundreds of years of light and soil and water and patient growth and hope and fire and loneliness and love and condensed it into an emotion as transparent and fragile as a new willow leaf. E let the sensation well up from e's taproot, through e's core and into e's limbs branches leaves and waver up into the sky. E let it go and the feeling came drifting down the breeze, shifting left then right, up then down and wafting into a circle and falling finally on to Enzo's crown, into his skull, his head, heart and whole body. Suffused by the power of such a vast life, Enzo gasped, drinking it in like a baby's first taste of air. This *ananda* was simultaneously delicate and strong, a whispery promise that in the face of death, only love lasts.

"This night will be as long as a whole life to you and then I will end," Tree asserted. Enzo saw green light and showers of white rays, sparks of gold and then black. Child and Tree knew that it would happen during the day, while he was at school. To himself, Enzo wished for the solace of an afterlife, or that police would answer his call for help or his parents might have some kind of last-minute epiphany, but he knew with a sick certainty what was going to come to pass. Time slowed down. Lifting a hand from the ground was a heroic act, taking millennia and the willpower of an army combined.

He understood Kobalt's raging fits and the American Revolution and kamikaze. He shivered trying to shake the dread off his person. Tree's voice came to him, a warm amused contralto. "Life is very long and very short. I must let go. I am Tree. My name is Tree." Recognizing e's first sentence from stories, Enzo started to cry. Tree took compassion on his little friend, remembering the loss of hot/light, the death of Univervia, the sweetness of life as Tree and the dearness of this flesh and blood walking plant named Enzo. Enzo could feel Tree urging him to make leaves and branches and limbs and roots, to grow tall and thrive. He nearly smiled.

Enzo could feel Tree retreating into the deep silence in which he had initially met it; a tree in a world of e's own, alive and self-aware, needing neither mobility nor language, happiness nor emotion, simply existing in a state of arboreal grandeur. Enzo understood that sinking into a state of beingness, existing in an illusion of timeless magnificence would make mortality bearable for such a great creature. But he was only a kid and he did not want to be abandoned. He grabbed the trunk in an embrace and pounded the hard wood with his small fists, bruising his forearms and scratching the flesh on the edge of his palms. He wanted something more, some connection, some passion, some final gift. He understood that death meant silence and this silence now felt like premature death. It was too much.

Enzo pleaded, "Tree, don't go. Stay." There was no word. No image. No breath of interconnection.

Enzo sat disconsolate for a long time. His mother came and dragged him to take a bath and go to bed. Later on he snuck out of bed and put on a ski parka and his mother's pink slippers that were beside the door and then he came back outside in the cold, wrapped in a blanket. He laid his head on the hard trunk, feeling acutely the absence of language between them. His eyes teared up with yearning.

It was very cold. The stars looked very far away. The light blinked off in his parents' room. The earth spun. He knew dawn would come. "Oh Tree," he said out loud.

Tree heard. For this little plant, for eself, e's core opened like a new leaf and a burst of memories came, flashcut at the speed of dragonfly life, then stretching to slow. Univervia, tall and green. María Marta in the embrace of her lover. Hot/light. The glint of the moon through stormclouds. Warm dirt. Groundwater in e's furthest root tips. The weight of acorns, so ripe, dropping off of branches. The urge to grow. The expectation of a hundred days times three for a hundred times two, three, four, even five, then suddenly the shock of one night left. A memory of rain pitter-pattering on e's leaves. The scent of wet from e's duff. The first time e felt the piercing loneliness from little Enzo and the simple happiness it gave Tree to drop joy into the boy's young core; the sweetness of receiving the child's love. Ah. That was it. That was the underlying melody in every thought and sensation, via every rock and plant and animal and sky and star, inside the water, from the dirt, through the light. And e found the exact words to speak just before Enzo fell into sleep. Tree told Enzo, "Only love lasts."

Tree spoke clearly, "Grow. And plant an acorn."

Besos to those who grew in my family before
and to those who will grow after.

Before and June Watts and now...
Stephen and Tess Watts
Rick Zeller, Z and Shannon Watts
Vincent Scott
Lucilla Mir Orton
Stephen Stanislaus Orton
...and after.

IN GRATITUDE

Tree *grew because many people helped to garden both the project and me. My first thanks goes to the members of my writing group Finish the Book, including Anika Colvin-Hannibal, Gerry Berns and Lee Michaelson and our one Brit, all of whom listened to* Tree *as it began.*

Thank you Ozzie Silna, may you rest in peace, for your belief in the value of my work and the gift of time that you gave me.

And... for the amazing people who funded Tree *via a Kickstarter campaign, your support of this project buoys me up every day. I cherish your gifts, dear Pam Suchman, Dr. Shelley Luce, Carolyn Hampton, Ronna Schary, Gregory Crouch, Melinda Barrett, Meredith McKenzie, Julie Du Brow, Gary Ananian, Sandra Albers, Roger Chong-Yi Lee, Emily Green, Ranlyn Hill, Jo O'Connell, Kian Schulman, Heidi Amundson and Rick Pearson, Catherine Malcolm, Jennifer Johnson, Nancy Miret, Jamie Rinehart, Debra Silbar, Gabriel Funzalida, Susan Hayden, Ross Porter, Stephen Svete, Lisa Zeller, Malaika, Sue Schmitt, Bonnie Clarfield-Bylin, Holly Forsyth, Phyllis Grifman, Drew Ready, Wendy Clarke, Paul Scott, Craig H. Foster, Douglas Jones, Maureen Tighe, Dana Roeber Murray, Chris Paine, Michael Wellborn, Isabelle Duvivier, Paula Henson, Jeff Sojka, Merrill Berge, Laurie Newman, Beth Pratt, Jillana Devine-Knickel, Kathryn Linehan, Anne Marie Cordingly, Stephen Davids, Pamela Conley Ulich, Jim Lamm, Nancy Steele, Jeff Harris, Kaitlin Worzalla, Ryan Maples, Christina Walsh, Larry Nimmer, Maria Pecci-Glass, Barbara from Malibu, Larry Crane, Jamelle Whitmore Griffin, Sojin Kim, Miguel Rodriguez, Susan Nissman, James Scott, Leslie Lewis-Oliver and Kelly Uchimura Kincaid.*

Many of the teachers in my life have been bright lights, including Mrs. Jörkan, Topanga Elementary, Lucilla, Mill Creek Stable, Mrs. Dengler, Dr. William Levy and Mrs. Sally Jordan, Viewpoint School, Dr. John Langdon, Marlborough School, Dr. Stanley Wolpert, UCLA and Sensei James Field, Santa Monica Japan Karate Association. Each of my many language teachers grew my world, while my children's music teacher Miss Annie of Cornerstone Music Conservatory, teaches me every time a child of mine is in her class. All of these people made me love research as much as writing.

My mother's obsession with gardening was my gateway into nature, while walking in Topanga made me the person I am today. Two visits as an adolescent to Yosemite Institute taught me how much I needed to learn, while an exercise in silence introduced me to Rock. The Children's Nature Institute naturalist program helped me to start to learn about our own native plants, along with a class on oaks by Rosi Dagit, to which I was referred by Dr. Travis Longcore. Thank you to all my many colleagues in the environmental world for teaching me and pushing me to do more and better. Casey Burns, Steve Williams, Jennifer Shelstead Parenteau,

Ken Widen, Delmar Lathers, each of you showed me great things about Topanga. I appreciate Dr. Randal Orton, whose commitment to science, hydrology and data made me look up the years for earthquakes and historic rainfall patterns. To members of the Chumash who introduced me to your culture and referred me to a brilliant Chumash scholar/writer who chose to make her comments private as she has her own novel coming out, kaqinas and I hope that I have written about your culture with reverence and love. To Jessica Hall, who knew that Mexican hot chocolate as we drink it today was not invented until the early twentieth century, thank you for all of your insights. I want to give a special note of appreciation to my mother's best friend forever, Mrs. Linda Porter, for her faith in me. While my grandfather Dr. Harold Watts is no longer here to read this, I know that my three children, Vincent Scott, Lucilla Orton and Stephen Orton will read Tree *on his behalf.*

And to Colleen, Linda and Irene Lye, Maria Gustavsson, Claudia Lange, Elizabeth Rhodes, Emily Johnson, Sandy Liddell, Tabitha Dileo, Kay Gabbard, Jude Brown, Elsje Kibler, Patty Meyer, Bridget Crocker, Kate Wulfsberg Townsend, Gail Chun, Tacy and John Currey, Alexandra Pisar, Betsey Lindsley, Amy Kazmin, Dena Moes, Tom Hicks, Suzanne Patmore Gibbs and Stuart Gibbs, Angelique Higgins, Nomi Kleinmuntz, Dennis Washburn, Jennifer Voccola Brown, Steve Kaminsky, Michael and Emily Haynes, Kickan Storer, Kristin Wells-Selby, Clara Sturak, Dr. Ken Rosenfeld, Irene Quinones, Ilona Strasser, Dr. Bolanile Akinwole, Flavia Potenza and many more, I am blessed by your friendship and patience. Martha / Marta Leticia Gonzalez, my roommate freshman year, wheresoever you may be, our conversations made me a much bigger human being and I miss you. I want to express core appreciation to some of my many inspiring employers, especially Peter Horton, Clyde Derrick, Dan Preece, Frank Marshall, Kathleen Kennedy and Brad Goodman. I adore my designers Phyllis Persechini and Nikki O'Connor, our print guru Steve Dreyer, gifted photographer Elizabeth Jebef and painter Jeff Sojka for making this book beautiful.

My parents Stephen and June Watts' commitment to inspiring their children to have intellectual curiosity gave me bibliophilia and a great education and I am always grateful for their care, as I am to the beautiful Tess Watts, my father's second wife, for her care for my father. My siblings Shannon Watts, Z Zeller and Ric Zeller are each consistently kind, a trait towards which I aspire.

The hero's move in taking the book from manuscript into print was made by Steve Davids.

Finally, once upon a time, as dusk fell to night, a large field of grass in front of the dormitories at the University of California San Diego spoke to me and I have to thank them blade by blade for sharing themselves with me. Poaceae.

ABOUT THE AUTHOR

MELINA SEMPILL WATTS

Melina Sempill Watts' writing has appeared in *Sierra Magazine*,
the *New York Times* motherlode blog, *Earth Island Journal* and
Sunset Magazine, in local environmental venues such as *Urban Coast:
Journal of the Center for the Study of the Santa Monica Bay*, the *Heal the Bay
blog* and in local papers such as *Malibu Times*, *Malibu Surfside News*,
VC Reporter, *Topanga Messenger* and *Argonaut News*.

Currently an environmental and media consultant, Watts began
her career in Hollywood as a development executive, writing consultant
and story analyst working for such luminaries Frank Marshall and Kathleen
Kennedy, Peter Horton and Dreamworks. She has worked as a watershed
coordinator, run a stable, shelved books at a library and created, marketed
and ran Starfish Catering. Watts graduated from UCLA with a degree
in history. She has three children and lives in California.

Photo by Elizabeth Jebef, Eyebright Studios